Law, Business and Human Rights

Law, Business and Human Rights

Bridging the Gap

Edited by

Robert C. Bird

Associate Professor of Business Law, University of Connecticut, USA

Daniel R. Cahoy

Professor of Business Law, Pennsylvania State University, USA

Jamie Darin Prenkert

Associate Professor of Business Law, Indiana University, USA

Edward Elgar

Cheltenham, UK • Northampton, MA, USA

Published by
Edward Elgar Publishing Limited
The Lypiatts
15 Lansdown Road
Cheltenham
Glos GL50 2JA
UK

Edward Elgar Publishing, Inc.
William Pratt House
9 Dewey Court
Northampton
Massachusetts 01060
USA

A catalogue record for this book
is available from the British Library

Library of Congress Control Number: 2014932525

This book is available electronically in the ElgarOnline.com
Business Subject Collection, E-ISBN 978 1 78254 662 7

MIX
Paper from
responsible sources
FSC® C013056

ISBN 978 1 78254 661 0

Typeset by Columns Design XML Ltd, Reading
Printed and bound in Great Britain by T.J. International Ltd, Padstow

Contents

Contributors

Robert C. Bird, Associate Professor of Business Law and Northeast Utilities Chair in Business Ethics, School of Business, University of Connecticut, USA

Norman Bishara, Assistant Professor of Business Law and Business Ethics, Stephen M. Ross School of Business, University of Michigan, USA

Daniel R. Cahoy, Professor of Business Law and Dean's Faculty Fellow in Business Law, Smeal College of Business, Pennsylvania State University, USA

Lucien J. Dhooge, Sue and John Staton Professor of Law, Scheller College of Business, Georgia Institute of Technology, USA

David Hess, Associate Professor of Business Law, Stephen M. Ross School of Business at the University of Michigan, USA

Janine S. Hiller, Professor of Business Law, Pamplin College of Business, Virginia Polytechnic Institute and State University, USA

Shannon S. Hiller, MPA Candidate, Princeton University, USA

Radu Mares, Raoul Wallenberg Institute of Human Rights, Associate Professor Faculty of Law, Lund University, Sweden

Kevin McGarry, Assistant Professor of Business Law, The School of Business Administration and Professional Programs, Texas Wesleyan University, USA

David Orozco, Assistant Professor of Legal Studies, The College of Business, Florida State University, USA

Marisa Anne Pagnattaro, Josiah Meigs Professor of Legal Studies, Terry College of Business, University of Georgia, USA

Stephen Kim Park, Assistant Professor of Business Law, School of Business, University of Connecticut, USA

Lydie Pierre-Louis, Associate Professor of Business Law, School of Management, University of San Francisco, USA

Jamie Darin Prenkert, Weimer Faculty Fellow and Associate Professor of Business Law, Kelley School of Business, Indiana University, USA

Preface

Robert C. Bird

HUMAN RIGHTS AND BUSINESS AT THE INDETERMINATE CROSSROADS

Multinational corporations have the potential to deeply impact human rights. Commerce can bring robust economic and social benefits to growing economies. As economic growth accelerates, an improving quality of life can follow, as well as in some circumstances, political freedom and democracy. Commerce also has the potential to degrade the human condition. With commerce can come environmental pollution, social upheaval, and political corruption that can suppress many fundamental human rights. The intersection of business and human rights is one with substantial economic, social, and political implications.

For decades, international organizations have tried to build a framework through which the responsibilities of business to human rights are more clearly understood. In 1976, the United Nations Commission on Transnational Corporations was tasked with drafting a Code of Conduct for Transnational Corporations. This code, which would have regulated various business practices on a global level, was beset with opposition from developed countries and other sources. Later efforts during the 1990s and early 2000s produced the Norms on the Responsibilities of Transnational Corporations and Other Business Enterprises with Respect to Human Rights (Norms). Endorsed by numerous NGOs, multinational corporations strongly resisted their adoption as they potentially bound corporations to a set of mandatory and ambiguous obligations. The U.N. ultimately decided that the Norms lacked legal standing and that no monitoring for compliance should be conducted.

In 2005, the U.N. tried again with the appointment of John Ruggie as a Special Representative of the U.N. Secretary General Ruggie's focus was different from his predecessors. He dismissed the norms and actively sought to engage numerous stakeholders impacted by the intersection of business and human rights. Notably, these stakeholders included multinational corporations and law firms to which any framework would be applied. Fourteen multistakeholder consultations, two dozen research projects, and 1,000 pages of documents later, Ruggie produced a final report in 2011 titled "Guiding Principles on Business and Human Rights: Implementing the United Nations 'Protect, Respect and Remedy' framework." The framework became a global and voluntary platform based upon "principled pragmatism" that articulates specific calls to action strengthening the protection of human rights while taking into account realistic competitive issues and interests important to most multinational corporations.

The "Protect, Respect and Remedy" framework has received both criticism and praise. Some contend that it represents an innovative platform for embedding stronger norms, while others perceive its voluntary nature as insufficient for protecting human rights in a global economy. An underexplored issue in this area is the need for convergence between global business enterprises and civil society groups that protect human rights. Much can be done, and much needs to be understood, to facilitate participation of business in the human rights dialogue through constructive and meaningful interaction. One can advance respect for human rights by illuminating the perspective and goals of multinational corporations who conduct business where human dignity is in peril.

It is from this perspective that this text takes a call to action. The business law group in the University of Connecticut School of Business hosted a colloquium titled "Bridging the Gap between Business and Human Rights." The event took place on May 14–15, 2013, at the University of Connecticut and was organized by Robert Bird, Associate Professor of Business Law in the School of Business and Northeast Utilities Chair in Business Ethics and co-sponsored by the Kelley School of Business at Indiana University. The purpose of this colloquium was to examine the potential for common ground between business and civil society groups in the area of human rights. Attendees at the conference explored how firms perceive and interact with human rights, examined how voluntary regulatory regimes can positively influence business behavior, and analyzed how multinational corporations can align their interests with human rights in their chosen markets. The result of this collaborative endeavor is found in the pages of this book.

This book, like the colloquium that inspired it, is not intended to serve as a comprehensive guide, but rather to explore business and human rights from a particular perspective. Participant authors who publish here are mainly business lawyers teaching at American business schools who have an abiding interest in the value-driven necessity of global commerce. These faculty are immersed in the language, practices, and goals of business academia. They speak the language of business schools, understand business school norms, and teach students whose goals are more often to maximize shareholder value than to serve a loftier goal of ethical leadership.

However, they are not merely servants of a profit-seeking philosophy. Law is the embodiment of social policy, and it is the impact of laws on our society to both facilitate commerce and remedy injustice that are an important focus. These authors mainly come from a legal background, with a firm grounding in fairness, justice, and advocacy of normative social policy. Their points of view shed light on the intersection of business and human rights in a unique and informative fashion. It is intended neither to be final nor definitive, but simply a perspective – one that would be modest in its goals but yet still contributing to an important idea. One hopes that this book will be only the beginning of a robust and engaging dialogue that bridges the gap and, in the process of doing so, helps change the world.

This book is divided into two parts. The first part focuses on the role of the multinational corporation in respecting human rights and its chapters examine the impact of human rights from the perspective of the corporations who have a significant ability to buttress or erode these rights in markets where they do business.

The book begins with a chapter by Radu Mares, of Raoul Wallenberg Institute of Human Rights and an Associate Professor Faculty of Law, Lund University. Professor Mares's work focuses squarely on one of the most important innovations in business and human rights – the protect, respect, and remedy framework developed by John Ruggie and his team. This chapter concentrates on the most relevant prong to business – the corporate responsibility to respect human rights. Professor Mares carefully examines what the "respect" label really implies, and explores the potential for a convergence of expectations around this relatively new, and potentially ambiguous, concept. He rightly notes the importance of the concept of due diligence as the defining idea, even over the responsibility to respect that headlines much of Ruggie's work. This is likely just the beginning of future research understanding the full implications of the framework and Ruggie's apparently deliberate choice of language familiar to corporate enterprises.

Chapter 2 is by Stephen Kim Park, Assistant Professor of Business Law at the University of Connecticut. This chapter shows how mandatory disclosure in human rights can be a catalyst for internally driven changes in tactical operations and strategic objectives. Mandatory disclosure can drive self-regulation, which can in turn improve performance. Viewing mandatory disclosure through the lens of Section 1502 of the Dodd–Frank Act, which requires firms to disclose if their products use minerals from certain conflict-plagued nations, Professor Park examines the benefits and costs of such disclosures, and identifies areas for future improvement.

The book continues with a chapter by Norman Bishara and David Hess, Assistant Professor of Business Law and Business Ethics and Associate Professor of Business Law, respectively, at the Stephen M. Ross School of Business at the University of Michigan. The authors explore one of the most pressing issues in international development – that of corruption of developing states. The chapter proposes that corporate impact on human rights will improve if business, human rights, and corruption are considered in tandem. Suppressing business-related corruption has many benefits but can also end the proliferation of human rights abuses that plague so many governments.

Lucien J. Dhooge, Sue and John Staton Professor of Law and Area Coordinator for Law and Ethics at the Scheller College of Business at Georgia Institute of Technology, contributes Chapter 4, focusing on the intersection between mandated disclosure regulations and the compelled speech doctrine embedded in the First Amendment to U.S. Constitution. Professor Dhooge reflects upon how disclosure regulations that can provide helpful transparency to government and civil society can potentially conflict with basic protections of expression guaranteed by national governments. The chapter reveals how the range of top-down regulatory solutions to human rights issues involving corporations are not limitless, and that uncertain boundaries in U.S. law between permissible disclosure requirements and unconstitutional compelled speech will make challenges to such regulation a continuing inevitability.

Chapter 5 is authored by Janine S. Hiller, Professor of Business Law at Virginia Tech, and Shannon S. Hiller, MPA Candidate at Princeton University. The authors squarely focus on the challenge of collaboration between two distinct groups – multinational corporations and the civil society groups who monitor them for human rights abuses. Using the protect, respect, remedy framework of John Ruggie as a springboard, the authors explore the risks of co-opetition between two disparate and often conflicting interests. While co-opetition has its risks, particularly for the civil society group that may find itself coopted by the corporate entity with which it too-closely affiliates, co-opetition can be a mechanism by which multinational corporations and the civil society groups genuinely partner to solve some of the most pressing global human rights problems.

Part II of this book takes a different tack, namely, the rights of vulnerable stakeholders and their erosion via direct or indirect corporate activity. Obligations for corporations to respect human rights are not merely motivated by *noblesse oblige* but based on empowerment held in the inherent dignity of each human person. The remaining chapters focus on human rights of individuals and groups impacted by corporate conduct and how meaningful communication and respect between business and civil society can produce mutually beneficial and rights-respecting outcomes.

This Part begins with a contribution by Marisa Anne Pagnattaro, Josiah Meigs Distinguished Teaching Professor at the University of Georgia. Professor Pagnattaro highlights the availability of legal tools that can be applied to improve the labor standards of the communities in which firms employ workers. This chapter is not simply about compulsion, however, and takes the intriguing perspective that implementation of voluntary labor standards can be a successful long-term sustainability strategy, citing research showing that high-sustainability firms have outperformed lower ones over time. While regulation may be necessary through a variety of means to protect worker rights, such regulation may not be an entirely zero-sum loss for firms subject to its requirements.

Chapter 7 focuses on the rights of indigenous peoples related to traditional knowledge that may be misappropriated by multinational corporations. David Orozco, Assistant Professor of Legal Studies and Florida State University, Kevin McGarry, Assistant Professor of Business Law at Texas Wesleyan University, and Lydie Pierre-Louis, Associate Professor of Business Law at University of San Francisco, examine how traditional U.S. legal doctrines have applicability to modern human rights problems. Such doctrines would speak to the access to remedy principle embedded in the protect, respect, and remedy framework.

In Chapter 8, Jamie Darin Prenkert, Weimer Faculty Fellow and Associate Professor of Business Law at Indiana University (Bloomington), explores some of the fundamental assumptions of the protect, respect, and remedy framework and the Guiding Principles. These are fundamentally conceived as a polycentric governance system, whereby a regulatory regime eschews top-down mandated rules in favor of a nonhierarchical and partially overlapping regime system. Using the work of Elinor and Vincent Ostrom, Professor Prenkert applies an institutional analysis and development framework to illuminate how polycentric governance can impact a voluntary regime like the Ruggie framework. Using the example of conflict minerals, Professor Prenkert reveals how polycentric governance can be a promising regime for successful implementation of the protect, respect, and remedy framework and the Guiding Principles.

In the final chapter, Daniel R. Cahoy, Professor and Dean's Faculty Fellow in Business Law at Pennsylvania State University, examines the intersection of the human right to food with the need for incentives to encourage innovation in agriculture through the use of intellectual property rights. Advances in technology protected by intellectual property can be a catalyst for substantial change, but also lock out food producers denied access in an environment of genetic diversity. This chapter balances compensation needs for innovators with the human right to access to food and also discusses the role of established legal doctrines in facilitating or impeding the human right to food.

When U.N. Special Representative John Ruggie completed his mandate to identify human rights standards for business, clarify their implications for business, and develop materials for impact assessments, he said that this was not the end of the process. Rather, it was the end of the beginning. A foundation of understanding regarding the intersection of business and human rights now exists, and it is the role of numerous participants, including academic commentators, to propel this understanding forward into practical and successful application. It is hoped that this book will be one of many helpful contributions toward making the aspirations of this mandate, and other mandates to come, a reality.

PART I

THE ROLE OF FIRMS IN RESPECTING HUMAN RIGHTS

1. "Respect" human rights: Concept and convergence

Radu Mares*

If one were tempted to affix labels on the field of business and human rights, a few words would come immediately to mind: contestation, distrust, illegitimacy, polarization, stalemate, incompatibility. Few moments pinpoint more eloquently the diversity of stakeholder expectations than the making – and demise – of the U.N. Norms on the Responsibilities of Transnational Corporations (Norms), shelved in 2004. The reasons for that demise were diverse, but one of them surely had to do with the way corporate responsibilities were conceived. According to the Norms, businesses were expected "to promote, secure the fulfilment of, respect, ensure respect of, and protect human rights" within their spheres of activity and influence (U.N. Commission on Human Rights, 2003, art. 1).

The mandate of the U.N. Special Representative of the Secretary-General on the Issue of Human Rights and Transnational Corporations and Other Business Enterprises (SRSG), entrusted to Professor John Ruggie, began in 2005, with one of its goals being explicitly to reduce polarization and find some common ground (U.N. Special Representative of the Secretary-General, 2011). In 2011, only seven years after the U.N. Norms debacle, the U.N. Guiding Principles on Business and Human Rights (GPs) simply reference "respecting" human rights: "the corporate responsibility to respect [human rights] is the basic expectation society has of business in relation to human rights" (Ruggie, 2011b, p. 4). This notion of corporate responsibility carries the weight of a document unanimously endorsed in the U.N. Human Rights Council and benefits from an unprecedented level of (declaratory) support coming from businesses, states, intergovernmental organizations, and numerous civil society groups.

Now that the U.N. has agreed, for the first time in its history, on a comprehensive business and human rights instrument, some questions arise. Does this watershed signify the genuine convergence of expectations that has eluded the field of corporate social responsibility (CSR) for so long? More narrowly, do we finally witness a real convergence around the corporate responsibility to respect (RtR) human rights as conceived in the GPs? Indeed, by his own account, the SRSG aimed to construct an "authoritative focal point around which the expectations and actions of relevant stakeholders could converge" (Ruggie, 2011b, p. 3).

That diverse parties in the business and human rights debate have held wider or narrower expectations about the extent of businesses' responsibility comes as no surprise, particularly in the case of multinational enterprises (MNEs), which have large concentrations of wealth and span the globe with their operations. With the positive and negative social, environmental, and economic impacts of MNEs, the widespread concern voiced by the corporate accountability movement is that MNEs are allowed to externalize risks, not least through the multitude of subsidiaries, contractors, and other affiliates. Indeed, the complex structures of these business groups and networks, operating transnationally or nationally, which are integrated economically but separated legally, have raised serious challenges for generations of lawyers in terms of how to regulate them effectively in a jurisdictionally divided world of national states (Blumberg, 1993). Furthermore, MNEs, which have been at the center of U.N. debates on CSR since the 1970s, have garnered even more attention recently, as MNEs have benefited handsomely from the wave of globalization since the 1990s.

This chapter subjects the corporate RtR human rights, as elaborated in the GPs, to a hard look. What do the GPs actually mean by *respect* human rights as *the* responsibility of businesses, that baseline, minimum expected from all companies in all situations? What are the implications and difficulties raised by applying this responsibility to MNEs, and how did the SRSG handle them? This chapter engages in an analytical and taxonomical effort to highlight a simple issue that is often and surprisingly obscured: what types of responsibilities do we really have in mind when we say, like the GPs do, that MNEs and corporate groups in general, like all other businesses, have a responsibility to respect human rights? What does respect entail under the GPs when it is applied to a specific subject, that is, the MNE, for the entities composing it?

Companies pursue strategies of subsidiarization and outcontracting to grow their operations and reach new markets. The interest in analyzing how the RtR applies to MNEs is to determine what is actually expected from those entities having the capacity, exercised or not, to influence or control affiliates. This inquiry is therefore relevant to parent companies in their relations with subsidiaries as well as to companies that contract out to entities in their value chains production or distribution functions. So the term "MNE" in this chapter covers both equity-based and contract-based enterprises.

The analytical focus herein is therefore on influential companies, companies with leverage over other entities in the enterprise. It should not be assumed, however, that influence (leverage) is concentrated in one or a handful of entities at the top of a hierarchically organized group (for example, the parent company based in an industrialized country with numerous fully owned subsidiaries in less-developed countries) or at the center of a business network (for example, the large retailer or brand with suppliers and distributors contracted to supply or distribute goods and services worldwide). It is true these are the parent companies and large buyer companies of the classic CSR cases of the 1990s (for instance, Nike, Shell, Chiquita);[1] we could call them "core companies" that are archetypal of influential companies. However, influence and leverage are distributed throughout the business enterprise; companies placed closer to the periphery of the enterprise might have real leverage in their small universe over their several local business partners. So, our inquiry into the meaning of RtR under the GPs is equally applicable to all types of influential companies – core companies dominating the enterprise or peripheral entities. It is the existence of a company's genuine leverage rather than its size or position in the enterprise that counts for the purposes of the present analysis. Therefore, the argument is not dependent on the existence of the archetypal core company and is applicable to a wide variety of business structures. Some display more integrated, hierarchical relationships among entities. Others are flatter, leaving more autonomy to diverse entities in the enterprise. It is important to keep this in mind because any discussion of the RtR applied to MNEs will immediately trigger thoughts of the "core company" association.

The companies with capacity to influence their partners might or might not have chosen to actually exercise their leverage. Indeed, the corporate accountability movement has challenged MNEs in both situations, either for exercising that capacity irresponsibly or for irresponsibly failing to exercise it when affiliate operations infringed human rights. Then the study of the GPs' treatment of MNEs and influential companies should answer the question, do the GPs envisage an additional responsibility for influential companies that is different in nature from the baseline RtR that applies to all types of companies, influential or not? If yes, how do the GPs justify this responsibility?

Finally, the analysis pursued in this chapter applies equally to business groups irrespective of their national or transnational character. Operations might span national borders or be more localized and confined to the borders of one state. Clearly, whether a responsibility deriving from leverage exists is relevant in both cases. Nevertheless, victims of corporate abuses have tried to reach corporate entities as well as audiences (courts, consumers, investors) abroad. It is this transnational dimension of rightholders seeking help and access to justice abroad that makes a distinct focus on MNEs justified and important. The MNEs, and influential entities within such multinational business groups or networks, are thus a distinct subject of RtR, and at times the analysis herein will be adjusted to reflect this distinctiveness. Perhaps here a reference to the core company concept is helpful, to distinguish the influential company based abroad, which might well respond to a different set of stimuli, from the nationally influential company.

The thesis of this chapter is that a careful reading of the GPs reveals that the RtR contains a clear responsibility to *protect* human rights included stealthily in the RtR. By *stealthily* I mean not only that a special and additional responsibility for influential companies exists despite that it was never labeled as such in the GPs, but also and more importantly that Ruggie has rejected any inference that something more than respect is asked from companies under the GPs. This chapter aims to prove that the nature of RtR in the GPs is not invariable, as the drafters insist, but that the GPs display a clear variation that encompasses both *respect* responsibilities grounded in the "do no harm" imperative and *protect* responsibilities grounded in the "reach out and help" proposition. Furthermore, the chapter aims to explain Ruggie's conceptual stance in the context of the GPs playing a decisive role in facilitating the convergence of stakeholder expectations and the emergence of a polycentric governance regime for CSR.

I. RESPONSIBILITY TO RESPECT HUMAN RIGHTS IN THE GUIDING PRINCIPLES: MERITS AND DIFFICULTIES

This section concentrates the analysis of the GPs on the situation of influential companies as distinct subjects of RtR. How did the SRSG account for corporate responsibilities in general? In particular, how does the RtR concept in the GPs handle business groups and this special entity, the influential company? And what responsibilities do the GPs actually place on it? As will be documented, the GPs propose a more extensive set of responsibilities than meets the eye.

First, this section summarizes the RtR concept in the GPs. Second, it pinpoints the uneasiness generated by the GPs concept.

A. SRSG's Responsibility to Respect Human Rights

Principle 11 lays down a corporate responsibility to respect human rights, which "means that they [business enterprises] should avoid infringing on the human rights of others and should address adverse human rights impacts with which they are involved." (Ruggie, 2011b, p. 13)

What the GPs expect from companies, including the influential companies and core companies in MNEs, is straightforward. GP 13 indicates that a responsibility exists in three broad situations: when a company causes, contributes to, or is associated through its business relationships with, adverse human rights impacts (Ruggie, 2011b, p. 14). The first two of the three situations – namely, cause or contribute – are not the focus of this chapter. Thus, the analysis herein focuses on the third situation in which a company's RtR arises not from its causing or contributing to harm but from its dealings with an affiliate who has adverse impacts on human rights.

Reading GP 13b and the commentary to GP 19 together clarifies the options a company has related to its business relationships, when it did not directly cause or contribute to harm. The responsibility is spelled out by GP 13b: "The responsibility to respect human rights requires that business enterprises … [s]eek to prevent or mitigate adverse human rights impacts that are directly linked to their operations, products or services by their business relationships, even if they have not contributed to those impacts" (Ruggie, 2011b, p. 14). The content of the RtR in this scenario is provided in the commentary to GP 19, which indicates three ways in which a company can act: by exercising leverage, by terminating the business relationship, and by continuing the relationship while being ready to pay a price and still making mitigation efforts (Ruggie, 2011b, p. 19). In a nutshell, under GP 13b there is a responsibility to act (i.e., the company cannot legitimately be a bystander as affiliates infringe rights), and under the commentary to GP 19 the "appropriate action" is specified.

Through GP 13b and the commentary to GP 19 the existence and content of RtR for a company that did not cause or contribute to harm are elucidated. The existence and content of the RtR still leave open the matter of its subject. In the SRSG vision, the subject of RtR is the business. According to GP 11, "Business enterprises should respect human rights" (Ruggie, 2011b, p. 13). No distinctions are needed for the purposes of RtR. The applicability of RtR does not vary with different types of companies. Whether a core company with vast resources and influence over the entire multinational enterprise or smaller affiliate with a handful of its own contractors at the periphery of the enterprise, both of these companies have the RtR and have to take appropriate action as described in the commentary to GP 19. Variations in the type of company are irrelevant for RtR purposes.

In the SRSG thinking, variations are only relevant when it comes to the implementation of the RtR. Adaptations are necessary, and it is here in which all variations of subjects and means of discharging responsibilities are factored. As GP 14 indicates about the means of discharging the RtR, "the scale and complexity of the means through which enterprises meet that responsibility may vary according to these factors [i.e., size, sector, operational context, ownership and structure] and with the severity of the enterprise's adverse human rights impacts" (Ruggie, 2011b, p. 14). About the subjects of RtR, the commentary addresses directly the interest taken in this chapter: "The means through which a business enterprise meets its responsibility to respect human rights may also vary depending on whether, and the extent to which, it conducts business through a corporate group or individually" (Ruggie, 2011b, p. 14). Further variations and adaptations are inherent in the concept of human rights due diligence, which is at the heart of operationalizing the RtR. *Due* implies variation of effort and resources necessary to address effectively adverse impacts in a particular context.[2]

B. The Problem

Surely this picture has much going for it. It is highly stable as the RtR remains the same (in existence and content) and does not vary with the subjects of the RtR. The coverage of companies is comprehensive (applicability is universal),[3] the content of the RtR is sound (appropriate action to be taken),[4] and the variations of the means used to implement the RtR show high adaptability to diverse contexts. There is even a unique term, or label, *responsibility to respect human rights*, encompassing it all. The label put on the corporate responsibility is also stable. It is about respecting human rights and only that. There is no mention of anything else, including a responsibility to protect, fulfill, secure, or realize rights even for the most influential companies.[5] As explained by the SRSG, companies respect human rights while states respect-protect-fulfill human rights. Furthermore, the *respect* label reflects a limited expectation fully in tune with "[t]he role of business enterprises as specialized organs of society performing specialized functions, [which are] required to comply with all applicable laws and to respect human rights" (Ruggie, 2011b, p. 6).

The RtR as constructed in the GPs seems to display great content with an appealing label. Is then the RtR concept beyond reproach? The content of the RtR (with its taxonomy and responsibility to take "appropriate action") as spelled out in GP 13b and the commentary to GP 19 is valuable. The label of *respect* seems appropriate and appears vindicated by the broad endorsement the GPs have received. At the same time, after reading closely the GPs, one is left reflecting on two issues. Is Pillar 2 strictly about business respecting rights or something more than that? How compatible truly is this RtR concept with lasting considerations of business organization and public policy? In other words, the preoccupation is whether the RtR concept is able to really withstand a challenge based on the organizational and legal separation of entities in a business group.

The issue of the RtR content and label is of much broader importance than just limited academic interest. Indeed, understanding the concept of RtR is consequential on three counts. First, a closer look at the label and content of RtR warns the GPs' advocates of a potential charge of misrepresentation coming from CSR skeptics. The analysis below explains the problem by showing the nature of the RtR in GP 13b as being something different from respect, and by problematizing the SRSG's claim of no variation in the nature of RtR.

Second, grasping the ways in which the SRSG built the container deepens our understanding of the GPs and the intricacies of Pillar 2 by revealing the techniques and methods Ruggie used so skillfully. The chapter pinpoints instances where the GPs reframe key concepts, use emphasis and de-emphasis strategically, and engage in complex drafting. Such instances demonstrate the ingenious ways in which the GPs managed to deliver an RtR more expansive than meets the hurried eye and to shelter it from a devastating blow. These insights will follow from a textual analysis of the GPs as well as a comparative analysis of the GPs included in the SRSG's final report in 2011 and previous versions (especially the 2008 Framework).

Third, understanding the purposes for which the GPs built the RtR container in the way they did opens a window into the very strategy of change that guided the SRSG in his acclaimed search for common ground, from polarization to a more effective governance regime protective of human rights. In a way this analysis gives a new meaning to the *principled pragmatism* term Ruggie used to define his approach as SRSG (U.N. Special Representative of the Secretary-General, 2006, p. 20; Ruggie, 2013, pp. xlii–xlvi). By understanding more fully the strategy displayed by the GPs one is better positioned to reflect on the evolution and dynamics of the emerging CSR regime and to assess the relative and genuine value of the GPs in time and context. The analysis below achieves this by refusing to lose sight of some lasting considerations of business organization and public policy, with emphasis on *lasting*. It is crucial to weigh as accurately as possible obstacles in the RtR path that reflect more than legal technicalities and idiosyncrasies of all sorts.

II. APPLICATION OF RESPONSIBILITY TO RESPECT TO BUSINESS GROUPS IN THE GUIDING PRINCIPLES

The remainder of this chapter is structured around the intricacies of the RtR concept in the GPs. The chapter discusses three building blocks that allowed the *protect* component to become rather stealthily part of the RtR and be accepted by stakeholders. In each block, the analysis will reveal the methods that the SRSG used. The first block, addressed in Part II.A, is about respect for human rights as defined by the SRSG and, based on that, about the charges of misrepresentation that can be levied against the RtR. The second block, discussed in Part II.B, is about the subjects of RtR and, based on those, about the ascendency of due diligence against "responsibility" (RtR) as the concept doing the heavy lifting in the GPs. The third block, addressed in Part II.C, is about the separation of entities as a towering obstacle that the SRSG had to deal with when applying the RtR to business groups.

Only after the three building blocks are explicated can the worth of the RtR concept be evaluated. Such assessment of RtR has to be done on two counts: its ability to deal conceptually with the separation of entities principle and its capacity to facilitate convergence of stakeholders' expectations. We come closer to the dilemma of justification that the SRSG confronted regarding the protect element: try to justify now conceptually (and clash head-on into the separation-of-entities principle) versus try to stimulate convergence and evolution of the field (if convergence occurs, the clash with the separation of entities principle will happen in a new and more favorable context) on which justification would eventually draw. The dilemma of justification that the SRSG faced on the *protect* component of RtR and the strategy of change animating the SRSG efforts is discussed in Part III.

A. Building Block 1: Respect Human Rights

Part I.A. introduced the concept of the RtR developed by the SRSG. This Part is devoted to clarifying what *respect* really means in the GPs.

Furthermore, this chapter insists that there is a clear responsibility to protect human rights included in the RtR. The following subsections take a closer look at both of the concepts of respect and protect to show where the responsibility to protect can be found in the GPs.

1. Respect

In tune with GP 11, the introduction to the GPs refers to "the corporate responsibility to respect human rights, which means that business enterprises should act with due diligence to avoid infringing on the rights of others and to address adverse impacts with which they are involved" (Ruggie, 2011b, p. 4).

Here are three aspects worth pondering. First, the definition of respecting human rights in the GPs is different from the 2008 Framework. Second, the definition is rather loosely formulated. And third, the definition is different from the international human rights law's (IHRL) use of the term *respect* as applied to the obligation of states to respect human rights.

Regarding the first aspect, comparing two key documents in the SRSG mandate – the final report containing the GPs from 2011 and the Respect, Protect, Remedy Framework from 2008 – reveals a shift in explanation. Actually the SRSG redefined altogether what *respect* means. The 2008 report explained respect as follows: "To respect rights essentially means not to infringe on the rights of others – put simply, to do no harm" (U.N. Special Representative of the Secretary-General, 2008, p. 9). The 2011 GPs explain that to respect human rights companies "should avoid infringing on the human rights of others and should address adverse human rights impacts with which they are involved" (Ruggie, 2011b, p. 13). On reflection, the 2011 definition is significantly more expansive than the 2008 definition and makes space for a protect aspect. While the 2008 concept of respect was single-pronged (i.e., not to infringe) the 2011 concept of respect is double-pronged (i.e., to avoid infringing and to address impacts with which they are involved). And *involve* is an expansive term indeed.

Regarding the second aspect, the reference to involvement (i.e., "adverse impacts with which they are involved") raises the question of what conduct of a company is not covered. Being involved could require that the company make some type of contribution to harm. Or it could envisage a mere association with a perpetrator of such harm. *Involve* is a comprehensive term or, one can say, an inherently ambiguous one.

Regarding the third aspect, the GPs use of *respect* is meant to resonate with the classic respect-protect-fulfill terminology used in IHRL. However, IHRL distinguishes precisely between responsibility of the state when its state organs and agents cause harm versus when third parties' activities (such as the activities of private actors) generate harm. For example, the definition offered by the U.N. Committee on Economic, Social and Cultural Rights reflects the classical understanding in IHRL:

> The obligation to respect requires States parties to refrain from interfering, directly or indirectly, with the enjoyment of the right to take part in cultural life. The obligation to protect requires States parties to take steps to prevent third parties from interfering in the right to take part in cultural life. (U.N. Committee on Economic, Social and Cultural Rights, 2009, p. 12)

Thus, in IHRL, *respect* refers to the harmful conduct of the state while *protect* refers to the harmful conduct of third parties. Protect is based on the failure of a state to adopt legislative and other measures to prevent and hold third parties accountable when they harm others. Thus, the way in which the GPs use *respect* in GP 13b covers responsibility for third parties' conduct, which is precisely what IHRL covers with its use of *protect*.

Notably, the redefinition of *respect* during the SRSG mandate cannot be explained as a result of operationalization, the new and different task entrusted to the SRSG in 2008 by the Human Rights Council after his first mandate was completed successfully. Neither can one say that the GPs superseded the former report, at least not on such a fundamental definitional issue as the definition of *respect*.

The 2011 expansive definition creates difficulties for the justification of the RtR provided in 2008. The 2008 definition was grounded squarely in a do-no-harm ethic and was in tune with rather uncontroversial ethical imperatives and tort laws. Respect as do no harm had a taken-for-granted quality. Nevertheless, in his first mandate the SRSG justified the respect requirement in multiple ways. For example, the SRSG severely criticized the U.N. Norms for going beyond a responsibility to respect, reasoned that "can does not imply ought," and emphasized the specialized function of business in society (U.N. Special Representative of the Secretary-General, 2008, pp. 16, 19–20; Ruggie, 2013, pp. 47–55). He still argues the latter, but the 2011 RtR is not consistent with the rest of the justification offered in 2008. Indeed, it is plainly contradictory to that justification. Apparently, the 2011 GPs quietly redefined and expanded respect; the SRSG acted as if the respect justification was settled in 2008 and there would be no need to again justify the RtR in 2011. So, between 2008 and 2011, the SRSG kept the respect label but stealthily moved the posts.

Interestingly, one searches in vain the GPs for the *do-no-harm* phrase. It has disappeared. How can this disappearance be explained? From the feedback that the SRSG received it is clear that the negative formulation in do no harm has unwarrantedly created the understanding that the RtR is a purely negative responsibility to avoid or to refrain in order not to harm, and thus would not require affirmative steps from the company. This perception by stakeholders reflects a misunderstanding. That the SRSG never contemplated such a refrain-type of RtR flows directly from the text of the 2008 Report, which expressly indicated that "'doing no harm' is not merely a passive responsibility for firms but may entail positive steps – for example, a workplace anti-discrimination policy might require the company to adopt specific recruitment and training programmes" (U.N. Special Representative of the Secretary-General, 2008, p. 17). Nevertheless this type of clarification by providing examples did not suffice. Therefore the SRSG preferred to change the terminology and renounce *do no harm* to dispel any potential misunderstandings that would shortcut the very idea of employing human rights due diligence as the way to address adverse impacts. That impresses beyond doubt that companies indeed have to act, to take positive steps, in order to respect human rights. Due diligence requires steps for "assessing actual and potential human rights impacts, integrating and acting upon the findings, tracking responses, and communicating how impacts are addressed" (Ruggie, 2011b, p.16). Furthermore, the 2012 Interpretative Guide directly addressed the question, "Why are policies and processes required if this is just a question of avoiding harm?" It answered, "Respecting human rights is not a passive responsibility: it requires action on the part of businesses" (U.N. Office of the High Commissioner for Human Rights, 2012, p. 23).

What started as a necessary clarification created an opportunity to expand the RtR without generating internal inconsistencies in the RtR. Not only did the removal of do no harm solve a misunderstanding of the RtR as a "negative", refrain-from-action responsibility, but also it offered a golden opportunity for the RtR to grow and encompass a protect component.[6] The do-no-harm reference invited the reader of GP 13b to ask the obvious question: how could a company's responsibility to act to address third parties' (affiliates') impacts be based on a do-no-harm basis when one did not cause or contribute to the harm in any way? By renouncing do no harm, the SRSG preempted a powerful objection that he was inviting with the 2008 do-no-harm definition of RtR. Thus, the disappearance allowed the 2011 conception of *respect* to be stretched enough to make a company responsible for what its affiliates do and to accommodate without internal inconsistencies the responsibility to act with due diligence in GP 13b and the commentary to GP 19.

2. Protect

GP 13b clearly states that companies must act when affiliate operations have adverse impacts on human rights, even when the company did not cause or contribute to that harm. So the company cannot legitimately be a bystander. GP 13b fulfills important functions in clarifying the corporate responsibility. It sets the expected conduct towards the purpose of prevention or mitigation and also places limits on this responsibility to act. What is most important for understanding the nature of this responsibility to act, however, is laid out not in GP 13b or its commentary: the nature of responsibility becomes clear only in the commentary to GP 19; only there will the reader find what type of action is required and will the reader be able to determine whether a respect or protect type of responsibility accrues. Under the commentary to GP 19, the company has three choices. Only two of those choices are truly fundamental: disengaging and exercising leverage. When dealing with an abusive affiliate, the company can either stay in a business relationship but exercise leverage or separate itself from the harm by ending the relationship.

Protect is an appropriate label for the option of exercising leverage, but it is surely not satisfactory for disengagement as a course of action. Indeed, the termination of relationship does not protect the rightholder but rather only separates the company from the abuse. On the contrary, exercising leverage has the purpose and the potential to increase protection for rightholders. So the RtR in GP 13b does not necessarily or exclusively have the character of a responsibility to protect, as the GP 19 allows for ending the relationship. Nevertheless, the protect element is of overwhelming importance. Indeed, according to the GPs, if the company has leverage, or the possibility to increase it, the company has to exercise it. As a result, the choice is not equal between leverage and disengagement. The former must be ineffective before disengagement becomes a legitimate choice.

While the SRSG is right to insist that the character of RtR in GP 13b cannot be reduced to protect, neither could he deny that a responsibility to protect exists. Moreover, the possibility cannot be downplayed conceptually given its great significance in the text of the commentary to GP 19 and from a human rights perspective. That means GP 13b lays down a responsibility to act with an irreducible and essential protect component, indeed a responsibility to protect human rights.

GP 19, in its guidance on appropriate action expected for a GP 13b situation, merges two prescriptions of appropriate action. One prescription resonates with do no harm, by instructing a company to separate from an abusive affiliate at the risk of being seen as contributing by enabling or benefiting the affiliate perpetrator otherwise. The other prescription resonates with reach out and help, by instructing a company to exercise leverage over an abusive affiliate at the risk of being seen as an inactive bystander refusing to extend help otherwise. This merging of prescriptions is able to obscure the nature of the responsibility in GP 13b, not to mention the entire GP 13 where GP 13a is clearly based in a do-no-harm ethic. The SRSG indicates there is nothing more in RtR than *respect*, yet if one has a proper taxonomy of situations and types of conduct covered by the RtR, the respect or protect nature of RtR appears clearly. What GP 13b establishes as RtR is a responsibility to act[7] when one could otherwise have been a legitimate bystander, and comprises both respect and protect components.

As discussed above, the SRSG treats all companies the same for purposes of RtR; it is meant to apply to all companies without distinction. The SRSG did not fall into the trap of defining the RtR by pairing additional responsibilities to certain positions in the enterprise – like powerful core companies in vast transnational enterprises – while assuming non-core companies have no influence and therefore a limited, if any, RtR. While this unitary treatment of RtR subjects solves the applicability of RtR, it does not settle questions about the nature of RtR. Actually, through the SRSG's context-driven approach to clarifying the RtR, which allows variations only in the means of discharging it, Ruggie insists that the respect nature of the RtR does not change. However, based on the analysis herein, what is presented in GP 14 as variation in the means is actually a variation in the nature of responsibility when GP 13b and GP 19 are read together: a protect responsibility to exercise leverage is a responsibility not based in do no harm, but in reach out and help.

Why insist so much on the nature of RtR? A responsibility to reach out and help (or protect) is not the same as a responsibility to do no harm (or respect). The former is exceptional in law for good reasons, and because of its nature, it has to be justified way more carefully than a do-no-harm obligation. We know from jurisprudence that this type of responsibility – the duty to act regarding third-party misconduct – is an exceptional one; therefore, its existence always needs to be justified and limited carefully. Otherwise there is no responsibility to act,[8] and remaining passive as harm unfolds is a legitimate course of action that rightly leaves it to others to prevent, mitigate, or remedy that harm. The GPs, however, display no reinforced justification for the protect situations, and this gives reason for concern. The GPs treat both types of responsibilities under the same banner of RtR. There is a ticking bomb under this part of RtR that has the potential to blow apart the apparent convergence of stakeholder expectations around RtR. It remains to be seen in the following sections how the SRSG attempted to defuse this bomb: what strategy he seems to have adopted and what methods he used.

There is a misalignment within the concept of RtR between its contents and the label. What appears to GPs supporters as a good enough approximation might well appear to GP skeptics as disturbing misrepresentation. The CSR proponents will hardly be disturbed given that the content – appropriate action – is right. However, the skeptics of CSR could take advantage of misalignment to score points against the RtR and possibly the GPs more generally. Mindful of these possibilities, this chapter, whose author counts himself among the GPs' supporters, reflects on the RtR intricacies in the context of convergence of stakeholder expectations (i.e., how it has been used to defuse potential objections to the RtR) and to explain how the methods through which the SRSG managed to avoid criticism (i.e., by employing a series of reframing and drafting techniques). Before continuing that analysis we could pause to reflect on whether the RtR is a satisfactory approximation or potential misrepresentation.

3. Far-reaching misrepresentation or satisfactory approximation?

Telling companies and governments that businesses are expected only to respect rights puts at ease such audiences that have been wary of expansive corporate responsibilities. The *respect* label on the RtR sends a reassuring message and is one of the selling points of the GPs as a reasonable, limited, realistic, pragmatic (and numerous other adjectives) approach to CSR. The elaborations through the concept of due diligence about how this RtR is to be implemented add indispensable guidance as well as familiarity, risk-management and process-friendly connotations to wary audiences. However, if there were a mismatch between the content of the RtR container and its label, the GPs would be subject to a significant critique; namely, the *respect* label on the container misrepresents the content of RtR.

The way GP 13 and GP 19 are drafted is interesting. There is not much in GP 13b that invites the reader to apply the 'protect' label. On the contrary, the responsibility in GP 13b is framed non-threateningly as an obligation of conduct ("Seek to"), it waives the remedy component of the RtR (prevent-mitigate-remedy[9]), it raises the threshold of relationship with affiliates to those with which the company is "*directly* linked," and it is formulated in the reassuring language of due diligence ("prevent or mitigate") (Ruggie, 2011b, p. 14). The protect element of the RtR comes into focus only when one notices the discussion of leverage. Still, leverage is treated under the due diligence title (GPs 17–21) and hidden in the body of the commentary to GP 19. One could wonder whether the

SRSG drafted the GPs in this way to put such protect-related provisions as far out of the way as possible from the principles laying down the key parameters of the RtR (GPs 11–14).

For the sake of argument, to preempt a charge of misrepresentation, the drafting of the GP 13b could have made the required action explicit. It would have sounded like this, if GP 13b and the commentary to GP 19 were merged: The responsibility to respect human rights requires that business enterprises: … (b) Exercise leverage, end relationship, or be prepared to pay the price for staying in the crucial relationship in order to prevent or mitigate adverse human rights impacts that are directly linked to their operations, products or services by their business relationships, even if they have not contributed to those impacts. Not only would such a formulation be clearer about the nature of the RtR and expected conduct, but it would also have been more consistent with the language of GP 13a, which requires companies to "[a]void causing or contributing to human rights impacts … and [to] address such impacts when they occur" (Ruggie, 2011b, p. 14).

GP supporters might perceive the problem of misalignment between content and label in the RtR concept as inconsequential misrepresentation or good enough approximation. Even so, it might still be worth understanding the problem and may then be possible to localize the damage if skeptics charge that the GPs display conceptual sloppiness and/or unacceptably far-reaching strategizing. For this reason a taxonomy effort is necessary, and this chapter takes a step in that direction. Furthermore, understanding why the SRSG was inclined to deliver his concept of RtR in this way requires us to understand the role of approximation in the process of facilitating convergence of stakeholder expectations in the CSR regime. Not only does this approximation have a role in facilitating the evolution of the CSR regime, but as described in Part III, it can also be corrected and vindicated retroactively once the convergence of expectations and regime-building have advanced enough.

The redefinition of respect between 2008 and 2011 and the renouncement of do no harm constitute the first building block that will be consequential in expanding the responsibilities of influential companies. While the renouncement created space for a protect component, the redefinition that went unobserved included, obliquely, the protect component in the very definition of RtR with which Pillar 2 begins. The now-expanded definition meant there would be no internal inconsistencies if GP 13b was added and supplemented by the commentary to GP 19. That, however, would be insufficient if the companies having to protect human rights – influential companies – were shielded by the separation-of-entities principle. The next section provides a closer look at how the SRSG accounted for the subjects of RtR and the situation of influential companies.

B. Building Block 2: Subjects of the Responsibility to Respect Human Rights

Under the GPs, the RtR applies to all companies irrespective of their characteristics. No variations in the subject can render the RtR inapplicable to some companies, not even the smallest, least resourceful, and least influential. Core companies and entities located at the periphery of the multinational enterprise alike must respect human rights and take appropriate action. By this treatment of the subjects, the content and applicability of the RtR are not problematized by jurisdictional or organizational boundaries, the latter being notoriously amenable to legalistic manipulation to preclude liability through legal separation strategies. The way the SRSG conceived the RtR is truly important and consequential: responsibility should follow the negative impacts of decisions even where such impacts occur in other jurisdictions and in the operations of other entities. Responsibility should follow operations. There are a number of methods through which the SRSG tried to promote this message.

1. Strategic ambiguity around subjects of RtR when applied to MNEs

Even after reading attentively the GPs one cannot say directly whether the subject of the RtR – "business enterprises" – refers to a business group or network in its entirety as a unitary actor or not. Only by reading GP 13b's references to business partners and relationships can one conclude that treating MNEs as a unitary actor (as proposed by theories of enterprise liability) might be contrary to the GPs. So GP 13 treats the company and its business partners as separate entities and separate subjects of RtR. But this treatment in GP 13b might not be determinative of how the entire GPs treat business groups because the SRSG reports nowhere define the term *business enterprise*; not even the 2012 Interpretative Guide offers such a definition in its special section explaining key concepts. Thus there is a strategic ambiguity on the subject of RtR when it comes to business groups and MNEs.

This ambiguity becomes even more evident when the reader searches to see how the GPs refer to subsidiaries[10] as subjects of RtR. Again, subsidiaries are nowhere mentioned in the GPs and are conspicuously absent from the list of example "business relationships" in the commentary to GP 13, which states that "'business relationships' are understood to include relationships with business partners, entities in its value chain, and any other non-State or State entity directly linked to its business operations, products or services" (Ruggie, 2011b, p. 14). One has to guess whether the GPs account for subsidiaries as a company's "own activities" or in terms of "business relationships." Still, the result of this choice is of real practical significance for a company given that impacts resulting from own activities have to be remediated while impacts from business relationships in GP 13b do not require remediation, as GP 22 makes clear. This ambiguity regarding subsidiaries, as one type of "business partners", is no mere oversight on the SRSG's part, given that subsidiary-parent company relationship is the instance most targeted by rightholders trying to move responsibility upwards in the business enterprise and hold the parent company accountable for its subsidiaries' harmful operations.

Not only is the SRSG strategically ambiguous on the subject of RtR in the ways described above, but the SRSG also explicitly said he never intended to put forward "a robust moral theory or a full scheme for the attribution of legal liability to underpin the Framework" (Ruggie, 2013, p. 107). Ruggie wrote, "I did not set out to establish a global enterprise legal liability model. That would have been a purely theoretical exercise" (Ruggie, 2013, p. 189). The SRSG mandate was not meant to elaborate how to assign legal liability in corporate groups. Therefore, when the reader thinks of corporate groups like MNEs as the subject of RtR and seeks to apply the RtR, he or she will see that the GPs are not a guide on how to impute or attribute responsibility to precise entities in corporate groups.

It appears that the SRSG deliberately refused to take a stance on the business group or MNE as a distinct subject of RtR, a stance that would have forced him to explain whether the group is seen as unitary for RtR purposes or atomized in a collection of entities, each being subject to RtR. That stance would have pushed the SRSG in a head-on collision with the separation-of-entities principle that would have crippled the entire RtR, even in GP 13a, and would have made it far more difficult for the SRSG to advance the responsibility to act (with its protect component) in GP 13b. It would have entangled the mandate in justificatory work and endless controversies about the existence and scope of RtR as currently defined in GP 13. Not only would that have been a tough fight, as the next section will show, to justify the existence of an expansive RtR, but it also would have sidelined the work on the implementation of RtR where the GPs contribute so much through due diligence elaborations.

In sum, the GPs were drafted in a way that maintains strategic ambiguity on the subject of the RtR. As the SRSG has defined the subject of RtR generically as business enterprises, the inquiries that the violations of human rights – instead of adverse impacts on human rights – would stimulate are neither hindered nor facilitated by the SRSG's concept of the RtR. The SRSG refused to pursue such inquiry, and he was preparing to offer a different conceptual account of corporate responsibilities. The reason is clear: the separation-of-entities principle, which lies at the core of business groups composed of multiple entities, was a formidable obstacle. And the SRSG needed to find a way to relate to it.

2. Violations of human rights and adverse human rights impacts

The terminology the GPs use regarding infringements of human rights is noteworthy. Before the SRSG mandate, CSR literature recurrently referred to "violations" of human rights (obligations) to depict corporate abuses. The SRSG however speaks of "adverse human rights impacts." Actually, after searching the GPs text, *violation* is a term that appears not more than two times in the GPs, and only in relation to states; thus, the two references are about the violation by states of their obligations and not about companies violating rights, which is a loose formulation widely employed in CSR.

What the SRSG managed, in addition to a more rigorous language, was a subtle shift from *violation* (of human rights) to *adverse impacts* (on human rights). The consequences of this reframing play a part in a bigger reframing task the SRSG undertook and which is explained below. *Impacts* focuses attention on operations rather than on specific entities that are often entangled in complicatedly structured business enterprises. *Violations* directs attention to the precise entity that committed the violation in order to hold it accountable. The next subsection focuses on this entity and revisits how the subject of the responsibility to respect is dealt with in the GPs.

3. Conceptual match: not "entity–responsibility," but "operations–due diligence"

The key conceptual match in the making of the RtR concept is not entity–responsibility, but operations–due diligence. The fine elaborations, the necessary distinctions, the creativity exhibited by the GPs are all dedicated to the latter match. In contrast, the former match is unremarkable and static. In it, all types of companies have the same responsibility under the same artificial label of respecting human rights. In his recent book, Ruggie wrote that his "aim was to prescribe practical ways of integrating human rights concerns within enterprise risk-management systems. … [T]here had been no authoritative guidance for how to manage risks of adverse human rights impacts" (Ruggie, 2013, p. 189).

Building the RtR along the entity-responsibility match would have created problems for the SRSG on both ends of the match. Regarding the treatment of entity, he would have had to account more directly for influential companies and define their specific responsibilities. The difficulties would soon arise as RtR would have put the spotlight on core companies of MNEs; these are the companies that, in the public imagination, are the epitome of influence and private power that came to define the CSR discourse regarding globalization's negative impacts on human rights. The SRSG absolutely did not contemplate his RtR to single out core companies in this way, as had been done from New International Economic Order in the 1970s to the U.N. Norms in the early 2000s, for convergence of stakeholder expectations reasons. Indeed, turning core companies into enemies would have taken the SRSG far away from what he set out to secure: unanimous endorsement by the Human Rights Council and broad support from all stakeholders groups (including business).

But also conceptually, pairing the RtR to the core company would have had two unfortunate consequences for its protect component. First, in the situation of less integrated MNEs with rather autonomous operations and affiliates, a core company, however defined, is hard to identify. This leaves the responsibility to protect without a subject and, thus, inapplicable. Second, the very assumption that leverage is placed at the top or center of corporate groups/networks where core companies reside would leave out of the picture the leverage spread throughout the enterprise. The concept of RtR, however, should be able to harvest leverage irrespective of the amount of leverage or its location closer to the periphery of the enterprise. Therefore, from a governance perspective, this treatment of leverage would have been counterproductive. Indeed, a wrongly placed analytical focus on the leverage of core companies would miss leverage present in other parts of the corporate group and, thus, would shortcut the practical possibilities to plug governance gaps and offer protection to rightholders.

Regarding the *treatment of responsibility*, a distinct focus on influential companies as subject of RtR would have brought into clear sight the uncomfortable justificatory dilemmas raised specifically by the situation of influential companies asked to act regarding abusive affiliates. These justification problems were highlighted in the previous section about the responsibility to "protect". By preferring the "operations–due diligence" match, the GPs strategically use soft focus for the "entity–responsibility" match, and thus deflect inquiries into the nature of the RtR that would question whether "respect" mutates stealthily into "protect" for certain subjects of RtR.

This section argued that the conceptual focus in Pillar 2 is on *operations* that generate adverse *impacts* rather than special *entities* within a business group or network that *violate human rights*. The RtR concept in the GPs begins to show the features of a highly creative, ingenious and valuable elaboration of the "operations–due diligence" match, but not of the "entity–responsibility" match. However, one should remember that enterprise–liability theories have, for a long period of time, explicitly drawn attention to a fundamental trait of business groups: they are integrated economically but separated legally. In other words, these theories of liability that challenged mainstream theory of entity liability (committed to the legal separation of entities principle) placed the analytical focus in a very similar way to the SRSG's: on the operations. The results, however, have not been encouraging, with enterprise liability confined to a few areas of law and no impact in tort law and corporate law. The SRSG argued just that – responsibility follows operations – but not bluntly through a theory of corporate group responsibility; instead he followed operations with the concept of "due diligence," whose connotations we noted already and to which we return in section III.C.

The SRSG made a strategic bet that the conceptual match "operations–due diligence", not "entity–responsibility", holds the key to the deadlock in CSR. To grasp the fuller significance of Ruggie's choice, we need to look into how it helped him to so slightly change course to navigate around, rather than crash into, a formidable obstacle confronting the RtR when applied to business groups and MNEs: the separation of entities principle.

C. Building Block 3: Separation-of-Entities Principle

The separation-of-entities principle lies at the core of any conceptual treatment of the RtR applied to business groups. The legally inclined reader will avidly search the SRSG reports for his position on the principle of legal separation of entities. Does the SRSG mention it or wrap this key issue for the RtR in silence? Does he challenge it in order to put it aside and out of the way in search of expansive responsibilities placed on influential companies? If not, how does he exactly position it in his conceptual architecture? Those readers will be relieved that Ruggie commented on this principle explicitly. He acknowledged its role as a key organizational principle for business activity in a globalized world but also voiced his concerns.

There is acknowledgement in the SRSG's work of the worldwide presence of the principle as a matter of law and policy.[11] Furthermore, in his recent book, Ruggie wrote:

> At the very foundation of modern corporate law lies the principle of legal separation between the company's owners (the shareholders) and the company itself, coupled with its correlative principle of limited liability. … This raises a fundamental question for business and human rights: how do we get a multinational corporation to assume the responsibility to respect human rights for the entire business group, not atomize it down to its various constituent units? (Ruggie, 2013, p. 188)

The GPs contain only one reference to the legal separation-of-entities principle. The commentary to GP 26, when discussing State-based judicial mechanisms, refers to "legal barriers" and exemplifies: "The way in which legal responsibility is attributed among members of a corporate group under domestic criminal and civil laws facilitates the avoidance of appropriate accountability" (Ruggie, 2011b, p. 23). It is in his previous reports that the SRSG commented extensively on the principle. In one report he wrote:

> [T]he legal framework regulating transnational corporations operates much as it did long before the recent wave of globalization. A parent company and its subsidiaries continue to be construed as distinct legal entities. Therefore, the parent company is generally not liable for wrongs committed by a subsidiary, even where it is the sole shareholder, unless the subsidiary is under such close operational control by the parent that it can be seen as its mere agent. (U.N. Special Representative of the Secretary-General, 2008, p. 5)

The SRSG further noted that "[i]n some jurisdictions, plaintiffs have brought cases against parent companies claiming that they should be held responsible for their own actions and omissions in relation to harm involving their foreign subsidiaries" (U.N. Special Representative of the Secretary-General, 2008, p. 23). However, there are obstacles, and "[m]atters are further complicated if the claimant is seeking redress from a parent corporation for actions by a foreign subsidiary" (U.N. Special Representative of the Secretary-General, 2008, p. 23). The SRSG took note of "challenges stemming from the complexity of modern corporate structures," particularly the legal challenge regarding "the attribution of responsibility among members of a corporate group." He writes that "applying those provisions [of civil or criminal law] to corporate groups can prove extremely complex, even in purely domestic cases" (U.N. Special Representative of the Secretary General, 2010, p. 20). Then he acknowledges various legal grounds for holding core companies accountable (under principles of negligence, complicity, and agency), before concluding, "In short, far greater clarity is needed regarding the responsibility of corporate parents and groups for the purposes of remedy" (U.N. Special Representative of the Secretary General, 2010, p. 21).

1. Separation of entities and shareholder limited liability principles, in context

This subsection evaluates how the GPs deal with the principles of separation of entities and limited liability. First, the precise applicability of the shareholder limited liability ('LL') principle to the MNE universe needs to be explained. Shareholder LL is often referred to as a corollary of the legal separation-of-entities principle; however, it is important to distinguish equity-based and networked-based enterprises, because two concepts are at play. On the one hand, shareholder LL applies to parent–subsidiary relations (equity relations) and protects the company that created and/or owns shares in the affiliate. It shields the parent company from liability despite its owning the subsidiary (or the subsidiary's shares) through the legal privilege of LL. On the other hand, for types of affiliates other than subsidiaries (non-equity relations), the company is not liable because these are third parties for whose conduct one has no responsibility, and the fiction of LL is not necessary or applicable. In this case, the legal separation of entities is genuine, not artificially induced through shareholder LL.

Thus the LL of shareholders (parent company) principle is relevant only in a particular organizational context, that is, in equity-based enterprises where a parent company is not liable for its subsidiaries' debts. For contract-based enterprises, it is the legal separation-of-entities principle, not shareholder LL, that shields the company from liability. Furthermore, LL is also relevant in a particular context of seeking compensation, that is, only when the assets of the affiliate appear to be insufficient to cover the damages. In that case, the plaintiff wants to access the (likely much larger) assets of the parent company (or the rest of the business group) to secure full compensation instead of being limited to the assets of the now insolvent subsidiary. In other words, the plaintiffs pursue the parent company to ensure full compensation for the damage suffered as the affiliate folds up. Hence, among all of the types of business enterprises the GPs cover, the shareholder LL principle is relevant only in equity-based groups and only when the affiliate has insufficient assets and becomes insolvent. For contract-based MNEs and subsidiaries with sufficient assets to be executed for compensation, shareholder LL is not an issue.

Showing that shareholder LL is not the key issue for RtR in the majority of CSR cases where harmed rightholders seek to hold the wider corporate group accountable requires careful consideration of the national/domestic and international/transnational litigation contexts.[12] Such CSR cases (transnational litigation cases) often involve equity-based MNEs but also can involve contract-based MNEs.[13] However, at a closer look, only in few of these cases is shareholder LL the obstacle. The problem is not the insufficient assets of the affiliate in the vast majority of transnational litigation cases. Instead, the problem is that the plaintiff cannot hold the affiliate accountable in local courts and/or the local law provides derisory compensation or fines for serious harms. Thus, the domestic legal system is unable either to justly compensate the plaintiff or to credibly deter corporate misconduct. In other words, it is an access to justice issue that compels the plaintiffs to seek justice in the courts of other states, where plaintiffs hope to get a fair hearing and fair compensation from a workable judicial system. This forces the plaintiffs to make a case against the entity in the corporate group over which the overseas courts have jurisdiction and can hold accountable – that, is the core company, meaning the parent company, the big brand or retailer, the influential company in the business enterprise that went for a strategy of subsidiarization or outcontracting. Compounding the focus on the core company is also the reality that such companies control or influence the operations of their affiliates, or at least have the capacity to do so, with negative effects.

Because transnational litigation arising in CSR cases has to do with access to justice and not insufficient assets of affiliates, the relevant issue is not the privilege of LL that shareholders (including the parent company) enjoy under corporate laws worldwide. Rather, the touchstone is the separation-of-entities principle. This is a fundamental principle of corporate law and business organization on which the existence of large corporate groups depends. For this reason the thrust of this section is to grasp firmly the organizational rather than the legal dimension of the separation-of-entities principle. Without full clarity on this aspect, the reader will not notice that the GPs skillfully framed the principle to emphasize its legal dimension with important consequences for the RtR concept; it is a skillful reductionist exercise that the SRSG performed, as will be demonstrated below. It is yet another concrete instance of reframing, a technique the SRSG used so successfully in the GPs in order to facilitate convergence of expectations.

The organizational dimension of the separation-of-entities principle is as simple to explain as it is important not to forget while discussing the RtR. The principle takes the burden off the company's managers to assess and manage the numerous risks posed by the operations worldwide and places that burden (or a significant part of it) on the managers of affiliates. The latter's managers assume risks, rights, and obligations based on the assets of the affiliate and have the responsibility and burden to manage those risks. Affiliate managers accomplish this in a number of ways, including by reducing the risks directly; by purchasing insurance; by further creating subsidiaries or contracting-out risky operations; by assuming the risk and deciding not to act in any way. The result for the business enterprise is a more efficient division of managerial tasks that allow companies to grow. As the size of business enterprises increases and their operations span more jurisdictions, this managerial burden becomes self-evident in its existence, size, and significance. While it is incontestable that companies use subsidiarization and outcontracting to externalize risks that harm rightholders, it is equally true that such separation strategies are also legitimate ways that allow enterprises to pursue risky endeavors that are socially beneficial and efficient. In sum, as the GPs apply the RtR to enterprises of varying sizes, the managerial burden is an aspect that grows in importance the larger the enterprise is.

It is here that the RtR runs into difficulties linked to its compatibility with the separation-of-entities-principle. The SRSG's RtR, through its risks-management orientation, captured in the notion of due diligence, reverses and re-imposes (at least partly) the burden to act regarding risks arising from affiliates' operations. Indeed the GPs ask companies to address adverse impacts, that is, for influential companies to prevent and mitigate impacts arising in affiliate operations. The entire Pillar 2, where the responsibility to act follows operations (not entities), is engaged in an elaborate, but straightforward, burden-shifting task. Pillar 2 works to the effect that part of the managerial burden that companies offloaded as they pursued subsidiarization and outcontracting strategies to operate worldwide has to come back to the company in the shape of a responsibility to act with due diligence.

This chapter is not engaged in an analysis of whether a shift of burden is desirable, under what circumstances it might be so, for which impacts a shift should occur, or to what extent. Rather, it just notices that due diligence and RtR function in this way in the GPs. It also asks an unavoidable question of whether the burden reversal is likely to be as unproblematic as the SRSG suggests. This is a question that any follower of the SRSG rooting for the success of the GPs wants to ask. This chapter depicts realistically the tension between the RtR and the separation of entities principle, documents the ingenious way in which the SRSG framed the issue, and tries to figure out why he proceeded in the way he did.

2. Shifting the risk-management burden: organizational contexts and likelihood

The analysis above placed the separation of entities and the limited liability principles in their proper organizational context and in a transnational accountability context. Both the legal and organizational efficiency dimensions of the separation-of-entities principle were pinpointed. The importance of the principle in any discussion about risk management and in any attempt to (partly) shift the managerial burden as Pillar 2 proposes becomes evident. The separation-of-entities principle emerges as a heavyweight challenger to the RtR. This subsection analyzes the relationship of RtR and due diligence with the separation-of-entities principle. In other words, it focuses on the separation-of-entities principle as an obstacle for RtR as applied to business groups and risk management as the approach the SRSG adopted. Ruggie wrote that "[s]eparate legal personality is rarely invoked in relation to enterprise risk management" and that the GPs provide "authoritative guidance for how to manage risks of adverse human rights impacts" (Ruggie, 2013, p. 189).

Parts I.A and II.B above established that the SRSG does not distinguish among subjects of RtR and the reasons behind that choice. Here, I distinguish tightly integrated and flatter enterprises in order to assess the real chances, the real promise of the due-diligence-, risk-management-based approach employed in the GPs. This dimension is different and should not be confused with differentiating between enterprises as either equity-based or contract-based; both types of enterprises will be covered. This will be a taxonomy exercise for the subjects of RtR that will help pinpoint where the chances of success are high or low and where the tension between the RtR and the separation-of-entities principles is acute. Therefore, it remains realistic about what incentives (legal or not) are needed to re-impose the managerial burden on the company. For both clarity in understanding Pillar 2 and for regulatory reform, such taxonomy can help.

Both equity-based and networked-based enterprises can be tightly integrated or not, meaning that affiliates might have more or less autonomy. The company may be in the position to exercise more or less control/influence over affiliates as a result. On the one hand, in more tightly integrated enterprises, the control or influence over affiliates is a given, and victims' attempts to trigger the responsibility of the controlling companies can draw on that. However, the control can be at the strategic – or general – level as distinguished from the operational level (of operations producing harm). The kind of control – strategic or operational – affects decisively the relation to the harm. In the case of strategic control, which limits the autonomy of the affiliate, responsibility can come from actions (being arguably a cause of harm in an indirect way) and arguably even for omissions to exercise control (as failure to prevent or minimize harms that were known or foreseeable by exercising influence). In the case of operational control, which governs closer-to-the-ground decisions and, thus, extinguishes the very autonomy of the affiliate (at least in relation to the harm in question), the harm is directly linked to the decision of the company. Therefore even legal liability is currently obtainable through piercing the veil in equity-based groups otherwise protected by the shareholder LL principle or by applying agency principles in contract-based enterprises.

Thus, for the most tightly integrated enterprises, where operational control is present, separation of entities poses neither an organizational nor even a legal impediment. Here, it is very easy for the GPs to speak of responsibility for a company's own conduct and draw on a do-no-harm justification for the RtR. It appears that GP 13a is readily available to cover operational control with its *cause* or *contribute* provision. On such a solid foundation for a responsibility to act, due diligence follows without constraint by any incompatibilities, because the company has actually not offloaded the managerial burden. Indeed, it chose to exercise control over affiliates' operations.

The picture changes in less tightly integrated enterprises where strategic control is present and the affiliate has a measure of operational autonomy that cannot be disregarded. The separation of entities is relevant both organizationally and legally. Indeed, the corporate veil will not be pierced based solely on a company's strategic control of an affiliate. However, one can still plausibly speak of a company's responsibility for its own conduct as it still exercised (commission) or failed to exercise (omission) influence over the affiliate. A responsibility to act can still be credibly advanced, even if not in a strictly legal way. GP 13a is available to cover strategic control, most likely with its *contribute* provision, given that the affiliate retained some autonomy. However, from an organizational efficiency perspective, there is a clear tension between the responsibility to act with due diligence prescribed by the GPs and the company's decision to offload much of the managerial burden (only strategic control is retained). One could say there is a tension more than an incompatibility that could be managed by the GPs, especially with the careful way the SRSG worked out due diligence (DD) and drew limitations on the RtR. Indeed, the presence of strategic control implies there are processes and structures already in place that are needed for strategic control, and this creates a good structural opening in which human rights DD may be plugged. Furthermore, the useful guidance the GPs provide regarding DD is able to lighten somehow the managerial burden. Indeed, Ruggie wrote, "My aim was to prescribe practical ways of integrating human rights concerns within enterprise risk-management systems. ... [T]here had been no authoritative guidance for how to manage risks of adverse human rights impacts" (Ruggie, 2013, p. 189).

On the other hand, for loosely integrated enterprises (whether equity-based or contract-based), the picture begins to change in fundamental ways. First, though, one should not assume that such loosely integrated enterprises cannot feature companies (parent company, buyer companies) causing or contributing to harm. They can be, and remain within GP 13a, responsible for their own conduct. Most commonly, such companies appear as accomplices in the harm inflicted by the main perpetrator. One recalls the numerous transnational litigation cases under the U.S. Alien Tort Statute that invoke the complicity ("aiding and abetting") of U.S.-based companies with their affiliates and other perpetrators. The company is then seen as accomplice or joint tortfeasor, and this may well attract legal liability for its own misconduct. Clearly, a company does not have to exercise strategic or operational control over an affiliate in order to cause or contribute to harm. Indeed the affiliate could be highly autonomous, or it could be a completely autonomous third party (private or even public entity). Notably, in such cases, legal separation and even shareholder LL offer no protection because they are irrelevant. This is a case of a company's responsibility for its own misconduct (affirmative conduct by contributing to harm). In the GPs, this is the case of GP 13a through its *contribute* or *cause* provisions. Needless to say, DD is fully compatible with the separation-of-entities principle, and the RtR in this case draws solidly on do no harm.

The genuine problem for the RtR appears for the loosely integrated enterprise (whether equity-based or contract-based) where the company did not cause or contribute to harm, that is, a GP 13b situation. There is neither operational nor strategic control present in this case. Here, to reflect on the relation of organizational separation of entities and risk management, one has to account for the choice of the company to pursue organizational efficiencies through subsidiarization and outsourcing that reflect genuine organizational separation. The managerial burden was offloaded, and this was done deliberately for genuine risk-management reasons. The responsibility in this situation is not based in do no harm. Further, the company's wrongful conduct in relation to harm cannot be pinpointed after reading the GPs' justificatory work. All these together make the DD prescriptions of the GPs fit uneasily with risk-management considerations, and there is a conflict with the separation-of-entities principle. The company chose not to carry the burden of managing the risks raised by affiliate's operations. The choice of the parent (holding) company was to allow subsidiaries to operate rather autonomously, and the choice of the company (the retailer or brand) was to contract out some activities by sourcing and distributing goods and services through value chains. Thus, the legal separation reflects a genuine organizational separation.

As a way of alleviating the managerial burden, the SRSG cannot rely on pre-existing processes and structures – as was the case with strategic control – in which human rights DD could insert itself; the only real thing the SRSG can count on is the usefulness of the guidance on DD he offers. So the RtR (yet to be justified conceptually by the SRSG) and the DD (offered as mere guidance) have to confront a matter of organizational efficiency on which the existence and growth of large business groups depend. From a tension between RtR and the separation-of-entities principle that could be managed the SRSG moved perilously close to an incompatibility; the RtR might well not survive the challenge. The next section analyzes the GPs' text and uncovers the "survival strategy" the SRSG devised, the way in which he managed this near incompatibility.

Summing up, based on the last two subsections, the problem for RtR and DD has become clear (shift of managerial burden), its exact location in the universe of business organizational arrangements was pinpointed (depending of the more or less integrated nature of the enterprise), and the severity of the problem was assessed (depending on the more or less autonomy the affiliate retained). The challenge for the GPs' prescriptions on DD comes from both the legal and organizational dimensions of the separation-of-entities principle. The SRSG attempted to relieve the managerial burden that he has just shifted by offering guidance on DD and by counting on processes and structures for risk-management already available in the enterprise. While commendable, the SRSG's strategy has limitations that he does not acknowledge in the GPs but that should prompt the reader to somberly reflect about existence of a mere 'tension' or something approaching 'incompatibility' between the RtR and the separation-of-entities principle.

3. Multiple reframings and drafting choices

The analysis above problematized the SRSG's risk management perspective. Ruggie explained the way he dealt with the separation-of-entities principle, stating:

> I did not set out to establish a global enterprise legal liability model. That would have been a purely theoretical exercise. My aim was to prescribe

> practical ways of integrating human rights concerns within enterprise risk-management systems. … Separate legal personality is rarely invoked in relation to enterprise risk management. But there had been no authoritative guidance for how to manage risks of adverse human rights impacts. (Ruggie, 2013, 189)

He also outlined the practical ways forward, through the concept of corporate culture and the oversight role of corporate boards of directors.[14] As we proceed with the analysis, it should be clarified from the outset that the SRSG's references to the separation-of-entities principle have nothing inaccurate in them. Not only that, but Ruggie also accounted for the weight of this principle in the business group context by referring to it as a "fundamental question for business and human rights" (Ruggie, 2013, p. 188). In dealing with this question, the SRSG adopted reframing techniques that he deployed systematically through the GPs.

The first reframing has to do with the emphasis the SRSG places on the legal separation-of-entities principle to the detriment of the equally important organizational-efficiency dimension. The SRSG tends to depict the separation of entities as a legal consideration that does not bind or constrain a SRSG mandate strategically oriented to capture and resonate with more diverse rationalities than the legal one. Ruggie chose his battlefield early on and decided not to produce a law-inspired account of corporate responsibilities. There are too many organizational arrangements, domestic legal systems filled with their own peculiarities, differing operational contexts, and industries for such an account to be workable. Thus, even though the RtR applies to MNEs, the SRSG never felt compelled to provide a scheme of attribution clarifying when a company is answerable for abuses occurring in affiliates' operations. Instead, such a major task would be one sitting properly before lawyers; would be dealt with domestically, as finding the right balance between the RtR and the separation-of-entities principle will necessarily differ depending on the domestic legal system; and would be due chronologically after the GPs were adopted and laid a foundation for the business and human rights field.

Although the SRSG correctly impressed the longevity and spread of legal separation worldwide, he did not take the reader behind the scenes of the legal separation principle. Much controversy has been taking place regarding shareholder LL. One could venture to say that the SRSG understood too well the nature of controversies. LL is a privilege, a subsidy that policymakers give to companies to stimulate their growth (Milton, 2007). It is a legal invention stimulating business growth that purportedly delivers net social benefits. Not only is LL artificially induced and smacking of privilege, but prominent economists (including law and economics scholars) (Hansmann and Kraakman, 1991; Mendelson, 2002; Harper Ho, 2012) and victim advocates alike have constantly challenged it. Critics of LL advocated for legal reforms that would eradicate or limit the applicability of LL, especially for involuntary creditors,[15] even on grounds of social inefficiency that LL produces. Such highly sophisticated attacks on LL failed to make a dent (Matheson, 2009), and the entity–liability model marches in jurisdictions across the globe (Ruggie, 2011a). That speaks volumes for the organizational efficiency and public policy considerations raised by LL and the separation-of-entities principle. The SRSG left this as a battle to be fought another day. What was more pressing for the SRSG mandate was for these organizational efficiency and public policy considerations not to disrupt the RtR in the GPs.

Turning to the second reframing, not only does the SRSG place emphasis on legal separation of entities, but he also frames it as a matter of access to remedies. As rightholders sought access to justice abroad against core companies, the separation of entities would be an important line of defense for companies denying responsibility for abuses in affiliate operations, particularly if the plaintiff could not pinpoint the company's own wrongful conduct causing harm. The SRSG accounted – accurately again – for the separation principle as an obstacle to rightholders' access to justice. No doubt mindful of the public policy considerations supporting the longevity and resilience of shareholder LL and separation-of-entities principles, the SRSG left it to states to consider lowering this obstacle and increasing access to judicial remedies for victims abroad. In his search to map and put forward in the GPs as many categories of remedies as possible – that is, state-based judicial and non-judicial grievance mechanisms and corporate operational-level mechanisms – the SRSG was naturally disinclined to expose the full range of public policy considerations. On the one hand the SRSG surely expects that human rights imperatives might counterbalance in some instances the traditional public policy objectives supporting the separation principle. On the other hand, the SRSG had no interest to let the separation discussion expand beyond the legal dimension toward public policy and soon after toward organizational efficiency aspects. When the latter is in focus, the DD concept based on risk-management will take a hit.

In this way the SRSG managed to account for some key facets of the separation-of-entities principle. The SRSG mostly emphasized the legal considerations but defined it out of the mandate's chosen way of constructing the RtR (a responsibility not outlining schemes of attribution of legal liability). The SRSG also implied the *public policy* considerations behind the principle, as he treated the separation of entities as a matter of access to judicial remedies, but limitedly, so that reconsidering/readjusting/rebalancing public policy considerations would be a battle to be fought contextually and after the SRSG mandate was concluded. What was most important for the GPs was that the *organizational efficiency* considerations were not brought under the spotlight as the clash between the responsibility to act with due diligence in GP 13b and the separation-of-entities principles would be unavoidable. *That* battle could not be left for another day, as the battles for defining legal schemes of attribution of liability and access to judicial remedies could be. The SRSG needed the silence and as high a firewall around the RtR and DD as possible to repel the charge from the separation-of-entities principle.

This brings us to the interesting drafting choice following these two reframings. The SRSG found a way to acknowledge the separation-of-entities principle, but move it as far away from the RtR and DD discussions as possible. The imperative was to get any discussion out of Pillar 2. The SRSG was ready to concede that "far greater clarity is needed regarding the responsibility of corporate parents and groups *for the purposes of remedy*" [emphasis added] (U.N. Special Representative of the Secretary General, 2010, p. 21). Following this train of thought, the GPs placed the (now legal) separation-of-entities obstacle as a matter of remedy in Pillar 3, not as an issue questioning the very existence of the responsibility to act – part and parcel of the RtR concept – in Pillar 2. The key gain for the RtR is that a major obstacle inherent in applying the RtR to MNEs gets removed from Pillar 2 and placed in Pillar 3 where it is framed as a matter of judicial remedy and of adjusting national liability regimes at a later date (post-SRSG mandate). The GPs keep the separation principle on the table but have moved it away as much as possible (in another Pillar) and framed it along two key dimensions (while de-emphasizing the third dimension of organizational efficiency).

By double reframing and ingenious drafting, the SRSG managed to insulate RtR from a devastating blow that unavoidably arises in the corporate group context. While apparently depicting a plausible account of responsibility, the SRSG managed to present the separation-of-entities principle as a feature of legal systems that hinders access to judicial remedies and is largely irrelevant ("rarely invoked") from a risk-management perspective. What the SRSG refrained from acknowledging was that this principle is much more than a legalistic obstacle. It appears to be a structural feature of business groups that raises challenges to the RtR because of the organizational efficiencies and societal wealth it creates and that ensure it strong public policy support.

4. Implications and limitations

It is the issue of efficient management of risks that is addressed here, not the issue of liability for damages. The SRSG may be correct that the enforcement aspect is a battle to be fought another day, not by the SRSG mandate and not to be settled conceptually in the GPs (in Pillar 3). Nonetheless, the organizational efficiency challenge cannot be similarly delayed. It is at the heart of Pillar 2 and has nothing to do with enforcement and liability, but with risk management and the very existence of the responsibility to act or legitimately be a bystander. And risk management is the framework that the SRSG explicitly and deliberately adopted, referring to "enterprise risk management" and providing "authoritative guidance for how to manage risks of adverse human rights impacts" (Ruggie, 2013, p. 189). The separation-of-entities principle, as a cornerstone of both organization of large business enterprises and corporate laws, will draw limitations more tightly around the RtR and DD and will follow a different dimension (tight or loose integration of the business enterprise containing less or more autonomous affiliates) than the RtR and DD concepts of the GPs indicate. As the SRSG did not elaborate this dimension in his account of RtR, it remains to commentators to keep it in mind and think more carefully about the genuine limitations of the RtR and DD concepts outlined in the GPs.

After analyzing the separation of entities principle, the picture becomes clearer. The GPs expect companies to act with DD in Pillar 2; however, this runs counter to the decision to offload the burden of managing risks related to affiliate operations. This tension is most difficult to handle in the situation of less-integrated enterprises featuring rather autonomous affiliates, be they equity-based or network-based. There is a genuine tension here that arises in a risk-management framework, not in a legal-liability or enforcement framework. The tension exists in Pillar 2, not in Pillar 3 as the SRSG encourages us to believe. As discussed above, DD is more or less compatible with diverse types of conduct in more tightly integrated enterprises and loosely integrated enterprises. The GPs ask companies to reverse (partly) the burden-offloading decision and deploy DD. Given that the SRSG did not offer a justification for RtR when the company did not cause or contribute harm, the promise that DD makes can go unfulfilled for reasons of business management reflected in the choice to offload risk management in the first instance. One is well advised to account realistically for the burden of risk management: this might draw a more severe limitation on the applicability of DD and RtR than the SRSG expects us to believe.

This analysis points to a limitation of DD as presented in the GPs: there has to be something to counterbalance the powerful incentive of organizational efficiency on which corporate groups thrive. That counterbalancing incentive cannot be a legal one under current liability regimes drawing on long-lasting corporate law and tort law principles, at least not for loosely integrated enterprises. The incentive is also unlikely to arise from adoption of new laws overriding legal separation as these laws would be criticized heavily for running counter to organizational efficiency. Nevertheless, even with legal incentives unlikely or exceptional, other incentives can come into play. The SRSG mapped them well as he tried to capture the multitude of rationalities that shape behavior: business incentives coming from social and market pressure placed on corporate groups to internalize more the risks they generate (from outside the management group) and moral imperatives acted upon voluntarily and drawing on the discretion afforded to them under corporate governance (from inside the management group).[16] Needless to say, these incentives may be present – indeed, are present – to a greater or lesser degree depending on the case at hand.

By employing reframing techniques, the SRSG ingeniously sheltered the RtR from an organizational efficiency challenge based on the separation-of-entities principle, which is unavoidable in a corporate group context, and crucially gave a demonstrable boost to the process of convergence of stakeholder expectations. For this reason, judgment should be withheld until the value of the SRSG's treatment of RtR can be assessed on two separate dimensions.

III. LOOKING BEHIND THE LABEL

As discussed earlier, my preoccupation is with the *respect* label applied on the contents (substance?) of RtR and with the insufficient justification the GPs offer to the *protect* component (the responsibility to act under GP 13b) given the tension with the separation-of-entities principle. So now, after grasping both the scale of the separation-of-entities challenge as well as the techniques the SRSG used, this Part asks the question, where is the above analysis leading the reader in the attempt to grasp the value of the RtR concept the SRSG put forward?

The reader might conclude that the RtR concept in the GPs does not solve the tension with the separation-of-entities principle and mislabels its content. Such mislabeling might encourage some to charge deliberate misrepresentation (hinting toward conceptual weaknesses and/or unacceptably far-reaching strategizing), or to more or less satisfactory approximation of content that nonetheless fails to be consequential in altering corporate behavior. Those who hoped that the SRSG's mandate would deliver more might be further aggravated in their perception that the SRSG's RtR works to move the spotlight away from some subjects of RtR (core companies of MNEs), that it overemphasizes process instead of result (effective protection of human rights), that it exudes the virtues of guidance instead of the constraints of accountability, and that more than respect should be expected from powerful companies.

This chapter puts forward an alternative take on the GPs's conceptualization of the RtR. The concept's value has to be assessed on two counts: on the one hand, its ability to deal conceptually with the situation of MNEs, wherein the separation-of-entities principle reigns and, on the other hand, its capacity to facilitate convergence of stakeholders' expectations.

A. Ability to Deal Conceptually with MNEs and Separation-of-Entities Principle

GP 13b put on the table a responsibility to act and, thus, countered the legitimate bystander option, while the commentary to GP 19 further laid down a responsibility to exercise leverage and thus foreclosed the cut-and-run approach of companies willing to distance themselves from harm fast by just ending relationships with abusive affiliates. This part of the RtR deserves conceptually a *protect* label. The SRSG should be commended for including such responsibility in his RtR. What is lacking from the GP account is a solid, principled justification for this protect component (part of the responsibility to act in GP 13b) that would enable it to stand a challenge from the separation-of-entities principle, which could well extinguish the protect component in its infancy.

What the analysis revealed was that the SRSG skillfully employed a battery of framing and drafting techniques to avoid a direct confrontation between the RtR and the separation-of-entities principle. But that leaves open the question of whether the SRSG avoided the confrontation and settled for a mere rhetorical exhortation on the protect element (GP 13b) or postponed the confrontation while meticulously preparing the ground for a latter confrontation. I would interpret Ruggie's approach as the latter. He deployed a battery of conceptual methods to develop an RtR concept of high ingenuity, fundamentally designed for a clear task: to ensure convergence of expectations and not to provide a principled, self-standing justification for the responsibility to act in GP 13b (Ruggie, 2013, p. 107).

B. Capacity to Facilitate Convergence of Stakeholders' Expectations

This thesis changes the justification equation fundamentally, as well as the assessment of the RtR concept's capacity to promote the protect element. It is not the SRSG mandate that could have ever provided a justification strong enough for GP 13b's responsibility to act to resist a challenge from the separation-of-entities principle; instead, it is the convergence of expectations that enables the avowed polycentric governance regime that would ultimately be able to support and institutionalize the responsibility to act in GP 13b and its protect element. Fundamentally, the SRSG appears to have calculated that, should the process of convergence advance, the justificatory battle around RtR would be carried in a new context where the GP 13b component would have a fairer chance against the separation-of-entities principle. His calculation clearly was that it is not worth mounting a direct conceptual attack on this principle, but instead approaching it politically by mobilizing and facilitating a social regulatory process. In my interpretation, the GPs were designed to facilitate a process that creates responsibilities that do not exist now. Indeed the RtR in GP 13b goes beyond what is currently accepted in law and business and is in tension with long-lasting considerations relevant to group organization and public policy supporting separation of entities.

The reading of the GPs that I espouse points towards an expectation of the SRSG that a responsibility to act as in GP 13b will be recognized – through a process of social regulation, possibly though not necessarily, facilitated by legal regulation – as an exception for human rights from the separation-of-entities principle. Indeed there is nothing in the SRSG reports indicating he favored, or hoped for, an enterprise theory model abolishing legal separation. Instead, GP 13b would appear as an exception from the legitimate bystander account of responsibility and would be a responsibility to act regarding abusive affiliates, just as the commentary to GP 19 indicates. How expansive that exception will be is not something that the GPs or the SRSG set out to determine. The SRSG mandate actually achieves a lot in this respect in that it ensured that the exception is on the table and, by achieving convergence and endorsement, set in motion a process that would determine the breadth of the exception. It is highly probable that the exception will end up being defined, like all exceptions, narrowly.

The SRSG commendably articulated an RtR concept of broad application and showed no inclination to predetermine the narrow contours of the exception, even though that would have resonated favorably with the business sector. Furthermore, the SRSG was also careful to design the GPs in a way that would not limit the applicability of the protect element (i.e., the responsibility to act in GP 13b) to powerful core companies in MNEs groups. Instead, by affirming a corporate responsibility to act regarding affiliates, the GPs mobilize the leverage of all companies over their partners, irrespective of the central or peripheral position of the company in the business enterprise. In addition, the GPs conceive the protect component of RtR in GP 13b as just one among other protective channels that we should not lose sight of, including state regulation under Pillar 1, self-help of victims empowered by access to grievance mechanisms under Pillar 3, and a manager's sense of professionalism and responsibility under Pillar 2. So, the SRSG positioned the responsibility to act in GP 13b in a governance context that he conceived in terms of an emerging polycentric regime (Ruggie, 2013, p. xliii).

The SRSG mandate proposes that the key to dealing with the separation of entities principle is not a Gordian-knot-cutting conceptualization of responsibility (and/or possibly followed by a push for the regulation of the enterprise liability model in law) but a good-enough, versatile concept of RtR, which is able to facilitate convergence. It is not clear what a better alternative of conceptualizing the RtR would have been. If the fate of enterprise liability theory and economists' efforts of reforming the LL regime offer any guidance, one will be hard pressed to identify a better alternative than the SRSG's in the governance context in which his mandate took place. The conceptual edifice the SRSG developed is impressive in its thrust to systematically reframe key responsibility-related concepts and to cluster them around the DD concept, which in turn would be instrumental in facilitating convergence of stakeholder expectations.

C. Potency of the Due Diligence Concept

The generic treatment of the subjects of RtR – the shift of focus from entity to operations in order to bypass jurisdictional and organizational boundaries; the stealthy redefinition of *respect* between 2008 and 2011; the renouncement of do no harm during the mandate, while still assuming the justificatory work for the RtR was completed; the emphasis on legal separation of entities instead of organizational separation; the placement of the separation principle discussion in Pillar 3 as remedy-related rather than in Pillar 2 as responsibility-related; and the insistence on the *respect* label attached to RtR despite the undeniable "protect" component – are some of the reframing and drafting maneuvers that the SRSG performed. The SRSG not only used reframing and drafting maneuvers as described above, but he also clustered them around the concept of DD instead of RtR in order to present a novel risk-management account able to guide companies rather than a classical responsibility-centered account to determine their liability. Add the simplicity of the three-pillared structure and the rather jargon-free language and the RtR concept shapes up as an elaborate package. The impact of the RtR is compounded by the way it was placed in a polycentric governance context, which the GPs and the SRSG portfolio of reports covered systematically and comprehensively to identify levers for changing corporate behavior.

This sketch implies more than saying that the SRSG grasped the potency of the DD concept and used it to sell the GPs to previously skeptical audiences by slapping the attractive DD label on RtR and CSR as we knew them. There is much more going on conceptually than that, and that might explain the unprecedented convergence of expectations – at a declaratory level – that happened in 2011. To some, the detailed textual analysis performed in this chapter might appear as speculative and textual nitpicking. One could argue that the relation between the RtR and DD has remained the same in both the 2008 and 2011 SRSG reports. Respect is the normative concept anchored in IHRL, while DD is the operational concept highly familiar to business executives, which is necessary for implementing the RtR. What this chapter calls elevation of DD is not more than a detailed elaboration of DD, which is hardly surprising given that the 2008 through 2011 SRSG mandate was expressly set up in order to operationalize[17] the more conceptual[18] Framework resulting from the 2005 through 2008 SRSG mandate (U.N. Human Rights Council, 2008).

Such a reading of the SRSG reports would merely scratch the surface. There is a subtle shift in emphasis taking place in Pillar 2, elevating the concept of *due diligence*. As Part II.A above showed, the GPs redefined what *respect* means. The SRSG kept the *respect* label from 2008, but in 2011 he stealthily moved the posts through which the DD balls could go. It looks like the definition of *respect* was expanded to make room for a concept of DD that outgrew the confines of the RtR as defined in 2008. While the 2008 responsibility to respect was single-pronged (i.e., not to infringe), the 2011 definition is double-pronged (i.e., to avoid infringing and to address impacts with which companies are involved). Thus, the presentation of the RtR as a responsibility to act rather than as a negative obligation began elevating the concept of DD in the economy of Pillar 2. Actually the reader finds the term *due diligence* mentioned in the very definition of RtR in 2011, as the GPs state that "the corporate responsibility to respect human rights, which means that business enterprises should *act with due diligence* [emphasis added] to avoid infringing on the rights of others and to address adverse impacts with which they are involved" (Ruggie, 2011b, p. 4).

Furthermore, GP13b's clear reference to RtR being triggered without a company contributing to affiliates' misconduct is absent from the 2008 Framework. This clarification actually appeared expressly only in a 2010 paper submitted to the OECD, which was hosting a roundtable on supply-chain responsibility (Ruggie, 2010). In the 2011 GPs, the RtR did acquire a protect component, which has been introduced stealthily, without openly wearing a *protect* label and apparently with limited efforts of justification from the SRSG. One could say that, when it comes to the protect component, as well as GP 13b in its entirety, the responsibility to respect works in the GPs as a label putting to rest company fears that unreasonably much is expected from business, while the DD concept delivers the cleverly disguised punch.

Reading the SRSG reports issued throughout the years suggests that the concept of DD cannot be seen merely as an operationalization-related concept in Pillar 2, as the implementation counterpart of RtR. Instead, it is a concept that works to expand RtR to encompass a protect component and shelter the RtR from a deadly blow from the separation-of-entities principle that jeopardized the very existence of a large part of the RtR. The DD approach the SRSG employed shelters the RtR in a twofold manner. First, it emphasizes the risk-management side of respecting rights and offers guidance in ways that ease the burden on managers seeking to "know and show" that they respect human rights. As the GPs provide authoritative guidance on risk management (Ruggie, 2013, p. 189), the DD approach makes a direct contribution to repelling the challenge from the separation-of-entities principle. Unfortunately, it is also only partly effective, as DD cannot justify the existence of an RtR but, at most, can only ease the burden for companies contemplating the voluntary adoption of the RtR. Second, and more interestingly, DD shelters the RtR by aiming to facilitate convergence of stakeholder expectations and governance regime evolution. If this aim is realized, the RtR will have more chances in a confrontation with the separation principle at a later date when the battlefield had changed. This is the indirect contribution that DD makes to the existence of the RtR.

The separation-of-entities principle is the iceberg in front of the RtR when this is applied to MNEs. The SRSG devised a concept of RtR able to navigate around the iceberg rather than crash into it. Crucially, the SRSG's reframing and drafting methods were employed not to build that elusive justificatory foundation under the RtR that would almost miraculously have made stakeholders finally agree on that unique justification of corporate responsibilities. Rather, the methods were used to secure a process of convergence. DD was the instrumental concept uniquely able to facilitate that process. In this light, DD is more than an attractive label and a concept encompassing the implementation stage of RtR. If GP 13b and the leverage paragraphs in the commentary to GP 19 did not exist, it is true that DD would have been just a fancy label. If the SRSG mandate were not deliberately and explicitly designed to reverse polarization and facilitate convergence of stakeholder expectations in a polycentric regime and if the SRSG did not spend half of his team's time selling the GPs to key institutions (Ruggie, 2013, pp. 159–66), it is also true that DD would have been a mere label, a well-known, hardly original term guiding implementation in yet another soft law document.

What we have witnessed in the 2011 GPs was a reversal in importance in the relationship between RtR and DD. As we saw throughout this article, the SRSG reframed key concepts and terms in the CSR discourse and clustered them around DD instead of clustering them around responsibility. This highly ingenious and conceptual maneuver delivers effects salutary for SRSG purposes, namely, to begin the convergence of stakeholder expectations and to lose the baggage that crippled other mandates bent on responsibility, which required precision on the responsibility's justification, subject, content and limits, and reviewer of compliance. Ruggie found the voice he was searching for in the early years as SRSG by focusing on sound process rather than responsibility. More than a fancy label applied on the RtR concept, DD came to redefine the very content of respect and offered the vehicle to try to shelter the RtR from a deadly challenge from the separation principle. DD became the key organizing concept for Pillar 2, able to facilitate the convergence of stakeholder expectations.

D. Post-GPs Developments

The elevation of the DD concept in Pillar 2 apparently created a new dynamic in how the corporate responsibility is conceptualized in both its existence and scope and how it is presented to stakeholders. The SRSG made a strategic bet that the conceptual match of operations and DD, not entity and responsibility, holds the key to the deadlock in CSR. This strategy surely paid off in facilitating the U.N. organizations' endorsement of the GPs. Is this strategy also able to deliver dividends in the post-GPs period, at the implementation stage of this groundbreaking U.N. instrument? In other words, does the SRSG strategy seem promising to facilitate regime building and consolidation, given that the issue that the SRSG skillfully dodged – the justification of a responsibility to act in GP 13b with a strong protect component in light of the separation-of-entities principle – is bound to re-emerge?

The SRSG aimed both to provide guidance on risk management and to gain multistakeholder endorsement. In this way the GPs stabilized expectations of what respecting human rights means. This in itself has important and welcome implications in destabilizing the incentives and enforcement. New actors and new synergies might become involved and in a more forceful manner after being stimulated and enabled by these newly stabilized expectations. The SRSG unequivocally counts on this happening. The mapping of remedies in Pillar 3 is illustrative, as is Ruggie's talk of a polycentric regime for CSR in a global governance context. For Ruggie, "[T]he GPs needed to be carefully calibrated: pushing the envelope, but not out of reach" (Ruggie, 2013, p. 107). This chapter's thesis is that the SRSG developed the RtR concept the way he did in order to postpone the justification of RtR and instead immediately stimulate convergence. And, in fact, the GPs have strategically postponed the justificatory battle. Although Ruggie set up his mandate to formulate a conceptual foundation for CSR, he delivered an RtR taxonomy and an RtR concept for convergence. He must have realized early on that the mandate could not deliver the conceptual foundation for an RtR prevailing over the separation-of-entities principle.

Nobody in the CSR community, not even Ruggie himself, ventured to foresee the success of the RtR and GPs in terms of implementation. This article explains one reason why this is indeed impossible to do: the responsibility contained in GP 13b is a true exception from the separation-of-entities principle. Like all exceptions, it will need its own justification, and its scope will be defined narrowly and contextually. The SRSG opened the door for this exception and skillfully assured it a place at the table; whether its justification will be provided and its scope will be not so narrowly defined to be practically irrelevant depends on the continuing convergence process that the GPs have set in motion. As Ruggie wrote, "Only time will tell if the Guiding Principles actually generate their intended regulatory dynamic" (Ruggie, 2013, p. 172).

IV. CONCLUSIONS

This chapter examined the application of the RtR to business groups and networks, especially multinational enterprises, and dissected the approach the SRSG took to bypass a high obstacle in his quest to establish an ambitious and properly broad concept of corporate responsibilities. The main thesis advanced herein is one that the Ruggie expressly denies, namely, that the RtR has a protect component. Thus, a part of the responsibility of a company that did not cause or contribute to harm to act as required under GP 13b has the demonstrable nature of a responsibility to protect human rights. The analysis not only substantiated this claim but also examined why and how the SRSG constructed the RtR in the way he did. The "why" is explained by the fundamental challenge coming from the separation-of-entities principle, unavoidable when the RtR is applied to multi-entity business enterprises. The analysis of the "how" reveals the SRSG systematically reframed concepts, employed ingenious drafting techniques, used silence strategically, and fully capitalized on the strength and appeal of an approach delivering operational and practical guidance.

Another thesis put forward herein is that, in the ingenious intellectual edifice the SRSG erected for the RtR, it is the concept of DD not that of responsibility that does the intellectual heavy lifting. DD should not be seen as an attractive label stuck to the implementation stage of the RtR; on the contrary, DD is instrumental in eventually justifying the existence and broad scope of the RtR as defined in GP 13b. The responsibility under GP 13b is currently so weakly justified as to be existentially threatened by a blow from the separation-of-entities principle. What the SRSG fundamentally did about this problem was to employ the power of the DD concept (with its risk-management connotations and guidance as the stated aim) to facilitate convergence of stakeholder expectations. The SRSG postponed the battle between the RtR in GP 13b and the separation-of-entities principle. Through the methods mentioned above and other ways, the SRSG meticulously worked on dismantling conceptual hurdles placed in the path of convergence and evolution of the CSR field. Once that began happening the clash would unfold on more favorable terms for the RtR and an exception from the separation-of-entities principle would be more likely to be accepted and institutionalized. The justificatory inadequacy currently plaguing the RtR in GP 13b would have been remedied.

In this plan, DD plays first violin. Not only does it play comforting notes of pragmatism, familiarity, guidance, and reasonableness to weary corporate executives, but it also crucially allows the SRSG to cluster around it key concepts that he worked on with framing and drafting methods. The way the SRSG managed to move the center of gravity from RtR to DD is remarkable. It is this shift of the center of gravity that allowed Ruggie to get rid of the baggage with which a responsibility-based elaboration inevitably comes, because it requires precision on the responsibility's justification, subject, content, and limits, as well as reviewer of compliance. In the GPs, the relation between RtR and DD has been reversed. It is the RtR that became the label for DD. Rather than a mere fancy label stuck to the implementation stage of the RtR, DD became the concept instrumental in achieving convergence and, thus, eventually in establishing the secure existence of a properly broad RtR. In turn, the RtR became a mere taxonomy device in the GPs.

Is the SRSG's strategy a masterful break of deadlock or a fleeting illusion of success? Ruggie aimed to construct during his mandate an "authoritative focal point around which the expectations and actions of relevant stakeholders could converge" (Ruggie, 2011b, p. 3). Judging by the endorsements the GPs have received, the SRSG managed spectacularly well. Still, what does the consensus around the GPs mean specifically on this issue of a company responsibility to act in GP 13b? Is the convergence of expectations real and profound or are disputes bound to explode after the declaratory stage is consumed, when action and actual implementation are required? Given that this is a foundational issue – that of deciding whether a company has to act or, to put it differently, that of a company legitimately remaining passive like the legendary tort law's cigar-smoking bystander watching someone drown – future disputes are unavoidable. The battle of the RtR with the separation of entities principle was not won, but was avoided and postponed to a date when the CSR field would have evolved and looked more favorable for the RtR. So the current consensus is bound to be severely tested precisely on the situation covered by GP 13b. It will be interesting to see whether Ruggie's strategy will play out in a way that makes the current weaknesses in the justification of RtR a moot point.

NOTES

* The feedback received from the anonymous reviewer, as well as Jonathan Bonnitcha and Sune Skadegård Thorsen, is gratefully acknowledged. Also my thanks go to the participants in the seminar organized by Professor Robert Bird at UConn in May 2013 for rewarding discussions.

1. Ruggie (2013, pp. xxxvi–xlii; 3–19) recounts the emblematic cases.
2. The SRSG and his team provided a definition of due diligence in the Interpretive Guide (U.N. Office of the High Commissioner for Human Rights, 2012, p. 6).
3. For example, the GPs prevent one from arguing that only large (core) companies have responsibility for affiliates' misconduct while entities at the periphery of the enterprise have no responsibility.
4. For example, one cannot maintain that appropriate action for entities at the periphery of the enterprise is limited to ending relationships; if leverage over partners exists, or could be increased, it has to be exercised.
5. The SRSG team's "Interpretive Guide" to the RtR included a discussion – in answer to the question "Do enterprises have any additional human rights responsibilities?" –

of its conception of when responsibilities extend, in exceptional circumstances, beyond respect (U.N. Office of the High Commissioner for Human Rights, 2012, p. 14).

6. Actually, at a September 2011 conference in London, after the GPs were endorsed in the Human Rights Council, I was present to hear a member of the SRSG team insist that the do-no-harm explanation was deliberately excluded from the GPs and should be seen as obsolete.
7. The corporate responsibility to respect human rights "means that business enterprises should *act* with due diligence to avoid infringing on the rights of others and to address adverse impacts with which they are involved" (Ruggie, 2011b, p. 4).
8. In a previous piece, I discussed more thoroughly the RtR as a responsibility to act (Mares, 2010, pp. 69–77).
9. As GP 11 states, "Addressing adverse human rights impacts requires taking adequate measures for their prevention, mitigation and, where appropriate, remediation" (Ruggie, 2011b, p. 13).
10. Subsidiaries are companies "owned" partially or fully by a parent company. In such equity-based relationships the parent owns shares in the subsidiary.
11. A multijurisdictional comparative report observed that "[s]ome form of 'separate legal personality' and 'limited liability' exist in all of the 39 jurisdictions" and concluded that "most of the surveyed jurisdictions have similar approaches to the concepts of separate legal personality and limited liability – it is rare for the 'corporate veil' to be pierced" (Ruggie, 2011a, pp. 10, 14).
12. Most such cases are litigated in the US under the Alien Tort Statute and before English courts applying tort law.
13. The Legal Accountability portal of the Business & Human Rights Resource Center provides exemplary cases (Corporate legal accountability portal, n.d.).
14. Ruggie advances two broad approaches: first, the concept of corporate culture, which can be recognized in law and policy and, second, the role of corporate boards, which should exercise oversight over human rights risks as part of their fiduciary responsibility to the company (Ruggie, 2013, pp. 190–2).
15. Involuntary creditors would be those harmed by corporate activities making a claim in tort law (Muchlinski, 2012).
16. Such discretion is epitomized by the business judgment rule and judicial self-restraint in second-guessing the wisdom of managerial decisions (Mares, 2008, pp. 40–52).
17. The Human Rights Council's Resolution 8/7 in 2008 asked the SRSG "to 'operationalize' the Framework – that is, to provide concrete and practical recommendations for its implementation" (Ruggie, 2011b, p. 4).
18. The 2008 Framework presents "a conceptual and policy framework to anchor the business and human rights debate, and to help guide all relevant actors" (U.N. Special Representative of the Secretary-General, 2008, p. 1).

REFERENCES

Blumberg, P. (1993), *Multinational Challenge to Corporation Law: The Search for a New Corporate Personality*. New York, NY: Oxford University Press.

Corporate legal accountability Portal (n.d.), "Business and Human Rights Resource Centre", retrieved from http://www.business-humanrights.org/LegalPortal/Home.

Hansmann, H. and R. Kraakman (1991), "Toward unlimited shareholder liability for corporate torts", *Yale Law Journal*, *100*(7), 1879–934.

Harper Ho, V. (2012), "Theories of corporate groups: Corporate identity reconceived", *Seton Hall Law Review*, *42*(3), 879–952.

Mares, R. (2010), "A gap in the corporate responsibility to respect human rights", *Monash University Law Review, 36*(3), 33–83.

Mares, R. (2008), *The Dynamics of Corporate Social Responsibilities*, Leiden, The Netherlands: Martinus Nijhoff Publishers.

Matheson, J. H. (2009), "The modern law of corporate groups: An empirical study of piercing the corporate veil in the parent-subsidiary context", *North Carolina Law Review 87*(4), 1091–156.

Mendelson, N. A. (2002), "A controller-based approach to shareholder liability for corporate torts", *Columbia Law Review, 102*(5) 1203–303.

Milton, D. (2007), "Piercing the corporate veil, financial responsibility, and the limits of limited liability", *Emory Law Journal, 56*(5), 1305–82.

Muchlinski, P. (2012), "Implementing the new UN corporate human rights framework: Implications for corporate law, governance, and regulation", *Business Ethics Quarterly*, *22*(1), 145–77.

Ruggie, J. G. (2013), *Just Business: Multinational Corporations and Human Rights*, New York, NY: W.W. Norton & Co.

Ruggie, J. G. (2011a, May 23), "Human rights and corporate law: Trends and observations from a cross-national study conducted by the special representative", Addendum 2 to the Report, U.N. Document A/HRC/17/31/Add.2

Ruggie, J. G. (2011b, Mar. 21), "Guiding principles on business and human rights: Implementing the United Nations "protect, respect and remedy" framework: Report of the special representative of the secretary-general on the issue of human rights and transnational corporations and other business enterprises", U.N. Document A/HRC/17/31.

Ruggie, J. G. (2010), "The corporate responsibility to respect human rights in supply chains", (Discussion Paper, 10th OECD Round Table Discussion on Corporate Responsibility). Retrieved from http://www.oecd.org/investment/mne/45535896.pdf.

U.N. Commission on Human Rights, Sub-Commission on the Promotion and Protection of Human Rights (2003, Aug. 26), "Norms on the responsibilities of transnational corporations and other business enterprises with regard to human rights", U.N. Document E/CN.4/Sub.2/2003/12/Rev.2.

U.N. Committee on Economic, Social and Cultural Rights (2009, Dec. 21), "General comment no. 21: Right of everyone to take part in cultural life (art. 15, para. 1(a), of the International Covenant on Economic, Social and Cultural Rights)", U.N. Document E/C.12/GC/21.

U.N. Human Rights Council (2008, June 18), "Mandate of the special representative of the secretary-general on the issue of human rights and transnational corporations and other business enterprises", HRC Res. 8/7. U.N. Document A/HRC/RES/8/7.

U.N. Office of the High Commissioner for Human Rights (2012), "The corporate responsibility to respect human rights: An interpretive guide", U.N. Document HR/PUB/12/02.

U.N. Special Representative of the Secretary-General (2011, Feb. 11), "Recommendations on follow-up to the mandate", retrieved from http://www.business-humanrights.org/media/documents/ruggie/ruggie-special-mandate-follow-up-11-feb-2011.pdf.
U.N. Special Representative of the Secretary-General (2010, April 9), "Business and human rights: Further steps toward the operationalization of the "protect, respect and remedy" framework: Report of the special representative of the secretary-general on the issue of human rights and transnational corporations and other business enterprises", U.N. Document A/HRC/14/27.
U.N. Special Representative of the Secretary-General (2008, April 7), "Protect, respect, remedy: a framework for business and human rights: report of the special representative of the secretary-general on the issue of human rights and transnational corporations and other business enterprises, delivered to the human rights council", U.N. Document A/HRC/8/5.
U.N. Special Representative of the Secretary-General on the Issue of Human Rights and Transnational Corporations and Other Business Enterprises (2006, Feb. 22), "Promotion and protection of human rights: Interim report of the special representative of the secretary-general on the issue of human rights and transnational corporations and other business enterprises", U.N. Document E/CN.4/2006/97.

2. Human rights reporting as self-interest: The integrative and expressive dimensions of corporate disclosure

Stephen Kim Park

Respect for international human rights increasingly hinges on awareness and knowledge concerning the activities of multinational corporations (MNCs) and their impacts. Concern about the effects of global business has led to calls to use mandatory disclosure to advance social goals, such as international human rights and environmental sustainability, under the rubric of corporate social transparency (Williams, 1999). By requiring MNCs to monitor their compliance with law and disclose the social effects of their activities, mandatory disclosure regimes place MNCs front and center in the regulation of international business.

The use of mandatory disclosure may be viewed as a means to bridge the processes of human rights due diligence and human rights reporting. Without sufficiently thorough human rights due diligence, corporate reporting will not adequately capture the human rights implications of MNCs' conduct. Just as importantly, without sufficiently robust reporting mechanisms, information gathered through internal corporate due diligence will be of no use if stakeholders are not adequately apprised of its existence and relevance. A failure to integrate due diligence and reporting impedes the ability of MNCs to respect human rights, regardless of their commitment to its principles. This raises a question that is largely missing from public debate on the relationship between business and human rights: how do we create mandatory disclosure regimes to meet the needs of MNCs themselves?

To answer this question, this chapter presents the concept of constructive discourse to help MNCs identify ways in which they might benefit from mandatory disclosure. Drawing on the insights of constructivist political theory and reflexive law, constructive discourse seeks to orient the purpose, scope, and application of the process of disclosure inward, to the firm. Disclosure as constructive discourse serves two distinct, yet interrelated purposes: one substantive and integrative, the other procedural and expressive. First, it identifies how the substance of information that MNCs collect in order to comply with mandatory disclosure requirements may help MNCs translate international human rights doctrine into operational scripts, with which MNCs can conceptualize the human rights impacts of their activities and integrate the values of business and human rights. Second, it shows how the interactive process through which MNCs share disclosed information may help them express their intent and adherence to global human rights principles, which then encourages and rewards further efforts by MNCs to respect human rights.

In the past couple of decades, MNCs have participated in the creation of a variety of voluntary reporting mechanisms with human rights and related social objectives, such as the Global Reporting Initiative (GRI) and the Extractive Industries Transparency Initiative (EITI). These public-private partnerships and industry-based initiatives contemplate the disclosure of certain specified social and environmental information on a voluntary basis. In contrast, this chapter focuses on mandatory disclosure regimes implemented by government regulators that are intended to address specific, narrowly defined social policy objectives. Due to its global scope and robustness, U.S. federal securities law is viewed as a particularly powerful mandatory disclosure regime to address international human rights. This is evident in arguably the most prominent example of human rights reporting required by U.S. law: the "conflict minerals" disclosure provisions in Section 1502 of the Dodd-Frank Wall Street Reform and Consumer Protection Act of 2010.

This chapter is organized as follows. Part I provides an overview of the purposes of corporate disclosure and mandatory disclosure regimes, in particular describing the appeal and limitations of securities disclosure as a means of promoting corporate social transparency. Part II outlines the concept of constructive discourse as an alternate construct of corporate social transparency, focusing on how MNCs may be able to use mandatory disclosure to their benefit. Part III applies the concept of constructive discourse to the disclosure provisions in Section 1502 of the Dodd-Frank Act. Part IV concludes by suggesting potential areas for future empirical research and reform.

I. HUMAN RIGHTS AND CORPORATE DISCLOSURE

A. The Purposes and Limits of Disclosure

Public disclosure is based on the power of information to influence private behavior. Rationales for disclosure may be understood as a balancing of public and private interests on instrumental and intrinsic grounds.

On an instrumental level, public disclosure may enhance social utility and, under certain conditions, also benefit firms. Regulators, along with investors, customers, and other parties with a direct economic interest in a firm, are commonly viewed as the primary beneficiaries of disclosure. The concept of corporate social responsibility (CSR) expands the scope of an MNC's obligations to a broader set of parties that are affected by its decisions, collectively referred to as stakeholders. Accordingly, disclosure provides these external parties with information necessary to reduce risks that they may face due to their direct or indirect interactions with a firm. As famously stated by Supreme Court Justice Louis Brandeis (1914, p. 92), "Sunlight is said to be the best of disinfectants; electric light the most efficient policeman."

Firms, particularly corporations, may have various incentives to provide information on a voluntary basis. From the perspective of firms as disclosers, the costs of disclosure are proportionate to the amount, scope, and/or level of detail of information provided to users while the benefits of disclosure decline as the amount of information disclosed increase (Fung, Graham, Weil, and Fagotto, 2006). If private optimality converges with social optimality, then disclosure will lead to the dissemination of all information that the public would find beneficial (Fox, 1999). This convergence between private and public interest does not necessarily mean that a firm derives the same benefits from disclosure that the public does – just that its cost-benefit analysis reaches the same result. Privately realized benefits of disclosure may be derived in a variety of ways. Investors may value a corporation's willingness to disclose information regarding its social impacts, resulting in shareholder support of management and increased interest from prospective investors. Disclosure may also improve morale among conscientious customers and employees (Stevelman, 2011). As a result of these factors, competitive pressures among corporations, as well as proactive efforts to avoid mandatory disclosure, may increase the quality and quantity of voluntary disclosure.

On an intrinsic level, public disclosure may itself have value as a commitment to transparency, a core element of CSR (Dhooge, 2004).

CSR broadens the scope of a corporation's obligations from a single-minded focus on maximizing its shareholders' return to capital to a broader set of ethical, social, and environmental considerations affecting its stakeholders (Bradford, 2012). Corporations may subscribe to CSR principles based on the perceived value of certain public goods, such as the environment (Case, 2005). Similarly, disclosure practices based on the social utility of certain information may be applied to human rights (Dhooge, 2004). Disclosure practices based on CSR obligations are typically implemented through adoption of codes of conduct, statements of best practices, industry guidelines, and similar legally non-binding instruments (Dhooge, 2004). Many MNCs have officially declared their adherence to voluntary CSR initiatives. Arguably the most ambitious, global, and inclusive initiative in the area of human rights is the Guiding Principles on Business and Human Rights: Implementing the United Nations "Protect, Respect and Remedy" Framework (U.N. Special Representative of the Secretary-General, 2011). Spearheaded by the Special Representative of the United Nations Secretary-General, John Ruggie, the Protect, Respect and Remedy Framework establishes a unified platform for implementing the human rights obligations of states and MNCs. A core element is the "know-and-show" paradigm, which requires MNCs to identify and communicate the human rights impact of their activities (Ruggie, 2013). Towards this end, the Protect, Respect and Remedy Framework emphasizes the importance of communication between MNCs and stakeholders through various modes of reporting, including corporate disclosure practices. Guiding Principle 21 states that reporting of adverse human rights impacts and responses must be accessible, sufficient, and not pose risks to any parties (U.N. Special Representative of the Secretary-General, 2011, p. 20).

B. U.S. Federal Securities Law as a Mandatory Disclosure Regime

Market forces or CSR, however, often do not provide sufficient incentives to voluntarily disclose, thereby leading to the systemic under-reporting of information. Firms may be deterred from disclosing due to the direct costs of gathering, analyzing, drafting, and disseminating information (Ripken, 2006). Indirect costs – which may include loss of proprietary information and the exploitation of information regarding a corporation's activities by its competitors, suppliers, or customers – may also discourage a socially optimal level of disclosure (Fox, 1997). Further, firms that engage, or are complicit, in violations of human rights may rationally choose not to disclose due to the possibility of incurring significant reputational costs or civil liability. Voluntary disclosure governed by codes of conduct and similar non-binding regimes are often hampered by a lack of operational utility due to vague, undefined terms and a lack of implementation and independent monitoring mechanisms (Dhooge, 2004). Due to these factors, voluntary corporate disclosure based on the convergence of public and private utility maximization and/or adherence to CSR principles is too inconsistent to serve as the sole basis for disclosure of the human rights impacts of business.

To address these shortcomings, mandatory disclosure is cited as a more robust means to ensure sufficient reporting by businesses. U.S. federal securities law is an example of "targeted transparency", a term used to collectively describe "public policies that … mandate disclosure by corporations or other actors of standardized, comparable, and disaggregated information regarding specific products or practices to a broad audience in order to achieve a specific public policy purpose" (Fung, Graham, and Weil, 2007, pp. 37–8). Due to the size of the U.S. capital markets, it has traditionally been the dominant regulatory regime in the international financial system (Brummer, 2011). Moreover, the scope of U.S. federal securities law – covering many of the largest and most prominent U.S. and foreign MNCs in the world – arguably makes it the single most influential and comprehensive form of business regulation. Accordingly, a brief summary of U.S. federal securities law is helpful in order to understand the role of mandatory disclosure in the business world.

Instead of "merit regulation" in which regulators determine the soundness of securities sold to the public, U.S. federal securities law seeks to ensure that issuers of securities disclose sufficient information so that investors can make their own decisions (Scott and Gelpern, 2012).[1] The Securities Act of 1933 (Securities Act) governs the disclosure requirements related to the issuance of securities in the primary markets, predominantly by requiring firms that wish to sell securities in the U.S. market to register with the SEC through the submission of a publicly available registration statement. The Securities Exchange Act of 1934 (Exchange Act) governs the trading of securities in secondary markets, and imposes ongoing disclosure requirements on an issuer through the filing of periodic reports with the Securities and Exchange Commission (SEC) that are made available to the public. Both registration statements under the Securities Act and periodic reports under the Exchange Act must include extensive information regarding an issuer's management, risks, operations, and financial condition, among other information.

To balance the benefits of disclosure to the market with its costs to issuers, the substantive scope of securities disclosure is circumscribed by the concept of materiality. Generally, corporate issuers are only required to disclose a given piece of information if there is a substantial likelihood that a reasonable investor would consider it important in making an investment decision. This provides a market-oriented test for determining what a corporation must disclose – i.e., what an investor would consider important information in an arm's length transaction to buy or trade a security.

C. Mandatory Disclosure as a Means of Achieving Social Goals

The concept of corporate social transparency broadens the scope of mandatory disclosure to account for information about the social, political, and environmental effects of corporate action (Williams, 1999). The use of mandatory disclosure to facilitate corporate social transparency is a response to a gap in global governance. On the one hand, the increasing scope of cross-border business activity and growing public awareness to the social impact of global business have coincided with calls for "shareholder democracy" through the exercise of shareholder rights by socially responsible investors (Stevelman, 2011). On the other hand, the absence of a global business regulator, the rejection by governments and MNCs of substantive requirements promulgated by international treaties, and inconsistent enforcement of social mandates through domestic regulation have spurred interest in transplanting the principles of mandatory disclosure to non-economic public issues.

How might U.S. federal securities law be used to advance international human rights? With respect to social concerns such as human rights, mandatory disclosure may influence corporate behavior by compelling corporate social transparency. Corporate management is motivated by reputational concerns that are triggered by the reaction from the market or the general public to disclosed information (Lynn, 2011). Reputational concerns may overlap with a corporation's desire to maintain share value; however, reputation may also be based on social norms. Mandatory disclosure of adverse human rights impacts, in particular, may have a salient effect on corporate conduct if corporate managers – or, for that matter, investors – seek to avoid moral disapprobation and act accordingly to avoid engaging in conduct that violates social norms (Skeel, 2001). That is, even if information that issuers disclose does not lead to any legal sanctions under U.S. federal securities law, issuers may seek to change their behavior if they believe that such information would lead to non-legal sanctions, such as reputational harm.

Historically, U.S. federal securities law accounted for the social and environmental impacts of an issuer's activities insofar as the disclosure of such impacts would be necessary to protect investors' financial interests

(Eisner, 2004). Under this principle, an issuer is not required to disclose activities that may have adverse social or environmental implications unless such conduct constitutes a material business risk. Regulation S-K,[2] which requires disclosure of certain material environmental and social information, reflects this risk-oriented approach to disclosure.

This, however, may be changing with the implementation of the "conflict minerals" disclosure provisions in Section 1502 of the Dodd-Frank Wall Street Reform and Consumer Protection Act of 2010 (Dodd-Frank, § 1502). Section 1502 requires issuers to report annually on their internal measures to exercise due diligence and chain of custody of minerals mined in the Democratic Republic of the Congo (DRC) or adjacent countries that have historically been linked to civil strife, human rights abuses, and violence. Unlike Regulation S-K and other reporting requirements under U.S. federal securities law, Section 1502 addresses a narrowly defined social objective through mandatory disclosure of specific non-financial information for the benefit of a range of non-investor stakeholders. It uses "information-forcing" rules, whose purpose is to move information from the actor best situated to hold or obtain such information (i.e., the firm) to the actors most likely to use it for the public good (i.e., regulators and civil society) (Ochoa and Keenan, 2011). Information disclosed under Section 1502 permits corporate outsiders (e.g., socially responsible investors, non-governmental organizations) to independently monitor and scrutinize corporations' internal management and decisionmaking (Backer, 2011). Section 1502 arguably constitutes the most prominent use of mandatory disclosure as an express means to further international human rights under U.S. federal securities law. Section 1502 is analyzed in detail in Part III of this chapter.

D. The Limitations of Mandatory Disclosure to Influence Corporate Conduct

Mandatory disclosure is typically premised on the interactive effects between disclosers and users triggered by the obligation to disclose, as shown in Figure 2.1.

Distinct functions arising out of the disclosure processes can be disaggregated and individually identified (Malloy, 2005). First, mandatory disclosure may enhance the ability of users of disclosed information vis-à-vis disclosers by reducing information asymmetries between managers and shareholders, thereby lowering agency costs that shareholders would otherwise incur to monitor corporations (Ripken, 2006). In addition, mandatory disclosure may alter the behavior of disclosers seeking to avoid the negative reaction of users (e.g., investors selling off

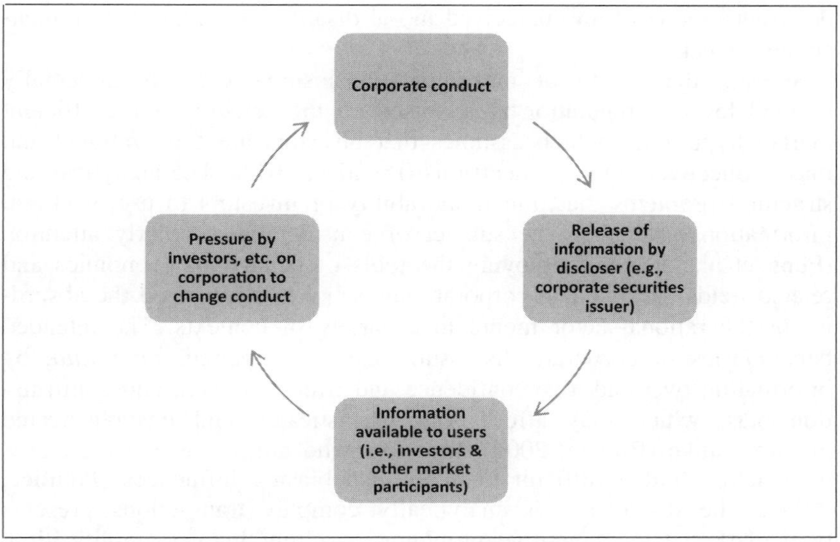

Figure 2.1 Mandatory disclosure regimes: compelled action and discretionary reaction

securities, customers declining to buy a product). This ex ante effect may be seen in the ways that managers might act more diligently and honestly due to the possibility of their actions being subject to public scrutiny (Ripken, 2006).

However, mandatory disclosure regimes may fall short in certain ways, as further described below, due to (i) weak compliance effects on disclosers; (ii) inconsistent informational value to users; and (iii) uncertain or even perverse incentives on disclosers.

First, mandatory disclosure may not sufficiently deter misconduct or incentivize virtuous behavior by firms. Disclosure in itself may not sufficiently persuade them of the need to change their *modus operandi* absent external enforcement (Ripken, 2006). Reliance on the reputational effects of disclosed information is arguably predicated on the existence of a moral community in which members share common values (Kahan and Posner, 1999; Skeel, 2001). This may pose a particular problem in respect of the activities of MNCs operating in a global, multicultural business environment, in which there may not be a commonly held sense of values regarding certain human rights principles. If MNCs have weak ties to a community and stakeholders do not have the capacity to react to disclosed information in the form of a social demand, then the deterrence value of any perceived moral disapproval might be commensurately weak.

Second, the ability of mandatory disclosure to ensure a socially optimal level of regulation is premised on the veracity of the efficient market hypothesis, which assumes that investors are fully rational and make collectively optimal decisions (Prentice, 2011). The analytical and structural problems that impair the ability of investors to use disclosed information have been the subject of considerable scholarly attention (Fung et al., 2006). Employing the tools of behavioral economics and related fields, finance and corporate law scholars have noted the absurdity of the rational actor model in a variety of contexts. The intended beneficiaries of corporate disclosure may be impaired, *inter alia*, by information overload, overconfidence and over-optimism, and confirmation bias, which may affect both sophisticated and unsophisticated investors alike (Ripken, 2006). Investors who are aware of such biases nonetheless find it difficult to undo such biasing influences (Prentice, 2011). The disclosure of analytically complex transactions presents particularly vexing cognitive problems, resulting in oversimplification, incomprehensibility, and ambiguity (Schwarcz, 2004). Aside from problems attributable to analytic complexity, the logistical complexity of analyzing complex transactions – such as organizing, sorting, and comparing enormous amounts of data – may unduly hamper the ability of investors to make use of information that they otherwise are capable of assessing (Bartlett, 2010).

On a related note, the direct costs of disclosure (such as the resources expended to translate complex and nuanced facts to a form compliant with mandatory disclosure requirements) as well as the indirect costs of disclosure (such as the concern that the dissemination of information will increase the risk of civil suits or administrative agency enforcement actions) may lead firms to use standard, cautious, and ultimately less useful language in their disclosure – i.e., the oft-maligned, but often useful, boilerplate (Schmidt, 2012; Manne, 2007).

Third, mandatory disclosure may fail to serve its purposes due to its perverse or otherwise less socially desirable incentives on disclosers. Absent a fiduciary obligation above and beyond disclosure, the very act of disclosing may free corporate agents to act in an even more self-interested way by permitting them to rationalize their behavior as morally justified (Prentice, 2011). Firms may deliberately act in a manner to satisfy disclosure requirements without making a good-faith effort to alter the substantive outcomes of their behavior (Weil, Graham, & Fung, 2013). A notorious example of this phenomenon is "greenwashing" – in which MNCs appear to promote environmental sustainability through selective positive disclosure while continuing to pollute the environment and otherwise act in violation of the spirit of sustainability (Cherry and Sneirson, 2011). A related concern arises from the possibility that unwanted conduct deterred by mandatory disclosure may lead to the worst of unintended consequences: a shift to even less desirable conduct (Manne, 2007). In the context of human rights reporting, for example, the requirement that MNCs disclose their interactions with oppressive regimes in a foreign jurisdiction could arguably deter their efforts to ameliorate human rights abuses through negotiation and persuasion or may create incentives for firms to shift their behavior towards other equally or more risky practices that are not subject to disclosure.

II. MANDATORY DISCLOSURE AS CONSTRUCTIVE DISCOURSE

A. The Concept of Constructive Discourse

The limitations of mandatory disclosure pose challenges to its use as a means to ensure corporate respect for international human rights. The distinct sets of principles that inform the business motives and the human rights aspirations of MNCs may be difficult to reconcile, thereby leading to a cognitive-like dissonance among corporate managers and agents.[3] This dissonance between MNCs' dual institutional selves – as profit maximizers, on the one hand, versus global citizens, on the other – may lead to doubt about what and how to disclose. Just as individual humans are neither pure manifestations of self-interested *homo economicus* or cooperative *homo reciprocans*, corporations as organizations must also grapple with competing allegiances.[4]

The conception of MNCs as binary, inert organizations fails to capture the catalytic potential of disclosure as social, interactive acts of MNCs. To augment the benefits of mandatory disclosure, this chapter presents the concept of constructive discourse. Constructive discourse draws on the insights of constructivist political theory and reflexive law as well as the experiences of MNCs with voluntary reporting initiatives. Whereas predominant rationales for mandatory disclosure invariably focus on the effects of external pressure on MNCs, the value of constructive discourse lies in the internal, firm-level value of disclosure. Under this concept, mandatory disclosure may help achieve the goals of human rights by facilitating MNCs' efforts to implement firm-level, internally generated change. By requiring MNCs to conceptualize their human rights obligations, a constructive-discourse approach facilitates the identification and reconciliation of the competing social values underlying human rights and international business. Therefore, ascertaining the value of disclosure depends on identifying how the act of disclosing can catalyze the corporate policymaking and self-regulation processes through which MNCs identify information concerning their human rights impacts, ascertain their significance and relevance, and reconcile them with other corporate objectives.

Mandatory disclosure as constructive discourse consists of two non-sequential, overlapping, and mutually reinforcing dimensions: an integrative dimension and an expressive dimension. The integrative dimension of constructive discourse concerns the substance of disclosed information, and what it reveals to MNCs in their capacity as disclosers. Many corporate codes of conduct, such as the United Nations Global Compact, are based on express commitments to human rights values by MNCs (Murphy, 2005). Nonetheless, there are cognitive gaps between the legalistic commitment of MNCs to human rights and their understanding of what is required to fulfill the principles set forth in codes of conduct (Murphy, 2005). The substance of the information that MNCs are required to disclose helps make tangible to MNCs the disjuncture between the rhetoric of MNCs and their action in respect of human rights – i.e., when confronting themselves with information regarding their conduct, MNCs may realize that they are not who they claim to be (Finnemore and Sikkink, 1998). Mandatory disclosure regimes may be viewed as "reflexion mechanisms," which facilitate internal self-critical reflection by MNCs about how to identify, substantiate, and fulfill normative understandings that they share with other MNCs and stakeholders (Teubner, 1983; Orts, 1995).

Disclosure may also provide MNCs with strategically valuable knowledge and expertise about the risks that they face in balancing business and human rights. Through the processes of collection, synthesis, and rationalization required to carry out disclosure, the underlying information is translated into the language of law. This legal formalization has two potentially transformative effects. It may broaden the perspective of local corporate managers by transforming specific, local narratives into normatively powerful international human rights. It may also facilitate the internalization of human rights norms within MNCs by making commitment to them a part of their business practices (Finnemore and Sikkink, 1998; Ruggie, 2013).

The expressive dimension of constructive discourse concerns the process through which MNCs communicate with each other as well as with stakeholders to identify and harmonize conflicts between business and human rights. The value of human rights to business is premised on the construction of organizational values in a social context, coupled with the ability of self-interested actors to persuade others and a willingness to be persuaded (Risse, 2000). As with states, the ideas, values, and beliefs of non-state actors such as MNCs may be shaped through social processes that generate shared understandings and mutual expectations (Ruggie, 1998; Finnemore and Sikkink, 1998). Processes of socialization among MNCs through their agents (i.e., senior management, influential shareholders, external legal counsel, etc.) may dictate how MNCs reconcile conflicting commitments between their "business" and "human rights" selves (Goodman and Jinks, 2004; Ochoa, 2011).

Further, MNCs can use the substance of disclosed information to generate a shared vocabulary with stakeholders to frame their normative views on how human rights objectives should be balanced with other corporate objectives (Park, 2013). By drawing from an array of particularized examples of ways in which they address the human rights impacts of their conduct, MNCs can more substantively engage in dialogue with civil society, regulators, shareholders, and other parties about what is appropriate and necessary (Abbott, 2008). In this sense, the process of communicating with external parties helps MNCs help themselves.

B. The Role of Lawyers in Constructive Discourse

The effectiveness of constructive discourse depends on the ability of MNCs to be able to engage with each other as well as with stakeholders. So how does disclosure facilitate organizational socialization by and among MNCs? The act of disclosing requires that the various divisions within MNCs coordinate with each other to create monitoring systems, implement industry best practices, modernize data collection, and strengthen internal controls and risk management functions (Bird and Dhooge, 2011). While these actions are a potential source of value to MNCs on their own terms, they also serve the purpose of signaling to other MNCs their willingness to reconcile business and human rights by following standardized, socially legitimated models of corporate behavior (Goodman and Jinks, 2004). Arguably in this vein, the proliferation of voluntary CSR certification schemes suggests that MNCs seek to expressly acknowledge their conformity to global human rights values by "joining the club" (Goodman and Jinks, 2004). In comparison to states, however, processes of socialization may require more formality and institutionalization due to the relative instability of individual MNCs (Ochoa, 2011).

The professional norms and training of lawyers are a potentially powerful mechanism to address these challenges. Disclosure hinges on the use of shared sets of beliefs and knowledge – or what is sometimes referred to as an "epistemic community". Just as international treaty making and policy coordination between governments have benefited from networks of specialists with shared beliefs in cause-and-effect relations, validity tests, and underlying principled values, corporate policymaking may benefit from the engagement of like-minded professionals who can converse in a shared vernacular (Haas, 1992). These gatekeepers are entrusted to carry out their "trust-but-verify" duties – specifically, to ensure that disclosure is honest, adequate, and complete, and to communicate the meaning of its information in a clear and even-handed manner.

In particular, lawyers in their capacities as in-house counsel to corporate issuers have a significant responsibility in determining what information should be disclosed pursuant to U.S. federal securities law, which implicates an individual, judgment-based decisionmaking process that requires a balancing of private corporate interests and the public interest (Schmidt, 2012). Further, in-house lawyers may be capable – due to their knowledge of legal lexicon, argumentation, and procedures – to communicate in the system-specific language necessary to influence corporate management (Buhmann, 2012). A key characteristic of this specific epistemic community of lawyers is that its group function and the individual obligations of its members are defined by mandatory disclosure regimes – that is, the authority of the epistemic community is driven by a combination of (i) a lawyer's professional training, (ii) externally imposed disclosure requirements to which the lawyer is subject, and (iii) the internally modulated judgment exercised by the lawyer to satisfy these externally imposed requirements in respect of a given set of facts. The effectiveness of disclosure ultimately depends on the ethical judgment of lawyers as well as their ability to control their clients (Schmidt, 2012). The effectiveness of this gatekeeping function heavily depends on the authority of in-house lawyers within a corporation, which may vary based on seniority, their relationship with senior corporate management, the deference accorded to in-house lawyers on discretionary decisions of a legal nature, and the extent to which disclosure-related duties are given instead to outside counsel. In addition, epistemic communities of corporate in-house lawyers can also serve as a forum for inducing compliance with group norms through peer pressure and reputational awards (Whitehead, 2006). Even if ties between MNCs and civil society are too weak and conflicted in many instances to constitute an epistemic community, the shared professional ties of their legal counsel may be strong enough to compel compliance through "soft" community-imposed sanctions.

C. The Strategic Benefits of Constructive Discourse

Constructive discourse may serve as a strategic corporate tool. The complexity of an MNC's relationships with its various stakeholders – defined by a web of overlapping, confusing, and sometimes conflicting legal obligations and social phenomena – leads to opportunities for mandatory disclosure to be the basis of competitive advantage (Bird, 2011). Constructive discourse may be applied strategically in a variety of ways.

A record of socially responsible disclosure practices may build trust with regulators, the investor community, and NGOs, thereby leading to potentially favorable legal treatment for MNCs. For example, regulators may grant greater autonomy to such firms in implementing internal reporting and due diligence regimes; socially conscious funds may add such firms to their selective lists of permitted investments; and NGOs may choose to share grassroots knowledge and credibility with MNCs in establishing non-profit partnerships devoted to human rights. Legal scholars define "relational contracts" as the penumbra of planning, trust, and solidarity norms that exceed the terms of the legal agreement between parties (Bird, 2011). The sharing of information, along with the attendant practices and rituals associated with such information sharing, constitute the basis for a particular kind of relationally based legal arrangement made possible by the act of disclosure.

The efficacy of corporate social transparency through mandatory disclosure may depend, at least on the margins, on the perception of MNCs that they stand to individually gain from the visibility of their efforts to properly and thoroughly disclose information regarding their human rights impacts. Therefore, the challenge is to inform MNCs of the broad-based nature of these potential gains. Voluntary CSR associations, established by MNCs in conjunction with human rights organizations and consumer groups, may play an important role in this learning process as agitators through the creation of targeted reporting and complaint mechanisms (Park, 2013). Another approach is through the use of privately trained and authorized audit and certification services to ensure corporate compliance with social standards that meet or exceed mandatory disclosure requirements. Among other objectives, third-party assurance services permit MNCs to signal to non-governmental organizations and socially responsible investors their commitment to social concerns (Blair, Williams, and Lin, 2008). The Mazars/Shift Project is an example of human rights assurance. The Mazars/Shift Project seeks to develop a twin set of standards for human rights reporting and assurance based on the Protect, Respect and Remedy Framework (Mazars and Shift, 2013). The reporting standard requires a participating company to articulate and make public its fidelity with the Protect, Respect and Remedy Framework while developing internal metrics to track its progress toward full alignment (Mazars and Shift, 2013). The assurance standard provides an external, third-party audit of the company's implementation of the Protect, Respect and Remedy Framework based on methodology developed by individual human rights assurance providers (Mazars and Shift, 2013).

III. CONSTRUCTIVE DISCOURSE IN PRACTICE: CONFLICT MINERALS REPORTING UNDER THE DODD-FRANK ACT

A. Legal Aspects and Operational Implications of Section 1502

The use of corporate social disclosure is evident in Section 1502 of the Dodd-Frank Act. Section 1502 amends Section 13 of the Exchange Act by enhancing disclosure requirements for producers of goods that include so-called "conflict minerals" from the DRC (Dodd-Frank, § 1502). The overarching purpose of Section 1502 is set out in its prologue, which states that it is intended to address:

> the exploitation and trade of conflict minerals originating in the Democratic Republic of the Congo [that are used to help] finance conflict characterized by extreme levels of violence in the eastern Democratic Republic of the Congo, particularly sexual- and gender-based violence, [that contribute] to an emergency humanitarian situation therein.

The human rights impact of conflict minerals directly and indirectly involves business (Ruggie, 2013). Local mining companies and their security providers may be directly or indirectly involved in human rights abuses, such as forced labor. Further, an array of firms – both locally based businesses and MNCs – that buy, trade, transport, process, and finance the purchase of conflict minerals may fund and thereby perpetuate the conflict in eastern Congo. Section 1502 seeks to curb the violence associated with the mining industry in the DRC and adjoining countries by exposing MNCs to public scrutiny, thereby incentivizing MNCs to implement socially responsible sourcing mechanisms. By cutting off access to mineral wealth, the ability of armed groups to fight and terrorize Congolese civilians would be diminished (Seay, 2012).

SEC reporting companies must be cognizant of the following considerations in respect of Section 1502:

> *What companies are subject to Section 1502?* Section 1502 requires companies to disclose annually whether any conflict minerals that are "necessary to the functionality or production of a product" that they manufacture originated in the DRC or any country that shares an internationally recognized border with the DRC (i.e., Angola, Burundi, Central African Republic, Republic of Congo, Rwanda, Sudan, Tanzania, Uganda and Zambia). Section 1502 designates columbite-tantalite (coltan), cassiterite, gold, or wolframite (or any of their derivatives) as conflict minerals if sourced from the DRC or contiguous countries. These minerals – commonly referred to as "3TG" (tin, tantalum, tungsten, and gold) in the mining industry – are typically acquired by MNCs indirectly through intermediaries for use in the manufacturing of a wide range of products, most notably consumer electronics (Seay, 2012; Taylor, 2012). Thus, if a company uses one or more minerals designated by Section 1502 either to produce a product *or* any such mineral is in a company product itself *and* such company is required to file mandatory reports under the Exchange Act, then the company must comply with Section 1502. There is no exception for *de minimis* use of 3TG minerals, nor grandfathering for any companies, products, or industries.
>
> *If a company is subject to Section 1502, what specific disclosure and due diligence requirements must it comply with?* If a company uses one or more 3TG minerals specified by Section 1502, it must follow a multi-step disclosure process. First, the company must conduct a "reasonable country of origin inquiry" into their source of origin. Second, on the basis of its country-of-origin inquiry, the company must explicitly state whether or not it uses conflict minerals and describe its inquiry in a special disclosure report on a new Form SD filed with the SEC. Third, if the company has determined that it uses conflict minerals, it must (a) exercise due diligence on "the source and chain of custody" of the conflict minerals and (b) arrange an independent private sector audit on the source and chain of custody of the conflict minerals through its supply chain. These measures, as applicable, must be disclosed in a Conflict Minerals Report filed with the SEC as an exhibit to Form SD.

Critics of Section 1502 raise a number of concerns. First, MNCs have criticized the costs of compliance (Woody, 2012). Its disclosure requirements involve various functions within MNCs, including legal counsel, financial reporting, audit and accounting, supply chain management and procurement, manufacturing quality control, and public relations. In addition to costs attributed to disclosure, the need to conduct supply-chain due diligence, third-party verification, external private audits, traceability schemes, and sourcing mechanisms require additional expenditures. Aside from these direct costs, it is plausible that the information disclosed by MNCs regarding their use of conflict minerals may impose a variety of indirect costs, such as economic sanctions, consumer boycotts, and potential litigation under human rights statutes (Ochoa and Keenan, 2011).

Further, Section 1502 may not satisfactorily improve conditions in the DRC. The reputational influence of conflict minerals' use is predicated on the salience of the issue with stakeholders. One way of viewing this dynamic is to consider the choices faced by consumers. Depending on the elasticity of global supply chains, there may be a trade-off between the price of a manufactured product and the use of "conflict-free" minerals. If the price differential is substantial, the benefit of using conflict free minerals will need to be commensurately higher. If Section 1502 successfully diminishes the use of conflict minerals, it may simply lead to a *de facto* embargo of all DRC minerals, in the process forcing Congolese employed in the mining industry out of work and damaging the Congolese economy (Woody, 2012).

More profoundly, critics charge that conflict minerals are a symptom of the conflict in the DRC, rather than a cause or aggravating factor, and thus "solving" the conflict minerals issue on its own terms will not end the violence. Warlords, military leaders, and foot soldiers in the ongoing civil conflict do not rely on the minerals trade to buy military equipment due to the ubiquity of weapons, and have access to other sources of revenue in the event that revenue from the conflict minerals trade ceases (Seay, 2012).

B. Conflict Minerals Reporting as Imperfect Constructive Discourse

Conflict minerals reporting under Section 1502 represents a momentous shift in the role of mandatory disclosure to address human rights objectives. However, Section 1502 falls short of constituting a perfect template for constructive discourse. Constructive discourse, along its integrative and expressive dimensions, seeks to re-orient disclosure in the following ways:

- From external pressure to *internal assessment based on enlightened self-interest*: Instead of acting only in response to external pressure, such as the threat of civil liability, MNCs should be able to use information from disclosure to engage in a continual process of self-assessment that takes into account the range of risks and strategic opportunities.
- From retrospective to *prospective*: Instead of merely telling what happened, MNCs should seek to draw from prior experiences to improve internal controls and contractual relationships.
- From static to *social*: Instead of viewing disclosure as a series of discrete, one-time events, MNCs should engage in a broad array of interactions with each other and their respective stakeholders in the context of their human rights impacts.
- From a bright-line distinction between disclosure and regulation to a *nuanced, case-by-case determination of the social utility of disclosure*: Instead of viewing mandatory disclosure as a blanket alternative to direct government regulation, regulators should have the discretion to permit the alternate use of voluntary reporting mechanisms created by MNCs on a case-by-case basis.

The procedural components of Section 1502 – namely, the country-of-origin inquiry, internal due diligence, and external audit requirements – have the potential to facilitate the integrative dimension of constructive discourse. If MNCs are able to use information collected through these fact-finding processes to understand their effects on the socio-political conflicts in the DRC, they may be better equipped to manage their commercial relationships with supply-chain intermediaries and third-party contract manufacturers in a way that curbs the illicit trade of conflict minerals. In this respect, the integrative function of Section 1502 would be enhanced by the creation of a central repository of information with which reporting companies could share information regarding their respective due diligence processes.

The expressive function of constructive discourse, however, may be hampered by Section 1502. Based on a hierarchical, rules-based approach to disclosure, Section 1502 may stifle meaningful dialogue between MNCs and stakeholders. Section 1502 imposes the obligation to disclose on issuers subject to Exchange Act reporting requirements, which are not best situated to obtain the information (Ochoa and Keenan, 2011). Issuers are required to extract information from suppliers along their conflict minerals supply chains, regardless of how operationally and legally attenuated their relationships may be. Stakeholder dialogue as well as shared governance among multiple governments and industry representatives has been credited with facilitating public–private certification schemes such as the Kimberley Process designed to prevent trade in conflict diamonds (Taylor, 2012; Woody, 2012). The failure of Section 1502 to adequately account for the role of MNCs in the design of reporting and due diligence schemes may undermine its ability to bridge the "credibility gap" among MNCs of the utility of changing their corporate behavior in order to respect human rights (Bird and Dhooge, 2011). In its current form, Section 1502 may jeopardize industry-based initiatives between MNCs, local companies, supply-chain intermediaries, governments, civil society, and multilateral institutions (Seay, 2012). The use of penalties for non-compliance with disclosure rules may inhibit, rather than facilitate, the goals of curbing mining-related violence in the DRC. On the other hand, MNCs may benefit from the industry-wide collection and sharing of information between MNCs regarding their respective supply chains, which would help MNCs mitigate the operational risks they face in the DRC. In order to more accurately take advantage of firm-level benefits, Section 1502 could be amended to grant mutual recognition to alternate voluntary schemes that fulfill similar substantive purposes.

IV. CONCLUSION: PATHS FORWARD FOR DISCLOSURE AND HUMAN RIGHTS

The observations in this chapter present a number of empirical questions concerning the use of constructive discourse. A fundamental precondition of constructive discourse that merits empirical study is the effect of in-house legal counsel on the success of MNCs in respecting human rights. A number of interrelated questions emerge for future research: How do in-house lawyers contribute to the veracity, clarity, and legitimacy of disclosure? Do their roles meaningfully differ from outside counsel tasked with preparing disclosure? Are the contributions of in-house lawyers any different in respect of mandatory disclosure regimes such as Section 1502 versus voluntary reporting mechanisms? What internal corporate conditions are necessary for ensuring the effectiveness of the gatekeeping function of in-house lawyers? Would targeted ethical training better equip lawyers to use disclosure to integrate the competing claims of business and human rights? How might an epistemic community of in-house lawyers facilitate the expressive dimension of constructive discourse?

Another area for empirical study concerns the effectiveness of voluntary industry certification schemes. Does the non-hierarchical nature of corporate self-regulation promote or inhibit compliance with human rights principles? In order to compare the effectiveness of public-private certification schemes versus regimes based on mandatory disclosure regimes such as Section 1502, it would be helpful to identify industries or regions that have been the focus of both approaches.

The use of mandatory disclosure as a means of facilitating human rights reporting reveals the challenges of global governance. Section 1502 has emerged in the context of an increasingly diverse, sometimes conflicting array of corporate social transparency reporting systems. The integrative and expressive dimensions of mandatory disclosure, evident in the concept of constructive discourse, suggest ways in which MNCs may be able to use mandatory disclosure regimes for their own benefit.

NOTES

1. Issuers subject to disclosure requirements under the Securities Act and/or Exchange Act include, most notably, corporations, but also may include other business entities and certain governmental entities.
2. Regulation S-K specifies the form and substance of the information that a company must disclose in its SEC filings.
3. The human rights aspirations of MNCs may range from a fear of negative publicity arising from gross violations of human rights to a deep-rooted normative commitment to human rights principles. In any event, there are potential conflicts between any such human rights values and other corporate objectives.
4. Although corporations as legally defined entities should not be casually attributed with human characteristics, their decision-making processes are driven by individuals and groups of individuals. Accordingly, processes of socialization within and between corporations and with other stakeholders influence how corporations act and on what grounds corporations justify their actions.

REFERENCES

Abbott, K.W. (2008), "Enriching rational choice institutionalism for the study of international law", *University of Illinois Law Review*, *2008*(1), 5–46.

Backer, L.C. (2011), "On the evolution of the United Nations' 'Protect-Respect-Remedy' Project: The state, the corporation and human rights in a global governance context", *Santa Clara Journal of International Law*, *9*(1), 37–80.

Bartlett, R.P. (2010), "Inefficiencies in the information thicket: A case study of derivative disclosures during the financial crisis", *Journal of Corporation Law*, *36*(1), 1–57.

Bird, R.C. (2011), "Law, strategy, and competitive advantage", *Connecticut Law Review*, *44*(1), 61–97.
Bird, R.C. and Dhooge, L.J. (2011), "Bridging the credibility gap between transnational corporations and human rights", retrieved from http://papers.ssrn.com/sol3/papers.cfm?abstract_id=1783579.
Blair, M.M., Williams, C.A., and Lin, L. (2008), "The new role for assurances services in global commerce", *Journal of Corporation Law*, *33*(2), 325–60.
Bradford, W. (2012), "Beyond good and evil: The commensurability of corporate profits and human rights", *Notre Dame Journal of Law, Ethics, & Public Policy*, *26*(1), 141–280.
Brandeis, L. (1914), *Other People's Money – and How Bankers Use It*. New York, NY: Stokes.
Brummer, C. (2011), *Soft Law and the Global Financial System: Rule Making in the 21st Century*. New York, NY: Cambridge University Press.
Buhmann, K. (2012), "Business and human rights: Analysing discursive articulation of stakeholder interests to explain the consensus-based construction of the 'Protect, Respect, Remedy UN Framework", *International Law Research*, *1*(1), 88–101.
Case, D. (2005), "Corporate environmental reporting as informational regulation: A law and economics perspective'", *University of Colorado Law Review*, *76*(2), 379–442.
Cherry, M.A. and Sneirson, J.F. (2011), "Beyond profit: Rethinking corporate social responsibility after the BP oil disaster", *Tulane Law Review*, *85*(4), 983–1038.
Dhooge, L.J. (2004), "Beyond voluntarism: Social disclosure and France's nouvelles régulations economiques", *Arizona Journal of International and Comparative Law*, *21*(2), 441–91.
Dodd-Frank Wall Street Reform and Consumer Protection Act, Pub. L. No. 111-203, 124 Stat. 1376–2223 (2010).
Eisner, M.A. (2004), "Corporate environmentalism, regulatory reform, and industry self-regulation: Toward genuine regulatory reinvention in the United States", *Governance: An International Journal of Policy, Administration, and Institutions*, *17*(2), 145–67.
Finnemore, M. and Sikkink, K. (1998), "International norm dynamics and political change", *International Organization*, *52*(4), 887–917.
Fox, M.B. (1999), "Retaining mandatory securities disclosure: Why issuer choice is not investor empowerment", *Virginia Law Review*, *85*(7), 1335–419.
Fox, M.B. (1997), "Securities disclosure in a globalizing market: Who should regulate whom", *Michigan Law Review*, *95*(8), 2498–632.
Fung, A., Graham, M., Weil, D., and Fagotto, E. (2006), "The effectiveness of regulatory disclosure policies", *Journal of Policy Analysis & Management*, *25*(1), 155–81.
Fung, A., Graham, M., and Weil, D. (2007), *Full Disclosure: The Perils and Promise of Transparency*. Cambridge, UK: Cambridge University Press.
Goodman, R. and Jinks, D. (2004), "How to influence states: Socialization and international human rights law", *Duke Law Journal*, *54*(3), 621–703.
Haas, P.M. (1992), "Banning chlorofluorocarbons: Epistemic community efforts to protect stratospheric ozone", *International Organization*, *46*(1), 187–224.

Kahan, D.M. and Posner, E.A. (1999), "Shaming white-collar criminals: A proposal for reform of the federal sentencing guidelines", *Journal of Law and Economics*, *42*(1), 365–92.

Lynn, D.M. (2011), "The Dodd-Frank Act's specialized corporate disclosure: Using the securities laws to address public policy issues", *Journal of Business and Technology Law*, *6*(2), 327–55.

Malloy, T.F. (2005), "Disclosure stories", *Florida State University Law Review*, *32*(2), 617–72.

Manne, G.A. (2007), "The hydraulic theory of disclosure regulation and other costs of disclosure", *Alabama Law Review*, *58*(3), 473–511.

Mazars and Shift (2013), "Developing global standards for the reporting and assurance of company alignment with the UN Guiding Principles on Business and Human Rights", retrieved from http://www.shiftproject.org/news/shift-and-mazars-launch-discussion-paper-comment.

Murphy, S.D. (2005), "Taking multinational corporate codes of conduct to the next level", *Columbia Journal of Transnational Law*, *43*(2), 389–433.

Ochoa, C. (2011), "Corporate social responsibility and firm compliance: Lessons from the international law-international relations discourse", *Santa Clara Journal of International Law*, *9*(1), 169–78.

Ochoa, C. and Keenan, P.J. (2011), "Regulating information flows, regulating conflict: An analysis of United States conflict minerals legislation", *Goettingen Journal of International Law*, *3*(1), 129–54.

Orts, E.W. (1995), "Reflexive environmental law", *Northwestern University Law Review*, *89*(4), 1227–340.

Park, S.K. (2013), "Talking the talk and walking the walk: Reviving global trade and development after Doha", *Virginia Journal of International Law*, *53*(2), 365–415.

Prentice, R.A. (2011), "Moral equilibrium: Stock brokers and the limits of disclosure", *Wisconsin Law Review*, *2011*(6), 1059–107.

Ripken, S.K. (2006), "The dangers and drawbacks of the disclosure antidote: Toward a more substantive approach to securities regulation", *Baylor Law Review*, *58*(1), 139–204.

Risse, T. (2000), "'Let's argue': Communicative action in world politics", *International Organization*, *54*(1), 1–39.

Ruggie, J. G. (2013), *Just Business: Multinational Corporations and Human Rights*. New York, NY: W.W. Norton & Co.

Ruggie, J.G. (1998), "What makes the world hang together? Neo-utilitarianism and the social constructivist challenge", *International Organization*, *52*(4), 855–85.

Scott, H.S. and Gelpern, A. (2012), *International Finance: Transactions, Policy, and Regulation* (19th ed.). New York, NY: Foundation Press.

Schmidt, P. (2012), "The ethical lives of securities lawyers", in Levin, L.C. and Mather, L. (Eds), *Lawyers in Practice: Ethical Decision-making in Context* (pp. 221–44). Chicago, IL: University of Chicago Press.

Schwarcz, S.L. (2004), "Rethinking the disclosure paradigm in a world of complexity", *University of Illinois Law Review*, *2004*(1), 1–37.

Seay, L.E. (2012), "What's wrong with Dodd-Frank 1502? Conflict minerals, civilian livelihoods, and the unintended consequences of Western advocacy",

Center for Global Development, Working Paper 284, retrieved from http://www.cgdev.org/publication/what%E2%80%99s-wrong-dodd-frank-1502-conflict-minerals-civilian-livelihoods-and-unintended.

Securities Act of 1933, 15 U.S.C. §§ 77a–77aa (2006 & Supp. IV 2011).

Securities Exchange Act of 1934, 15 U.S.C. §§ 78a–78lll (2006 & Supp. IV 2011).

Skeel, D.A. (2001), "Shaming in corporate law", *University of Pennsylvania Law Review*, *149*(6), 1811–68.

Stevelman, F. (2011), "Global finance, multinationals and human rights: With commentary on Backer's critique of the 2008 report by John Ruggie", *Santa Clara Journal of International Law*, *9*(1), 101–45.

Taylor, C.R. (2012), "Conflict minerals and SEC disclosure regulation", *Harvard Business Law Review Online*, *2*, 105–20.

Teubner, G. (1983), "Substantive and reflexive elements in modern law", *Law & Society Review*, *17*(2), 239–86.

U.N. Special Representative of the Secretary-General (21 March 2011), "Guiding Principles on Business and Human Rights: Implementing the United Nations 'Protect, Respect and Remedy' Framework", U.N. Document A/HRC/17/31.

Weil, D., Graham, M., and Fung, A. (2013), "Targeting transparency", *Science, 340*, 1410–11.

Whitehead, C.K. (2006), "What's your sign? International norms, signals, and compliance", *Michigan Journal of International Law, 27*, 695–741.

Williams, C.A. (1999), "The Securities and Exchange Commission and corporate social transparency", *Harvard Law Review*, *112*(6), 1197–311.

Woody, K.E. (2012), "Conflict minerals legislation: The SEC's new role as diplomatic and humanitarian watchdog", *Fordham Law Review*, *81*(3), 1315–51.

3. Human rights and a corporation's duty to combat corruption

Norman Bishara and David Hess*

In the last decade, the debate over corporations' human rights obligations has become a central topic in the fields of corporate social responsibility (CSR) and international law. Developments such as the United Nation's *Norms on the Responsibilities of Transnational Corporations and Other Business Enterprises with Regard to Human Rights* in 2003, and lawsuits filed against corporations in the United States under the Alien Tort Statute (ATS) (sometimes called the Alien Tort Claims Act) for alleged human rights abuses abroad, led to the United Nations appointing John Ruggie as a Special Representative for Business and Human Rights (U.N. Commission on Human Rights Subcommittee, 2003). In 2011, the U.N. Human Rights Council endorsed his recommendations, which were promulgated as the *Guiding Principles on Business and Human Rights* (U.N. Special Representative of the Secretary-General, 2011). These principles have been well received and established corporations' obligation to "respect" human rights.

During this same time, combating corruption in international business was also gaining prominence. The major developments included the OECD Convention on *Combating Bribery of Foreign Public Officials in International Business Transactions* coming into force in 1999, and then the United Nations *Convention against Corruption* in 2005. Of more direct importance to the business community is the U.S. Department of Justice's increased enforcement of the Foreign Corrupt Practices Act in the last several years through well-publicized settlements and guilty pleas of major corporations, such as Siemens, Daimler AG, and Pfizer. Other potential enforcement activity, such as the U.K. Anti-Bribery Act in effect from 2011, has made controlling the supply side of corruption through the criminal law an important, and highly controversial, topic (Barta and Chapman, 2012).

Increasingly, there is awareness that these two topics – corruption and human rights – are intimately connected: high levels of corruption in a country prevent the realization of human rights and fuel human rights abuses. However, the debates and reform proposals on improving corporations' social performance in these two areas are often treated as separate concerns. To combat corruption, corporations focus on ensuring that their employees or agents do not pay bribes by adopting compliance programs that are likely to be effective in ensuring that anti-bribery laws are not violated (or, at least, adopting the appearance of compliance programs that satisfy external demands). With increased enforcement of anti-bribery laws in the U.S. and elsewhere, combating corruption is increasingly becoming seen by corporations as primarily, or solely, a legal compliance issue. Likewise, business and human rights efforts recognize the harms of corruption, but treat it as a separate issue. In many ways, corruption seems to be viewed as something present in the local business environment that is a separate legal issue from the CSR issues surrounding human rights and therefore is not a direct concern of initiatives to improve human rights outcomes.

This chapter argues that corporations will have a more positive impact on human rights if these issues – business and corruption, and business and human rights – are considered together. CSR initiatives aimed at improving corporations' human rights performance must directly consider the impact of corruption and how combating corruption can improve human rights outcomes. In other words, combating corruption should not just be considered as an end in itself, but also as a means for preventing human rights abuses.

In Part I we begin by discussing the background of the relationship between corruption, CSR and human rights. We provide an explanation of the goals of fighting corruption and protecting human rights before presenting the existing international and domestic frameworks that have begun to address these issues for both business and society. In Part II we discuss the Ruggie "Protect, Respect and Remedy" framework in greater detail, as well as the notion of corporate complicity in human rights violations, and then present several theoretical perspectives from the debate over a corporation's positive duty to act. In Part III, we argue for a dynamic conceptualization of addressing these goals that goes beyond mere compliance with legal frameworks to combat corruption and promote human rights, all alongside a corporate social responsibility view of corporate action. To move in this direction we advocate a multi-prong approach within a framework of developing and implementing effective policies, procedures, publication, and stakeholder participation. We ultimately sum up our arguments and the model of corporate action in a brief conclusion.

I. BACKGROUND ON THE CORRUPTION, CSR, AND HUMAN RIGHTS RELATIONSHIP

In this Part we first lay out the issues of corruption and human rights, then discuss how they are connected to each other and MNCs' activities in emerging economies. In addition, we discuss the rise and evolution of key business accountability efforts, such as the U.N. Global Compact and the Global Reporting Initiative, and show how corruption, once a neglected CSR issue, is now a part of those frameworks. We also explain that the CSR and especially the legal literature related to corruption often view corruption as *something done to the corporation* in terms of demands from corrupt officials, rather than *something the corporation is doing* to the citizens of the developing country. Throughout, we examine how corruption and human rights are interrelated issues, how corruption compares to other human rights concerns, and why it has not been a central part of the business and human rights discussion. We also show that only recently has corruption been seen as an important issue of corporate social responsibility.

A. International Frameworks and Other Instruments Related to Corruption and Human Rights

As noted by many scholars, corruption is an ancient problem that has been condemned widely throughout history, including by all major world religions (Nichols, 2004, 2009). With an increasingly globalized economy, the harms of corruption to economic development are now more fully appreciated. Moreover, as the U.N. Global Compact has concluded:

> It is now clear that corruption has played a major part in undermining the world's social, economic and environmental development. Resources have been diverted to improper use and the quality of services and materials used for development seriously compromised. The impact on poorer communities struggling to improve their lives has been devastating, in many cases undermining the very fabric of society. It has led to environmental mismanagement, *undermining labor standards and has restricted access to basic human rights*. (U.N. Global Compact, 2013)

This recognition of the harms of corruption[1] by leaders in all sectors of society has moved corruption from being an issue that was not openly discussed to a major topic of international policy.

Early evidence of an appreciation for the supply side of corruption is Transparency International's Bribe Payers Index (BPI), which was first published in 1999. Unlike the CPI, which ranks countries based on perceptions of the level of corruption, the BPI "ranks the world's wealthiest countries by the propensity of their firms to bribe abroad and looks at which industrial sectors are the worst offenders" (Transparency International, 2013a). In part, the BPI challenged beliefs that corruption existed in developing countries and MNCs had no choice but to comply if they wanted to do business there, and encouraged interested parties to examine how MNCs from clean countries on the CPI "exported corruption" (Hess and Dunfee, 2000, p. 598).

In fact, labeling the payment of bribes by the private sector as the "supply side" may be misleading and not reflect the exportation of corruption. A recent example illustrates this. Wal-Mart de Mexico managers used bribes to gain building permits for stores in numerous locations in Mexico. Some of the alleged bribes were used to speed up approval processes or to move ahead of other companies in priority lines for government services. This appears to be in line with the company supplying the bribe demanded by a corrupt government official. However, some of the alleged bribes paid by Wal-Mart to Mexican officials allowed construction on sites – including within a previously-designated sensitive archeological zone around the Mayan pyramids of Teotihuacán – that had previously been denied (Barstow and Bertrab, 2012). In another instance, "thanks to eight bribe payments totaling $341,000, for example, Wal-Mart built a Sam's Club in one of Mexico City's most densely populated neighborhoods, near the Basílica de Guadalupe, without a construction license, or an environmental permit, or an urban impact assessment, or even a traffic permit." As a result of even larger bribes "totaling $765,000 … Wal-Mart built a vast refrigerated distribution center in an environmentally fragile flood basin north of Mexico City, in an area where electricity was so scarce that many smaller developers were turned away" (Barstow and Bertrab, 2012). Such actions were apparently condoned by senior Wal-Mart managers, at least implicitly by not taking corrective action once learning of the payments, and appear to show an example of a MNC bribing to get what it wants and not simply giving in to bribe demands (Barstow, 2012). Overall, the investigative journalists at the *New York Times* concluded:

> Wal-Mart de Mexico was not the reluctant victim of a corrupt culture that insisted on bribes as the cost of doing business. Nor did it pay bribes merely to speed up routine approvals. Rather, Wal-Mart de Mexico was an aggressive and creative corrupter, offering large payoffs to get what the law otherwise prohibited. It used bribes to subvert democratic governance – public votes, open debates, transparent procedures. It used bribes to circumvent regulatory

> safeguards that protect Mexican citizens from unsafe construction. It used bribes to outflank rivals. (Barstow and Bertrab, 2012)

For a significant amount of time, only the U.S., through the adoption of the Foreign Corrupt Practices Act (FCPA) in 1977, used the criminal law to attempt to control the supply side of bribery in international business. However, it was rarely enforced for the first 25 years of its existence. Although there were non-binding anti-corruption guidelines for MNCs in Europe, it was the 1997 OECD anti-bribery convention that brought nations toward an international consensus on regulating the supply side of corruption through government enforcement (OECD Convention on Combating Bribery of Foreign Public Officials in International Business Transactions, 2011). Another important step in pushing countries to regulate the supply side of corruption, and also for acknowledging the importance of corruption as an economic development issue, was the United Nations Convention against Corruption, which entered into force in 2005 as the "first globally-agreed anti-bribery instrument" (U.N. Global Compact, 2013).

The voluntary U.N. Global Compact initiative created a further advancement in recognizing the role of MNCs in contributing to corruption that imperils human rights. Started in 2000, the Global Compact initially focused on corporations' responsibilities for human rights, labor, and environmental issues (U.N. Global Compact, 2011). In 2004, an additional tenth principle was added that required corporations to "work against corruption in all its forms" (U.N. Global Compact, 2013). Thus, although corruption was initially not viewed as a part of a corporation's social responsibilities, it was added later, at least in part, due to a recognition that meaningful progress on the other issues, such as human rights, could not be made if corruption was not controlled.

In addition to the Global Compact, other major initiatives have also started to connect combating corruption with MNCs' social responsibilities. One such major initiative is the Global Reporting Initiative (GRI). For the last decade, the non-profit organization GRI has produced the leading standards on sustainability reporting (Global Reporting Initiative, 2013b). Like the U.N. Global Compact initiative, the GRI's standards did not initially designate corruption as a key area of concern, but subsequent standards have made it an important topic. Another major initiative, which is specific to resource extraction MNCs – a broad industry of natural resource-related MNCs known for a high incidence of corruption – is the Extractive Industry Transparency Initiative (EITI) (Extractive Industries Transparency Initiative, 2013). In short, the EITI involves a centralized reporting structure that allows interested parties to track contracts and payments between MNCs and the countries where the resources are located. By increasing transparency on the transfer of payments concerning the resources extraction activities it is hoped that these proceeds end up benefiting citizens in the developing nation and not in the foreign bank accounts of corrupt officials.

Overall, the policy developments and multi-stakeholder initiatives described are significant developments in recognizing the importance of controlling the supply side of corruption as a part of a corporation's social responsibilities. Although these developments were able to move forward due, at least in part, to a recognition of the impact of corruption on human rights and sustainability more generally, they do not do much to move past the view that a corporation's only obligation is to prohibit its employees from paying a bribe. As stated earlier, the attention given the U.K. Bribery Act and increased enforcement of the FCPA also encourage that limited view. Underlying this view seems to be an assumption that corruption abroad is something that MNCs have done to them. That is, MNCs do not bring a corrupting influence to the country ("exporting corruption"), but they are unwillingly forced into situations where they need to decide whether or not to give into a demand for bribes.

This is a different perspective from that of MNCs in the areas of human rights. Concerning labor conditions, for example, a motivating force behind policy developments and multi-stakeholder initiatives is the view of MNCs as exploiters of developing countries' low-wage workers and weak labor laws. Likewise, with respect to the environment, MNCs are viewed as *causing* the environmental damage. This difference in underlying views potentially changes how MNCs' view their obligations. That is, MNCs are more likely to take a broader view of their responsibilities and expand from "avoid the harmful activity" to "work for positive change in the local environment to prevent the harmful activity from occurring." One example may be the *Accord on Fire and Building Safety in Bangladesh*. Another could be the work of IKEA to combat child labor in India and other countries, by not only prohibiting its use, but also seeking to mitigate the root causes of child labor in those countries, such as through providing opportunities for meaningful education for the children.

In this chapter, our primary focus is on making combatting corruption a central part of MNCs' obligation to respect human rights. Certain social responsibilities of MNCs may be independent – such as avoiding child labor and protecting the environment – but combatting corruption is different. The social responsibility to combat corruption is not an end in itself, but in developing countries with high levels of corruption, it should be an integral part of an MNC's efforts to meet any of its responsibilities.

There is some movement in this direction. For example, in the US, the Dodd-Frank Act is essentially an attempt to mandate the requirements of the voluntary EITI (Dodd-Frank Wall Street Reform and Consumer Protection Act, 2010). This is movement beyond the FCPA's prohibition on bribery, and is an attempt to establish a system – based in part on an MNC's disclosure obligation – that reduces the likelihood of corruption in a country that harms that country's citizens. Thus, this is an example of combatting corruption through the law beyond simply requiring a corporation to ensure it does not pay bribes. In the realm of voluntary CSR initiatives, the World Bank Institute, Transparency International, and others, have engaged in efforts to encourage MNCs to work through collective action efforts to reduce corruption in particular business environments (World Bank Institute, 2008). This chapter seeks to build upon these efforts and ensure that combatting corruption is a central part of the business and human rights movement. As some further background on this is needed, the next section provides an illustration of how many of the human rights challenges that companies face throughout their supply chain cannot be fully addressed without first adequately addressing the issue of corruption.

B. Corruption as a Business and Human Rights Problem

At the time of this writing, the labor safety issues in the garment industry in Bangladesh are a primary ongoing example of a business and human rights problem. Since 2007, over 700 workers have died in fires at garment factories in various developing countries such as China and Bangladesh (Most, 2013). In April of 2013, an eight-story building that housed several garment factories collapsed, causing the deaths of over a thousand workers (Manik and Yardley, 2013; Accord on Fire and Building Safety in Bangladesh, 2013). These deaths likely could have been prevented if corruption did not allow workplace safety violations and building code violations to go unchecked (Manik and Yardley, 2013).

Corruption allows factories to remain in operation even if inspectors find numerous safety violations (Keeping and Zaman, 2012). Likewise, as was the case with failing bridges in China, for example (Hess and Dunfee, 2000), corruption is likely to be the culprit that allowed the building in the Bangladesh collapse to be constructed in violation of building codes (Yardley, 2013).[2] This lack of building code enforcement has been connected to the devastating situation where countries that suffer a relatively high level of perceived corruption also have a high percentage of earthquake-related deaths from collapsed structures. This correlation may be attributable to the existence of poorly constructed and often illegal buildings that are made possible because of corrupt officials shirking their oversight duties. This has included the extensive loss of life from collapsed buildings during the 2010 Haitian earthquake (Ambraseys and Bilham, 2011).

The point is that anti-corruption efforts cannot focus only on MNCs refusing to pay bribes. Collapsing buildings and avoidable factory fires where MNC's suppliers operate are due to corrupt transactions that may not have directly involved the MNC apparel company, but that company is impacted by them and has (or should have) responsibility for the problem. Similarly, where a MNC uses bribery to gain construction approval that leads to environmental and cultural degradation, that company should not be without some level of responsibility for the impact stemming from the corruption. Overall, MNCs know, or should know, that corruption greatly erodes their ability to respect human rights. Awareness of how corruption impacts human rights throughout the MNC's supply chain is essential for conducting "human rights due diligence" (U.N. Special Representative of the Secretary-General, 2008).[3] Thus, preventing corruption from creating human rights concerns for workers in their supply chain should be a top priority of MNCs.

To accomplish this goal, MNCs should not only ensure that their employees and agents do not pay bribes, but that corruption is not standing in the way of their suppliers meeting human rights obligations. In addition, this may also include a responsibility to work towards reducing the enabling environment that allows corruption to thrive in that location. This duty goes beyond legal compliance with the FCPA or other national anti-bribery laws and must be central to the discussion of corporations' human rights obligations. With this in mind, it is useful to revisit existing thought on an MNC's obligation to respect human rights, as well as the debate over whether MNCs have a positive obligation to protect human rights.

II. CORRUPTION AND HUMAN RIGHTS PERSPECTIVES AND JUSTIFICATIONS

The long-standing debate over the role of the corporation in society, particularly multinational corporations operating abroad, continues today and is generally framed as a debate over CSR. In this section we focus on three nuanced approaches to explaining and justifying corporate action – of varying degrees – in the context of an MNC's impact on human rights. We first discuss the Protect, Respect and Remedy framework promoted by former U.N. Special Representative John Ruggie. In that section we focus on the framework's concept of due diligence. In the second section we discuss the idea of corporate complicity in allowing or even facilitating human rights abuses. In the third section we turn to a review of the prominent theoretical arguments for an MNC's duty to act beyond merely following any applicable legal rules and regulations and to proactively improve human rights conditions. Throughout this section, we raise the issue of more directly including the issue of corruption in these business and human rights approaches.

A. Due Diligence Under the Protect, Respect and Remedy Framework

The Guiding Principles endeavor to set up a workable framework that simultaneously requires states to act under an obligation to protect human rights and that creates a mechanism that will encourage private actors (i.e., businesses) to participate in human rights protection by first respecting them. For business, the seemingly passive duty to "respect" is actually presented in terms of a corporate responsibility. The first action, therefore, for businesses is derivative of that duty to respect: mobilizing to avoid human rights infringement and addressing the "adverse human rights impacts with which they are involved" (U.N. Guiding Principles, p. 13).

One powerful way to turn what could be seen as a negative duty of respect (that is, refraining from infringing rights) is for the principles to put the respect element into a proactive business duty of due diligence. This creates a powerful rhetorical tool for the framework's advocates by putting the duty in terms that businesses understand. In other words, the concept of due diligence places the respect duty into an accountability and business process context that companies can recognize and even treat as a source of risk that must be addressed. In Chapter II ("The Corporate Responsibility to Respect Human Rights") the principles explicitly make this link between CSR and due diligence investigation into the corporation's impact on human rights.[4] The due diligence process businesses should implement is set out in the guiding principles, particularly with principles 16–21. As spelled out in the commentary to Principle 15 – commitment to human rights, identification of "actual and potential human rights impact," remediation of violations as needed, and, in some cases, communicating the effectiveness of these efforts to external stakeholders. This is the so-called "know and show" duty related to human rights impact.

Specifically, Principle 17 "defines the parameters for human rights due diligence, while Principles 18 through 21 elaborate its essential components." The commentary to Principle 17 is enlightening. Due diligence is needed not only to protect the company from being involved in a human rights violation, but is also needed to build a process designed to prevent a violation against those individuals holding the right:

> Human rights risks are understood to be the business enterprise's potential adverse human rights impacts. Potential impacts should be addressed through prevention or mitigation, while actual impacts – those that have already occurred – should be a subject for remediation (Principle 22) ... Human rights due diligence can be included within broader enterprise risk- management systems, provided that it goes beyond simply identifying and managing material risks to the company itself, to include risks to rights-holders. (U.N. Special Representative of the Secretary-General, 2011, pp. 17–18)

Overall, the due diligence framework seeks to take the business profit maximization strategy of reducing sources of costly risk and use it for promoting the social good of protecting human rights. The examples of the factory fire and building collapse in the Bangladeshi garment industry are useful in understanding how business risk, corruption, and human rights converge. In retrospect the risk and subsequent business cost in terms of adverse publicity from the high-profile disasters are obvious, but market incentives failed to spur the necessary safety changes beforehand. The proactive approach of executing due diligence obligations could have helped avert such tragedies on business grounds once the risk was formalized. Greater due diligence and reporting by western companies with regard to the garment supply chain could have identified the human rights risks and created an opportunity for positive action to protect the violations, including those resulting from the corruptly-facilitated disasters. The guiding principles can help make these connections clear for business decision-makers and in a way that goes beyond simply making moral claims by explicitly framing human rights as a business issue.

As discussed further below, corporations conducting due diligence should not simply look for violations of labor rights or safety regulations at a supplier, for example, but understand how corruption is potentially impacting compliance with such rights and regulations. This will require that any auditors used to conduct an inspection of the supplier are trained in these matters and can help identify when corruption is impacting operations. It will also require that a supplier in a high-risk environment is trained on anti-corruption laws and their behavior is monitored appropriately. Without the inclusion of the corruption issue, the due diligence process will be incomplete.

B. Corporate Complicity in Human Rights Violations

Principle 2 of the UN Global Compact states that, "[b]usinesses should make sure they are not complicit in human rights abuses" (U.N. Global Compact, 2013). Likewise, the ISO 26000 guidance on social responsibility states that an "organization should avoid being complicit in the activities of another organization that are not consistent with international norms of behavior," including human rights (Int'l Org. for Standardization, 2010). In addition to the legal meaning, which is to knowingly provide some form of assistance to the commission of a wrongful act, a corporation "may also be considered complicit where it stays silent about or benefits from such wrongful acts" (U.N. Guiding Principles, 2011; Int'l Org. for Standardization, 2010, p. 26).

The Global Compact and ISO 26000 further divide complicity into direct, beneficial, and silent. Direct involves knowing assistance to the violation of a human right. Beneficial complicity "involves an organization or subsidiaries benefiting directly from human rights abuses committed by someone else," with one example being "an organization benefiting economically from suppliers' abuse of fundamental rights at work." Silent complicity "can involve the failure by an organization to raise with the appropriate authorities the question of systematic or continuous human rights violations, such as not speaking out against systematic discrimination in employment law against particular groups" (Int'l Org. for Standardization, 2010, p. 26).

Under this perspective, there are many situations where corporations know (or should know) that they are benefiting from corruption that either facilitates or directly supports the violation of human rights. Consider again the apparel industry in Bangladesh. Corporations in the apparel industry know (or should know) that corruption allows the violation of building safety codes that imperil human rights at their suppliers' factories. Thus, corporations are arguably beneficially or silently complicit in those actions. This is not to say that those corporations should have legal liability, but they have a moral responsibility to take some action to reduce corruption that is directly impacting the rights of the workers in the suppliers' factories. Under current practices, it seems that corporations will rely on safety audits and local government inspections and – knowing that corruption is endemic to many developing countries such as Bangladesh – simply hope for the best; or worse, turn a blind eye to the problem.

C. The Debate over a Corporate Duty to Act

In the last few decades, formalized conceptions of a corporate duty to stakeholders and the larger society beyond mere profit-making for shareholders has become a well-established feature of both academic and practitioner oriented research (Freeman, 2002; Freeman, Velamuri, and Moriarty, 2006). In that time the definition of who or what will qualify as a stakeholder, and thus necessitate consideration by corporate decision makers, has also expanded (Fassin, 2009). In a broad sense, these ideas can all be placed under the umbrella of CSR (Dahlsrud, 2008).

Since CSR concepts began taking form in the 1970s critics have argued that business has no social responsibility beyond representing the interests of shareholders (Friedman, 1970; Karnani, 2012). Others argue that CSR is not a tension between business and society, but rather an opportunity to provide the greatest benefit to society and the corporation, and that the corporation should integrate CSR into its business strategies for its own interests (Porter and Kramer, 2006). Critics of this perspective, however, point out that these management-driven conceptions of CSR end up as risk-management tools that focus only on the corporation, such as protecting its reputation (McCorquodale, 2009). In addition, these conceptions create the view that CSR involves only voluntary responsibilities (McCorquodale, 2009). These concerns frame the debate on a corporation's human rights responsibilities, as human rights obligations should be focused on the risks to the right holder not the corporation (as seen in the commentary to Guiding Principle number 17 quoted above), and are not voluntary (McCorquodale, 2009).

The U.N. Norms on the Responsibilities of Transnational Corporations and other Business Enterprises with regard to Human Rights (the Norms) catalyzed an intense, public debate about these issues. The Norms were controversial because they imposed direct obligations on corporations to protect human rights (Kinley, Nolan and Zerial, 2007). Although the debate on the Norms revolved around placing a legal obligation on corporations to protect human rights, there is also significant debate on the extent of a corporation's moral obligations, which has been reignited by the Ruggie framework. While the Ruggie "Protect, Respect, and Remedy Framework" places MNCs in the role of respecting human rights and recognizes the role of governments to respect *and* remedy, others have argued that a corporate duty to act is feasible and is supported under ethical theories (Ruggie, 2008). This recent work by leading scholars in business ethics and law has re-energized the theoretical justifications for why multinational corporations must act in certain circumstances.

When and how MNCs must act, including with regard to protecting human rights, is often evaluated in terms of Rawlsian conceptions of justice and fairness. One leading scholar in this area, Nien-hê Hsieh, roots this discussion in notions of justice developed by John Rawls, particularly in *The Law of Peoples*. In one instance Hsieh specifically examines the positive obligations contemplated in the Global Compact. He begins by presenting three principles, the Principle of Assistance, the Principle of Limited Scope, and the Principle of Accountability, which, in turn, describe the conditions where a MNC is obligated to act, the limits of the required assistance, and when MNCs "have an obligation to support mechanisms that enable those affected by [MNC] activities to contest corporate decisions in areas that related to the fulfilling of those obligations." He concludes that there is a duty for MNCs to assist those in need, including an obligation to alleviate the conditions under which human rights are imperiled (Hsieh, 2004, p. 645). Moreover, there are also arguments that rebut the shareholder primacy account of why MNCs should refrain from assisting stakeholders in need.

In another article, Hsieh focuses on the duty of MNCs to promote just background institutions (Hsieh, 2009). As with the earlier debates on an MNC's duty to act with regard to human rights, this assertion lends support to the notion that MNCs should go beyond simply respecting human rights and take an active role in supporting just institutions. Thus, it plausibly follows that MNCs can be held to a standard that connotes an obligation to not only refrain from bribery, but also to fight corruption, especially when human rights are at stake.

Other scholars have also recently engaged with the question of if or when MNCs have affirmative duties to stakeholders. For instance, in the CSR context, Florian Wettstein argues for CSR efforts to go beyond a mandate that MNCs refrain from causing harm and for a positive responsibility to society. He sees human rights as a "blind spot" in CSR, meaning that human rights has "played a peripheral role" in CSR debates (Wettstein, 2012a, pp. 745–6). In effect, he calls for MNCs to take a capability based minimum approach to remedial obligation to protect human rights. He concludes MNCs have a duty to assist in *realizing* human rights – thus to improve the human rights situation where they operate. He adds that to limit MNCs only to a duty to do no harm, or remediate harms when capable, endangers "the prospect of achieving holistic collaborative solutions for today's large-scale human rights challenges in serious jeopardy by letting one of the most powerful parties in the mix off the hook" (Wettstein, 2012a, p. 759).

In a slightly different framing of his argument Wettstein applies this corporate imperative to human rights violations that are within the purview of corporations and asserts that MNCs have a duty to speak up when those violations occur (Wettstein, 2012b). This essentially turns the idea of corporate personhood back on itself with the implication being that if MNCs have political power and rights of their own like individuals or even governments, they will also necessarily have a duty to denounce human rights violations and support the achievement of human rights.

Stephan Wood's work adds another voice to the debate over if and when MNCs must act regarding human rights issues. In essence, his defense of the leverage-based approach is determined by the power and influence that corporations have in a given situation as a determinant of their level of duty (Wood, 2012). This role of the MNC to act is also related to the relationships it enjoys that contribute to its level of potential positive influence.

This brief summary just gives a sample of the rich debates on an MNC's moral obligation to protect human rights and how well Ruggie's framework provides guidance on meeting that moral obligation. Of course, on the other side, others have argued for limitations on how far MNCs must go in addressing human rights where they operate. For example, MNCs may be constrained by their nature and expertise, and the necessary reservation of certain powers and obligations to governments and not corporations (Bishop, 2012).[5] The basis for the Protect, Respect and Remedy framework has also been critiqued on several grounds, including the capacity and private orientation of corporations (Cragg, 2012).

Overall, for purposes of this chapter, it is important to note a few issues emerging from this literature. First, the Ruggie framework is not built on a consensus of what an MNC's positive duties should be to protect human rights. There is still significant debate on these matters. Second, with respect to the topic of this chapter – business, corruption and human rights – there is much room for development of these ideas. Hsieh (2009) is the only author who begins to addresses these issues in any depth when he argues that corporations have a moral obligation to "build local capacity as a way to overcome impediments to well-ordered societies that may arise from the social and economic circumstances of burdened societies" (Hsieh, 2009, p. 262). Those arguments relate directly to the central focus of this chapter. That is, when does corruption prevent MNCs from being able to respect human rights, and what are MNCs' obligations to provide assistance to reduce that specific impact of corruption? The next section sets out a basic framework for encouraging corporations to fully consider these issues, and, as they struggle with these issues, open up new debates on the extent of a MNC's positive duty to combat corruption to be able to meet its obligation to respect human rights.

III. PROMOTING HUMAN RIGHTS BY COMBATING CORRUPTION

Increased enforcement of the FCPA and other anti-bribery legal developments have created a sea change in how much attention corporations pay to combating corruption. The next step is to move corporations away from viewing anti-corruption as solely a compliance issue, and to see these efforts as a matter of CSR, especially as it relates to business and human rights. This means that corporations should focus not just on ensuring that their employees and agents do not pay bribes, but that they should also use their resources to assist the efforts to reduce the levels of corruption in those developing countries with significant governance problems. In short, companies must see combating corruption and promoting human rights as connected and complementary moral duties in the countries where they operate.

The necessary evolution in corporate action requires that corporations change their mindsets in at least two different ways, which require deviating from the usual corporate governance and compliance script. First, corporations must not view anti-corruption as an end in itself (for example, avoiding the payment of bribes that would create FCPA liability), but instead view anti-corruption as an essential part of their efforts to respect human rights. Second, corporations must treat anti-corruption as a matter of CSR, and not simply legal compliance. The legal department must be involved in the corporation's anti-bribery efforts, as the current FCPA enforcement practices create significant legal risks for companies. In addition, as enforced, the FCPA's provisions are complex and require expert legal advice. However, those in the corporation responsible for human rights issues, and CSR more generally, must also be involved. Anti-corruption cannot be isolated from those other CSR activities.

To work towards reducing corruption in a country – as it relates to a company's business activities in that country and as it relates to its obligations to respect human rights – corporations generally need to evolve along the lines of the model developed by Simon Zadek (Zadek, 2004). According to Zadek, firms typically first take a very defensive view of a particular social or environmental issue and they deny any responsibility for having to solve the problem. When they do accept responsibility, the focus initially is on risk mitigation with respect to legal liability and harm to their reputation in the market. With respect to corruption, it seems that many corporations are at this stage.

In the next stages, corporations should recognize that the adoption of compliance programs is not sufficient to address the problem of corruption. They should realize that they must take a more comprehensive view of the problem and perhaps make operational changes to correct the problem. The final stage for socially responsible corporations in Zadek's view is the "civil" stage. At this stage, corporations are committed to solving the problem and seek draw in others (e.g., other industry members, civil society organizations, and governments) to work together to raise the standards of the industry. This stage is, thus, crucial to establish a proactive approach to CSR and to general sustainable social returns.

The following outlines what is necessary to push corporations to enter the "civil" stage as it relates to combating corruption for the purposes of respecting human rights. These actions can be categorized as policies, procedures, publication, and participation (Hess and Dunfee, 2000). These are actions that corporations should voluntarily implement to meet their obligations with respect to corruption and human rights. In addition, there is also a role for governments, civil society organizations, social investors, and others, to push corporations to meet these requirements.

A. Policies

Policies refer to the corporation's commitment to combating corruption. Through codes of conduct, corporations instruct their employees on the standards the corporation expects them to follow. In addition, these codes demonstrate the company's commitment to ethical behavior to its stakeholders. In this way, codes of conduct are part of the stakeholder dialogue on what constitutes corruption and what obligations corporations have to protect against it. Thus, if corporations explicitly link corruption and human rights obligations in their codes of conduct, then this dialogue is pushed further ahead and the foundations of progress are set.

From a business and human rights perspective, corporations' policies should not focus simply on compliance with the FCPA or U.K. Anti-Bribery Act, for example. Instead, the focus should be expanded to understand what policies are needed to ensure that corruption does not prevent the ability of the corporation to respect human rights. Likewise, the company's human rights policies should be integrated with its anti-corruption policies.

B. Procedures

The concept of procedures refers to the implementation of the company's policies. Surprisingly, despite the attention given to anti-bribery laws, many corporations still have not implemented procedures that allow the corporation to identify corruption risks and then protect against those risks. For example, one survey found that only "40 percent of respondents believe their controls are effective at identifying high-risk business partners or suspicious disbursements" (PricewaterhouseCoopers, 2008, p. 5). If many corporations are not appropriately protecting against their own direct involvement in corruption, it is quite likely that even fewer are addressing corruption as it relates to human rights issues.

Thus, as with policies, when corporations develop and implement human rights due diligence procedures, those procedures must be sure to include anti-corruption. One way corporations conduct due diligence is through external certification. For example, companies seek SA8000 certification of their suppliers to ensure those suppliers use safe workplaces and meet minimum standards of decent working conditions (Social Accountability International, 2013a). Corporations should work to ensure that those organizations take anti-corruption into account as it relates to those standards. For example, due in part to a 2012 factory fire at a factory in Pakistan that was SA8000 certified, Social Accountability International states that it is in the process of updating its standards to better account for the harms of corruption (Social Accountability International, 2013b).

C. Publication

Publication involves the disclosure of the corporation's managerial efforts to combat corruption (its policies and procedures) and how well it is meeting those standards. As stated above, although early versions of the GRI (the leading standards for sustainability reporting) left out reporting indicators on anti-corruption, those standards now include such matters. More recently, the U.N. Global Compact and Transparency International have published guidelines for reporting on anti-corruption efforts (U.N. Global Compact and Transparency International, 2009). Consistent with what was stated above, these indicators focus on the corporation not being a participant in wrongful payments.

The next step should include integrating the anti-corruption reporting indicators with the corporation's efforts on other matters of human rights. This will not only encourage corporations to more fully consider these issues, but also facilitates learning. As stated in the U.N. Global Compact guidance, "[R]eporting on anti-corruption activities based on a consistent reporting guidance enables different stakeholders to share information, raise awareness, learn from each other and improve practices" (U.N. Global Compact and Transparency International, 2009).

D. Participation

For both corruption and human rights, multi-stakeholder initiatives are needed to address the problems. In both areas, multi-stakeholder initiatives have made significant progress in driving forward the agenda and allowing corporations to work together (and with governments and civil society organizations) to begin implementing possible solutions. The next step is for existing multi-stakeholder initiatives – or the development of new multi-stakeholder initiatives – to focus on the relationship between corruption and human rights. Such initiatives can push corporations to find those ways where they can improve human rights by helping to reduce corruption (as opposed to just not being an active participant in a corrupt transaction) and then share best practices. Through the collective voice of a multi-stakeholder initiative, corporations can influence governments and find ways to help reduce the corrupt environment surrounding the corporation's activities (either direct activities or in its supply chain) in any particular country.

Such initiatives can become the "institutional entrepreneurs" that bring about the necessary changes needed. As Misangyi and colleagues state:

> anticorruption reforms must be championed by institutional entrepreneurs who possess the requisite capabilities for doing the institutional work necessary to successfully establish the new institutional order. Such entrepreneurs must have a critical understanding of the existing institutional order and must be able to construct a new anticorrupt institutional logic – a new collective identity that defines anticorruption roles and practices in a legitimate manner and that legitimates the social resources necessary to have the anticorrupt order prevail. (Misangyi, Weaver and Elms, 2008, p. 766)

In sum, we advocate for a proactive, cohesive approach by MNCs to both act against corruption and to promote human rights, all under the umbrella of CSR. To accomplish this effort we find that a policies, procedures, publication, and participation framework is a promising mechanism to organize and promote these actions.

IV. CONCLUSION

While not without its critics, the push to raise awareness and promote corporate action to fight corruption and protect human rights continues to gain momentum. Although the recognition that corruption negatively impacts human rights has fueled the anti-corruption movement, the movements to encourage corporations to respect human rights and to combat corruption have proceeded in parallel. These two movements must be brought together if we are to achieve meaningful, sustainable improvements in the human rights impact of business. This suggests a more expansive role for corporations to combat corruption, rather than simply taking efforts to ensure that their employees or agents do not pay bribes. To promote these goals, this chapter set out a multi-prong approach for corporations. This approach proceeds within a framework of developing and implementing effective policies and procedures that is marked by the transparency of a publication regime. The framework also involves participation in multi-stakeholder initiatives to achieve the benefits of collective action.

NOTES

* An earlier version of this chapter was presented as a paper at the *Bridging the Gap between Business and Human Rights Colloquium*, University of Connecticut, Storrs, CT in May 2013. That version also received the 2013 Maurer Award for the best-submitted ethics paper at the Academy of Legal Studies in Business annual meeting. The authors thank the colloquium participants and organizers for their valuable comments and Raine Richards for her helpful research assistance, as well as several anonymous reviewers. All remaining mistakes and omissions remain the authors' responsibility.

1. In this chapter, we use the broadly accepted definition of corruption proffered by the prominent anti-corruption non-governmental organization Transparency International (TI): corruption is "abuse of entrusted power for private gain" (Transparency International, 2013c). Through tools like its Corruption Perceptions Index (CPI), TI applies this definition to both the private and public sectors, thus taking the definition beyond the traditional realm of criminalized bribery where one of the participants must be a public official (Transparency International, 2013b). TI's definition is relatively expansive and others have begun to look at private-to-private corruption and otherwise begun to see corruption as a major issue for the multi-national business community (Argandoña, 2003).
2. In an article discussing the reasons behind illegal construction in one developing area in India, the author states that "politicians preferred to keep colonies vulnerable so that residents remained more beholden to them for even incremental improvements." One business owner located in an illegally constructed area told the reporters that, "petty officials routinely demanded bribes to allow new construction projects. Others said that the police routinely required payoffs, too."
3. Ruggie frames the need for corporate due diligence related to human rights by asking, "Yet how do companies know they respect human rights? Do they have systems in

place enabling them to support the claim with any degree of confidence?" He concludes that "[m]ost do not" have such systems and argues that, "What is required is due diligence – a process whereby companies not only ensure compliance with national laws but also manage the risk of human rights harm with a view to avoiding it," adding that "[t]he scope of human rights related due diligence is determined by the context in which a company is operating, its activities, and the relationships associated with those activities" (p. 194).

4. Principle 11 states that, "Business enterprises should respect human rights. This means that they should avoid infringing on the human rights of others and should address adverse human rights impacts with which they are involved."
5. Bishop agrees with Ruggie to an extent, regarding corporate duties to refrain from human rights violations and to avoid complicity in human rights violations, but he concluding that, "[c]orporations have no obligation to ensure human rights. To have such obligations, corporations would need many rights that ought to be reserved only for governments" (p. 141).

REFERENCES

Accord on Fire and Building Safety in Bangladesh (2013, May 12) retrieved August 29, 2013, from http://www.workersrights.org/linkeddocs/Accord%20on%20Fire%20and%20Building%20Safety%20in%20Bangladesh%205.12.2013.pdf.

Ambraseys, N. and Bilham, R. (2011, Jan.) "Comment: Corruption kills", *Nature, 469*, 153.

Argandoña, A. (2003) "Private-to-private corruption", *Journal of Business Ethics, 47*(3), 253–67.

Barstow, D. and Bertrab, A.X.V. (2012, Dec. 17) "The bribery aisle: How Wal-Mart got its way in Mexico", *New York Times*, A1.

Barstow, D. (2012, April 21) "Wal-Mart hushed up a vast Mexican bribery case", *New York Times*, A1.

Barta, J.A. and Chapman, J. (2012) "Foreign Corrupt Practices Act", *American Criminal Law Review, 49*, 825–58.

Bishop, J.D. (2012) "The limits of corporate human rights obligations and the rights of for-profit corporations", *Business Ethics Quarterly, 22*(1), 119–44.

Cragg, W. (2012) "Ethics, enlightened self-interest, and the corporate responsibility to respect human rights: A critical look at the justificatory foundations of the UN Framework', *Business Ethics Quarterly, 22*(1), 9–36.

Dahlsrud, A. (2008) "How Corporate Social Responsibility is defined: An analysis of 37 definitions", *Corporate Social Responsibility and Environmental Management, 15*(1), 1–13.

Dodd-Frank Wall Street Reform and Consumer Protection Act, Pub. L. No. 111-203, 124 Stat. 1376 (2010).

Extractive Industries Transparency Initiative (2013) (n. d.) *What is the EITI?* retrieved August 29, 2013, from http://eiti.org/eiti.

Fassin, Y. (2009) "The stakeholder model refined", *Journal of Business Ethics, 84*(1), 113–35.

Foreign Corrupt Practices Act of 1977, Pub. L. No. 95-213, 15 U.S.C. § 78. Amended by Omnibus Trade and Competitiveness Act of 1988, Pub. L. No.

100-418, 15 U.S.C. § 78, and International Anti-Bribery and Fair Competition Act of 1998, Pub. L. No. 105-366, 15 U.S.C. § 78.

Freeman, R.E. (2002) "A stakeholder theory of the modern corporation", in Donaldson T., Werhane , P. and Cording, M. (eds), *Ethical Issues in Business: A Philosophical Approach*, (8th ed.), Upper Saddle River, NJ: Pearson.

Freeman, R.E., Velamuri, S.R. and Moriarty, B. (2006) "Company stakeholder responsibility: A new approach to CSR", *The Business Roundtable Institute for Corporate Ethics Bridge Paper Series* retrieved from http://www.corporate-ethics.org/pdf/csr.pdf.

Friedman, M. (1970, Sept. 13) "The social responsibility of business is to increase its profits", *New York Times Magazine*. 32–3.

Global Reporting Initiative, The (2013a) (n. d.) *Anti-corruption Working Group – Background* retrieved August 29, 2013, from https://www.globalreporting.org/reporting/g4/g4-developments/g4-working-groups/Pages/Anti-corruption.aspxttps://www.globalreporting.org/reporting/latest-guidelines/g4-developments/g4-w.

Global Reporting Initiative, The (2013b) (n. d.). *What is GRI?* retrieved August 29, 2013, from https://www.globalreporting.org/information/about-gri/what-is-GRI/Pages/default.aspx.

Hess, D. and Dunfee, T.W. (2000) "Fighting corruption: A principled approach; the C2 Principles (combating corruption)", *Cornell International Law Journal, 33*(3), 593–625.

Hsieh, N. (2004) "The obligations of transnational corporations: Rawlsian justice and the duty of assistance", *Business Ethics Quarterly, 14*(4), 643–61.

Hsieh, N. (2009) "Does Global Business Have a Responsibility to Promote Just Institutions?" *Business Ethics Quarterly, 19*(2), 251–74.

International Organization for Standardization. (2010) *ISO 26000: Guidance on Social Responsibility*, 13, 26.

Karnani, A. (2012, June 14) "Editorial: The case against corporate social responsibility", *Wall Street Journal* retrieved from http://online.wsj.com/article/SB10001424052748703338004575230112664504890.html.

Keeping, J. and Zaman, I. (2012, Dec. 20) "Bangladeshi factory fires, corruption and the rule of law", *Troy Media* retrieved from http://www.troymedia.com/2012/12/20/bangladeshi-factory-fires-corruption-and-the-rule-of-law/.

Kinley, D., Nolan, J. and Zerial, N. (2007) "'The Norms are Dead! Long live the Norms!' The politics behind the UN Human Rights Norms for Corporations", in D. McBarnet, A. Voiculescu and T. Campbell (eds.), *The New Corporate Accountability: Corporate Social Responsibility and the Law* (pp. 459–75), United Kingdom: Cambridge University Press.

Manik, J.A. and Yardley, J. (2013, Apr. 25) "Western firms feel pressure as toll rises in Bangladesh", *New York Times* retrieved from http://www.nytimes.com/2013/04/26/world/asia/bangladeshi-collapse-kills-many-garment-workers.html?pagewanted=all.

McCorquodale, R. (2009) "Corporate social responsibility and international human rights law", *Journal of Business Ethics*, *87*(2), 385–400.

Misangyi, V., Weaver, G. and Elms, H. (2008, July 1) "Ending corruption: The interplay among institutional logics, resources, and institutional entrepreneurs", *Academic Management Review, 33*(3), 750–70.

Most, M. (2013, Jan. 27) 'Another factory fire kills more garment workers", *ABC News* retrieved from http://abcnews.go.com/Blotter/factory-fire-kills-garment-workers/story?id=18327767.

Nichols, P.M. (2004) "Corruption as an assurance problem", *American University International Law Review, 19*(6), 1307–49.

Nichols, P.M. (2009) "Multiple communities and controlling corruption", *Journal of Business Ethics, 88*(4), 805–13.

Organization for Economic Co-operation and Development. (2011) "Convention on combating bribery of foreign public officials in international business transactions", retrieved August 29, 2013, from http://www.oecd.org/daf/anti-bribery/ConvCombatBribery_ENG.pdf.

Porter, M.E. and Kramer, M.R. (2006) "Strategy and society, the link between competitive advantage and corporate social responsibility", *Harvard Business Review, 84*(12), 78–92.

PricewaterhouseCoopers (2008) "Confronting corruption: The business case for an effective anti- corruption programme", retrieved August 29, 2013, from http://www.pwc.com/anti-corruption.

Rawls, J. (1999) *The Law of Peoples*, Cambridge, MA: Harvard University Press.

Ruggie, J. (2008, Spring) "Protect, Respect and Remedy: A framework for business and human rights", *U.N. Innovations, 3*(2), 189–212.

Social Accountability International (2013a) (n. d.) *About SAI* retrieved August 29, 2013, from http://www.sa-intl.org/index.cfm?fuseaction=Page.ViewPage &pageId=1365.

Social Accountability International (2013b , Mar. 11) "Fire safety a key focus in SA8000 Revision", retrieved from http://www.sa-intl.org/index.cfm?fuseaction =Page.ViewPage&PageID=1435#.Uh-4s_IrE0U.

Transparency International (2013a). (n. d.) "Bribe payers index – Overview", retrieved August 29, 2013, from http://www.transparency.org/research/bpi/ overviewAugust.

Transparency International (2013b) (n. d.) "What is the Corruption Perceptions Index (CPI)? – 3. What is corruption and how does the CPI measure it?" retrieved August 29, 2013, from http://www.transparency.org/cpi2011/in_ detailAugust.

Transparency International (2013c) (n. d.) "Who we are, FAQs – 1. How do you define corruption?" retrieved August 29, 2013, from http://www. transparency.org/whoweare/organisation/faqs_on_corruption/2/.

United Nations Commission on Human Rights Subcommittee, 55th Session (2003, Aug. 13) "Norms on the responsibilities of transnational corporations and other business enterprises with regard to human rights", U.N. Document E/CN.4/Sub.2/2003/12/Rev.2.

United Nations Global Compact (2013) (n. d.) "Transparency and anti-corruption", retrieved August 29, 2013, from http://www.unglobalcompact.org/ AboutTheGC/TheTenPrinciples/anti-corruption.htmlAugust.

United Nations Global Compact (2011) "Corporate sustainability in the world economy", retrieved from http://www.unglobalcompact.org/docs/news_events/ 8.1/GC_brochure_FINAL.pdf.

United Nations Global Compact and Transparency International. (2009) "Reporting guidance on the 10th principle against corruption", retrieved August 29,

2013, from http://www.unglobalcompact.org/docs/issues_doc/AntiCorruption/UNGC_AntiCorruptionReporting.pdf.

United Nations Special Representative of the Secretary-General (2011, Mar. 21). "Guiding Principles on Business and Human Rights: Implementing the United Nations "Protect, Respect and Remedy" Framework", U.N. Document A/HRC/17/31.

Wettstein, F. (2012a) "CSR and the Debate on Business and Human Rights: Bridging the Great Divide", *Business Ethics Quarterly, 22*(4), 739–70.

Wettstein, F. (2012b) "Silence as complicity elements of a corporate duty to speak out against the violation of human rights", *Business Ethics Quarterly, 22*(1), 37–61.

Wood, S. (2012) "The case for leverage-based corporate human rights responsibility", *Business Ethics Quarterly, 22*(1), 63–98.

World Bank Institute (2008) "Fighting corruption through collective action: A guide for business", retrieved August 29, 2013, from http://info.worldbank.org/etools/docs/antic/Whole_guide_Oct.pdf.

Yardley, J. (2013, Apr. 27) "Illegal districts dot New Delhi as city swells", *New York Times*, A6.

Zadek, S. (2004, Dec.) "The path to corporate responsibility", *Harvard Business Review, 82*(12), 125–32.

4. The First Amendment, compelled speech and disclosure regulations

Lucien J. Dhooge

Government regulation of business in the United States is ubiquitous and inescapable. Although regulation may take many different approaches, one common form is based upon disclosure. These regulations may engender conflict between the government's interest in full and meaningful disclosure and business interests in shielding certain types of information, the disclosure of which could prove harmful to an industry and its individual members.

These conflicts have recently manifested themselves in numerous judicial challenges by individual companies and trade associations utilizing the prohibition upon compelled speech. Courts have applied a variety of standards by which to determine the constitutionality of these regulations. This chapter analyzes recent challenges to disclosure regulations in the context of the type of speech and the appropriate level of constitutional scrutiny. The discussion is particularly relevant to disclosures that relate to human rights issues.

I. THE FIRST AMENDMENT AND COMPELLED SPEECH

The First Amendment to the U.S. Constitution states, in part, that "Congress shall make no law … abridging the freedom of speech" (U.S. Constitution, amendment I). The right to speak and the right to refrain from speaking are "complementary components of the broader concept of individual freedom of mind" enshrined within the First Amendment (*Wooley v. Maynard*, p. 714, 1977). This "freedom of mind" protects individuals and corporations against governmental action compelling speech. The value of this prohibition to speakers is readily apparent. The prohibition upon compelled speech also serves listener interests in receiving information free from government compulsion and potential distortion. The resultant exchange of ideas results in "genuine, robust expression that (listeners) can use for belief formation" (Royal, p. 210, 2012). In this manner, an uninhibited marketplace of ideas is secured.

Compelled speech cases have traditionally focused on the recitation of political or ideological messages and statements of opinion on controversial issues. However, the U.S. Supreme Court has held that compelled factual recitations are legally indistinguishable from statements of opinion and may violate the First Amendment. First Amendment interests also are implicated in circumstances where the government compels a speaker to disseminate the views of other individuals or organizations to which the speaker objects or disagrees, especially when such forced accommodation impacts the speaker's own message.

Commercial speech also is arguably subject to restrictions on government compulsion. In *United States v. United Foods, Inc.* (2001), the U.S. Supreme Court reviewed a subsidization provision within the Mushroom Promotion, Research, and Consumer Information Act, which required handlers of fresh mushrooms to pay assessments to a government-appointed council to fund industry promotion, research, and consumer information. Applying case law dating back to 1943, the Court invalidated the subsidies as compelled contributions to speech. Although the decision is part of a compelled subsidy of speech line of cases, the Court's holding implicitly created a compelled commercial speech doctrine (Pomeranz, 2009). However, the Court did not elaborate upon factors to determine the existence of compelled commercial speech or the applicable constitutional framework.

II. SPEECH AND APPLICABLE CONSTITUTIONAL STANDARDS

Content-based restrictions on core-protected speech (such as speech relating to political, economic and social matters) are subject to constitutional analysis utilizing the strict scrutiny standard. Strict scrutiny is the proper standard in such circumstances as "[t]he freedom of speech … guaranteed by the Constitution embraces at least the liberty to discuss publicly and truthfully all matters of public concern without previous restraint or fear of subsequent punishment" (*First National Bank v. Bellotti*, p. 776, 1978). Such restrictions are subject to a rigorous two-part test. The government must first demonstrate that the restriction serves a "compelling state interest." An exact definition of "compelling state interest" remains elusive. Nevertheless, the U.S. Supreme Court has recognized compelling interests relating to public safety; the effective functioning, stability and integrity of the national government; voting rights; discrimination; national defense; and the protection of minors. The restriction or burden on speech also must be narrowly tailored to achieve the compelling state interest. A restriction on speech is not narrowly tailored to serve a compelling interest if there is a less restrictive alternative available.

Strict scrutiny is also applicable to circumstances involving compelled speech. For example, strict scrutiny may serve to invalidate statutes compelling individuals to express or subsidize messages with which they disagree, or that alter the content of their own messages or infringe on rights to political association or belief. The factual rather than ideological nature of a mandated disclosure does not exempt it from strict scrutiny analysis. However, strict scrutiny is not applicable to "routine disclosures of economically significant information designed to forward ordinary regulatory purposes" (*Pharmaceutical Care Management Association v. Rowe*, p. 316, 2005).

A less stringent standard of constitutional review is utilized in instances of content-neutral government regulation of speech. Courts analyzing such regulations utilize an intermediate scrutiny standard consisting of two separate inquiries. The initial inquiry is whether the regulation at issue furthers "an important or substantial governmental interest unrelated to the suppression of free speech" (*Turner Broadcasting System, Inc. v. FCC*, p. 186, 1997). Assuming such important or substantial interests are implicated, the second inquiry requires determination of whether any restrictions contained within the regulation "burden substantially more speech than is necessary to further those interests" (*Turner Broadcasting System, Inc. v. FCC*, p. 186, 1997). Content-neutral regulations furthering important or substantial government interests that do not unnecessarily burden speech will be upheld.

Restrictions on commercial speech are subject to a different intermediate scrutiny test set forth in *Central Hudson Gas & Electric Corporation v. Public Service Commission* (1980). In this case, the Court reviewed a New York regulation prohibiting public utilities from placing promotional advertising in their monthly billing statements. The Court concluded this prohibition violated the First Amendment and, in so doing, fashioned a four-pronged intermediate scrutiny test by which to evaluate such restrictions. First, a court must determine whether the expression is one that qualifies for First Amendment protection. This requirement is satisfied if the speech concerned lawful activity and was not misleading. Second, a court must determine whether the asserted governmental interest is substantial (a wide variety of government interests have been deemed substantial by the U.S. Supreme Court, including the health, safety and welfare of citizens and privacy interests). The court must examine the government's stated interest and cannot substitute its own justifications for the restraint. The third prong requires a court to determine whether the regulation directly advances the asserted governmental interest. This prong has been described as requiring the government to produce factual evidence that the regulation directly and materially advances its stated interest and would be effective in addressing an identified problem.

The final prong of the *Central Hudson* standard requires the government to demonstrate that the regulation is not more extensive than necessary to serve the government's interest. This prong requires courts to evaluate whether there is a "reasonable fit between the legislature's ends and the means chosen to accomplish those ends, a means narrowly tailored to achieve the desired objective" (*Lorillard Tobacco Company v. Reilly,* p. 556, 2011). This fit need not be perfect or the least-restrictive means, but speech-related measures will fail if the government could achieve its interests in a manner that does not restrict speech or restricts less speech.

The *Central Hudson* standard has been applied in the context of compelled speech. In *R.J. Reynolds Tobacco Company v. FDA* (2012), the U.S. Court of Appeals for the District of Columbia Circuit concluded the graphic warnings required by the Family Smoking Prevention and Tobacco Control Act of 2009 (FSPTCA) as implemented by the FDA failed the *Central Hudson* standard. It was undisputed that the cigarette packaging and labeling requirements related to lawful activity, and there was no misleading or fraudulent behavior; thus, the court's primary focus was on the substantiality of the government's interest and whether the use of such warnings directly advanced this interest. The court identified the FDA's stated interests in adopting the graphic warnings requirement, specifically, encouraging current smokers to quit and dissuading future consumers from purchasing and using tobacco products. The court noted that the U.S. Supreme Court had implied the existence of a government interest in reducing smoking rates due to the associated health consequences. However, the court concluded the government failed to meet its burden of offering substantial evidence that the graphic warnings directly advanced these interests to a material degree. Such evidence was "critical" in order to prevent the government from interfering with commercial speech "in the service of other objectives that could not themselves justify a burden on commercial expression" (*R.J. Reynolds Tobacco Company v. FDA,* p. 1219, 2012). "Ineffective or remote support" and "mere speculation or conjecture" were insufficient to meet this burden, which the court described as "not light" (*R.J. Reynolds Tobacco Company v. FDA,* p. 1218–19, 2012).

Applying this standard, the court concluded the FDA had failed to provide "a shred of evidence – much less … 'substantial evidence' … showing that the graphic warnings will 'directly advance' its interest in reducing the number of Americans who smoke" (*R.J. Reynolds Tobacco Company v. FDA,* p. 1219, 2012). The FDA's reliance on international consensus concerning the effectiveness of graphic warnings in directly causing material decreases in smoking rates was at best questionable. The FDA could not demonstrate the reduction in smoking rates in countries utilizing graphic warnings such as Canada were directly attributable to such warnings rather than other smoking control initiatives. The FDA's own Regulatory Impact Analysis conceded the lack of direct evidence directly linking graphic warnings to substantial decreases in smoking rates and described its own methodology as failing to account for other contemporaneous factors contributing to the decrease in smoking rates such as stringent smoking bans, advertising restrictions, and higher prices. Other studies relied upon by the FDA failed to demonstrate that graphic warnings would directly and materially advance the cause of reducing smoking rates. This lack of supporting data "strongly implie[d] that such warnings [were] not very effective at promoting cessation and discouraging initiation" (*R.J. Reynolds Tobacco Company v. FDA,* p. 1220, 2012).

Finally, government-imposed restrictions upon commercial speech may be analyzed utilizing the reasonable relationship test set forth in *Zauderer v. Office of Disciplinary Counsel* (1985). In this case, the Court reviewed a state court determination requiring advertisements for legal services offered on a contingent fee basis to disclose whether the percentages allotted to attorneys for their fees were net of costs in order to prevent consumer deception. Zauderer failed to comply with this requirement and was sanctioned by the Ohio Office of the Disciplinary Counsel. The Court concluded the cost disclosure requirement was not of the magnitude of earlier cases relating to compelled speech in the context of politics or religion. Ohio "attempted only to prescribe what shall be orthodox in commercial advertising … [by requiring disclosure of] purely factual and uncontroversial information about the terms under which [Zauderer's] services will be available" (*Zauderer v. Office of Disciplinary Counsel,* p. 651, 1985). This factual disclosure did not restrict speech nor compel public discourse in contravention of the First Amendment but instead served listeners' interests in receiving additional information. These interests and the purely factual nature of the information minimized the speaker's interest in not providing disclosure.

These considerations justified less rigorous constitutional scrutiny. The Court devised a five-part test for determining the constitutionality of government-required disclosures. First, the compelled disclosure must be purely factual. Second, the factual information subject to compelled disclosure must be "uncontroversial" and truthful. The third requirement is the presence of a legitimate government interest in compelling disclosure. And fourth, the disclosure must be reasonably related to this government interest. The element requires a rational connection between the purpose of the disclosure and the means employed to achieve the purpose. Finally, the required disclosure must not be unjustified or unduly burdensome.

The Court revisited its holding in *Zauderer* 25 years later in *Milavetz, Gallop & Milavetz, P.A. v. United States* (2010). The speech at issue in *Milavetz* was the requirement contained in the Bankruptcy Abuse Prevention and Consumer Protection Act of 2005 (BAPCPA) that debt relief agencies include "clear and conspicuous" disclosures in their advertisements of bankruptcy assistance services (BAPCPA, § 528(a–b), 2005). Milavetz challenged these disclosures as unconstitutionally compelling speech pursuant to the *Central Hudson* intermediate scrutiny standard.

The Court rejected this challenge utilizing *Zauderer's* reasonable relationship test. The Court concluded that the challenged provisions shared essential features of the rule at issue in *Zauderer,* specifically, the intent to "combat the problem of inherently misleading commercial advertisements," in this case the promise of debt relief without reference to the costly process of filing for bankruptcy (*Milavetz, Gallop & Milavetz, P.A. v. United States*, p. 249, 2010). The disclosures entailed only accurate factual statements and did not prevent debt relief agencies from conveying additional information. This lack of limitation upon additional speech served to distinguish BAPCPA from other instances where the Court applied the *Central Hudson* framework.

The Court discounted the lack of evidence that the advertisements were in fact misleading by noting that advertisements for professional services pose "a special risk of deception" (*Milavetz, Gallop & Milavetz, P.A. v. United States*, p. 251, 2010). The possibility of deception rendered it unnecessary to survey the public in order to determine actual deception or the tendency of the advertisements to mislead consumers. Milavetz failed to adduce any evidence that the term "debt relief agency" was confusing or misleading to consumers. To the contrary, the identification of law firms such as Milavetz's firm as "debt relief agencies" provided interested parties with "pertinent information about the advertiser's services and client obligations" such as assistance with bankruptcy filings. (*Milavetz, Gallop & Milavetz, P.A. v. United States*, p. 251–52,

2010). The Court thus concluded BAPCPA's required identification of "debt relief agencies" and disclosure of information regarding their services relating to bankruptcy were reasonably related to the government's interest in preventing consumer deception as required by *Zauderer.*

III. THE FIRST AMENDMENT AND DISCLOSURE REGULATIONS

A. Disclosure Regulations and Strict Scrutiny: A Case of Corporate Overreach

Strict scrutiny as the standard by which to judge disclosure regulations has been utilized or urged upon courts in several recent cases. The plaintiffs in *R.J. Reynolds Tobacco Company v. FDA* (2012) urged the court to apply strict scrutiny to the graphic warnings required by FSPTCA and its implementing regulations. Similarly, in *National Association of Manufacturers v. Securities and Exchange Commission* (2013), the petitioners urged the district court to apply strict scrutiny to Dodd-Frank's conflict minerals disclosure requirement. The Dodd-Frank Wall Street Reform and Consumer Protection Act (Dodd-Frank) and its implementing regulations require companies subject to Securities and Exchange Commission (SEC) reporting to disclose whether "conflict minerals" (specifically, tantalum, tin, tungsten and gold) that are "necessary to the functionality or production of a product manufactured" by such companies originated in the Democratic Republic of the Congo (DRC) or nine adjoining states (Dodd-Frank, 15 U.S.C. § 78m(p)(1)(A), (2)(B), 2010; Conflict Minerals, 77 Fed. Reg. 56,274, 2012). Disclosing companies must conduct a "reasonable country of origin inquiry" into the source of any such minerals (Conflict Minerals, 77 Fed. Reg. 56,311, 2012). If such minerals did originate in the DRC or adjoining states or if a company cannot determine the source, then it is required to submit a report to the SEC describing due diligence measures taken to determine the source and supply chain of such minerals and products manufactured or contracted to be manufactured that are not "DRC conflict free" (Conflict Minerals, 77 Fed. Reg. 56,311, 2012). The report must be filed with the SEC and posted on the company's website. (Dodd-Frank, 15 U.S.C. § 78m(p)(1)(E), 2010; Conflict Minerals, 77 Fed. Reg. 56,362-63, 2012).

The petitioners contended that the government had no legitimate interest with respect to the origin of conflict minerals as the subject matter was outside of the SEC's expertise relating to the regulation of securities markets. To the extent the government could identify a compelling interest in promoting peace and security in the DRC and depriving armed groups of revenue derived from trade in conflict minerals, the regulation did not advance these interests as the SEC failed to assess the degree to which disclosure would achieve these goals, quantify the benefits of disclosure, and identify reliable empirical evidence regarding the rule's effects. The petitioners further alleged the regulation was unduly burdensome due to the pervasive presence of the minerals in a multitude of products; the large number of manufacturers utilizing such minerals; the extensive and largely unknown supply chain; the inability to trace potential conflict minerals to their source of origin and proceeds derived from their trade to specific armed groups; and the absence of de minimis exceptions.

In a related challenge, the petitioners in *American Petroleum Institute v. SEC* contended that strict scrutiny should be the applicable standard by which to determine the constitutionality of the section of Dodd-Frank requiring publicly listed members of the extractive industry to disclose payments to foreign governments relating to the commercial development of oil, gas and mineral resources. "Resource extraction issuers" were required to include in their annual reports information relating to any payment made by them, their subsidiaries or entities under their control to foreign governments for "the purpose of the commercial development of oil, natural gas, or minerals" (Dodd-Frank, 15 U.S.C. § 78m(q)(2)(A), 2010). Examples of payments subject to disclosure included "taxes, royalties, fees (including licensing fees), production entitlements, bonuses, and other material benefits, that the [SEC] … determines are part of the commonly recognized revenue stream for the commercial development of oil, natural gas, or minerals." (Dodd-Frank, 15 U.S.C. § 78m(q)(1)(C)(ii), 2010; Disclosure of Payments by Resource Extraction Issuers, 77 Fed. Reg. 56,378–79 2012). Specific disclosures with respect to such payments included the total amount of the payment by category, the currency utilized, the financial period in which the payment was made, the business segment making the payment, the identity of the recipient government, and the project with which the payment was associated. (Dodd-Frank, 15 U.S.C. § 78m(q)(2)(A)(i–ii), 2010; Disclosure of Payments by Resource Extraction Issuers, 77 Fed. Reg. 56,393, 2012). The SEC refused to grant exemptions for smaller issuers and foreign private issuers; compliance with foreign laws prohibiting disclosure; confidentiality provisions in contracts relating to natural resources; and protection of commercially or competitively sensitive information. The petitioners contended that the empowerment of citizens of resource-rich countries with respect to accounting and utilization of monies received from members of the extractive industry was not a compelling interest, and the disclosure requirement was not narrowly tailored to further U.S. interests in influencing social and political conditions in other countries.

These attempts to apply strict scrutiny to overturn disclosure laws are misguided. Strict scrutiny has never been applied to laws requiring disclosure of factual and non-ideological information. Nor was strict scrutiny applied in the determination of these challenges. However, there are other reasons that render it unlikely that courts will apply strict scrutiny to such laws in future cases.

Courts will go to extraordinary lengths to avoid the application of strict scrutiny to disclosure regulations. For example, the court in *R.J. Reynolds Tobacco Company* described the graphic warnings to be placed upon tobacco packaging as symbolism highly susceptible to misinterpretation by consumers, nonfactual due to their primary intent to evoke shock, disgust and other emotional responses in viewers, inaccurate, biased, inflammatory and provocative. There was no evidence to support the FDA's conclusion that such warnings would be effective in reducing domestic smoking rates and contrary evidence suggesting that such warnings were not effective at promoting cessation and discouraging initiation. Nevertheless, despite the presence of compulsion to host a governmentally drafted message, the highly biased nature in which it was to be presented to consumers, and the absence of supportive evidence linking the message to its purported goal, the court overturned the district court's application of strict scrutiny.

Similarly, in *National Association of Manufacturers v. SEC,* the district court applied intermediate scrutiny to the conflict minerals disclosures due to their commercial nature. The disclosures were commercial given that they encompassed "material representations about the efficacy, safety, and quality of … [a] product, and other information asserted for the purpose of persuading the public to purchase the product" (*National Association of Manufacturers v. SEC* , p. 55 n.27, 2013). The mere fact that the disclosure linked a product to ongoing debate about a controversial topic did not transform the disclosure to compelled non-commercial or ideological speech. Accordingly, the court had "no trouble concluding that the disclosures – which consist of information regarding a company's supply chain and sourcing practices for its products – comfortably fit within the realm of commercial speech" (*National Association of Manufacturers v. SEC* , p. 77 n.27, 2013).

Another factor distinguishing cases warranting the application of strict scrutiny is the absence of compelled political or ideological expression by those subject to reporting. The disclosures in cases in which strict scrutiny has been urged by petitioners are a far cry from speech to which such a rigorous standard has been deemed applicable. The information subject to disclosure does not touch or concern topics essential to citizen participation in self-governance such as politics, religion and matters of opinion. Companies subject to these regulations are not suffering an infringement of their rights to political association or belief nor being denied "the autonomy to choose the content of [their] own message" (*Hurley v. Irish-American Gay, Lesbian & Bisexual Group of Boston*, p. 573, 1995). Such companies also are not being required to embrace state-sponsored viewpoints or serve as mobile billboards for the government's ideological viewpoint. They are simply required to disclose specific factual information regarding discrete aspects of their business operations. Affected companies may be reluctant to disclose some or all of this information, but such reluctance does not equate to forced expression or subsidization of political or ideological messages with which they disagree.

That some of this information touches upon matters of current public debate is irrelevant absent compelled ideological recitations of belief. For example, the court in *National Association of Manufacturers v. SEC* dismissed the contention that the linkage between the conflict minerals disclosure requirement and the public debate surrounding events in the DRC mandated the application of strict scrutiny as "unavailing" and "miss[ing] the mark" (*National Association of Manufacturers v. SEC,* p. 77 n.27, 2013). The U.S. Supreme Court reached a similar conclusion in *Bolger v. Youngs Drug Products Corporation* in which it concluded that "advertising which links a product to a current public debate is not thereby entitled to the constitutional protection afforded noncommercial speech" (*Bolger v. Youngs Drug Products Corporation,* p. 68, 1983). It is worth noting the disclosure bearing the closest resemblance to compelled recitation of an ideologically based government message, specifically, the graphic warnings regarding the consequences of tobacco use, were not deemed political or ideological thereby warranting strict scrutiny. If such biased and provocative messages as those conveyed by the graphic tobacco warnings were not sufficiently ideological in nature as to trigger strict scrutiny, it is difficult to ascertain how less inflammatory messages could cause a court to determine their constitutionality utilizing such a rigorous standard.

Compelled factual speech is entitled to review utilizing strict scrutiny if there are elements of intertwined commercial and non-commercial speech pursuant to the U.S. Supreme Court's opinion in *Riley v. National Federation of the Blind of North Carolina, Inc.* The Court applied strict scrutiny to that portion of the North Carolina Charitable Solicitations Act requiring professional fundraisers, prior to an appeal for funds, to disclose to potential donors the percentage of charitable contributions collected in the previous 12 months that were actually turned over to charity. Strict scrutiny was necessary as speech does not retain its commercial character in circumstances where it is "inextricably intertwined" with "fully protected" and "informative and perhaps persuasive speech" that would not occur in the absence of solicitation (*Riley v. National Federation of the Blind of North Carolina, Inc.*, p. 796, 1988). The "lodestars" in deciding which level of scrutiny to apply were the "nature of the speech taken as a whole and the effect of the compelled statement thereon" (*Riley v. National Federation of the Blind of North Carolina, Inc.*, p. 796, 1988). However, the Court also held purely commercial speech to be more susceptible to compelled disclosure requirements.

The nature of the disclosure regulations to which strict scrutiny has been sought to be applied is, taken as a whole, commercial rather than political. The absence of fully protected speech in the context of the challenged disclosure regulations renders strict scrutiny inapplicable on the basis of *Riley's* intertwined commercial and non-commercial speech standard. Furthermore, the compelled disclosure of facts, such as payments to foreign governments and utilization of conflict minerals, will not terminate or significantly interfere with protected speech. It is highly unlikely that affected companies would cease exercising their commercial and non-commercial speech rights as a result of disclosure regulations. In fact, it likely such companies would engage in greater amounts of speech in an effort to explain and contextualize the disclosed information. Additionally, commercial disclosure regulations have the opposite effect of their counterpart in *Riley* by making important information available to the public rather than depriving the public of such information. Given these distinctions, the regulations subject to judicial challenge to date fit within *Riley's* increased susceptibility to compelled disclosure requirements.

However, the absence of political or ideological expression does not automatically render such speech commercial in nature and subject to a lesser degree of scrutiny. This has created a gap which industries have sought to exploit. These industries have argued that strict scrutiny must be utilized to analyze any disclosures that are not commercial in nature, specifically, that are not related to a proposed or consummated commercial transaction. For example, in *American Petroleum Institute v. SEC*, the petitioners urged the court to apply strict scrutiny as the compelled disclosure did not "propose a commercial transaction and … is not part of any commercial transaction between covered entities and foreign companies" (Memorandum of Points and Authorities in Support of Plaintiffs' Motion for Summary Judgment, p. 32 n.7, 2013). Proponents have been successful in convincing several courts, including the U.S. Courts of Appeals for the Sixth and Seventh Circuits, that regulations requiring disclosure beyond specific business transactions are no longer commercial in nature and require the application of strict scrutiny.

This argument and the opinions that have endorsed it have created an all-or-nothing approach in which the government's interest in disclosure must be directly related to identifiable commercial transactions (and thus subject to the reasonable relationship test) or suffer strict scrutiny. The result is overly restrictive definitions of commercial speech and possible government interests beyond identifiable transactions. This approach also completely ignores a readily available compromise framework of intermediate scrutiny as established by *Central Hudson*. It is incumbent upon the courts to eliminate this confusion.

The district court's opinion in *National Association of Manufacturers v. SEC* is a significant step forward in this regard. The court rejected the all-or-nothing approach advocated by the petitioners and defined commercial speech as "not limited to purely economic speech or speech proposing a commercial transaction" (*National Association of Manufacturers v. SEC*, p. 77 n.27, 2013). The district court's definition correctly recognizes that commercial speech may relate to broader economic interests and motivations of the speaker. It is particularly important to separate advertising from commercial speech as not all advertising necessarily proposes an economic transaction and not all commercial speech is advertising. A broader definition also is more closely aligned with government interests. Governmental interests in commercial speech transcend advertising to include a number of other interests such as labeling, product use and safety warnings, and factual disclosures directed at investors, all of which implicate the economic interests of the speaker. This definition is also consistent with court opinions, which have taken a broader view of commercial speech, including the opinion of the U.S. Supreme Court in *Central Hudson*.

This is not to contend commercial speech is that which has any economic implications for the speaker whatsoever. Every utterance, be it a voluntary statement, a compelled disclosure or silence, carries with it economic implications. Such a definition would swallow all business-related speech wholesale including content-based restrictions and compelled political and ideological statements clearly meriting application of strict scrutiny. Rather, the argument is simply that courts recognize a wider range of speech as commercial beyond specific transactions. In the compelled commercial speech area, these communications would fall somewhere between factual statements designed to prevent consumer deception subject to review utilizing *Zauderer* and the automatic default standard of strict scrutiny for any other type of compelled communication. This is a preferable approach to the current standard which is court-specific and invites more First Amendment challenges to disclosure regulations.

One additional area in need of greater consensus and breadth is whether the government interest at stake is sufficient to justify compelled disclosure. Government interests alleged to justify disclosure to date have almost exclusively focused on the U.S. population. This domestic focus changed upon the adoption of Dodd-Frank and its conflict minerals and foreign government payments disclosure requirements.

Government interests in compelling disclosure to primarily serve the interests of foreign populations have been questioned in subsequent judicial challenges. However, the U.S. undoubtedly has an interest in the stability of foreign governments, the prevention of discord and upheaval in foreign states and transparency efforts in a wide variety of areas. Such interests should be treated no differently from a constitutional standpoint than the government's domestic interests. A limitation upon compelled disclosure to purely domestic interests would hamstring government regulation in an increasingly global marketplace. Such a limitation would be inconsistent with the power of federal agencies over the international operations of U.S. companies and the reach of federal administrative regulations. Such a result also places companies challenging disclosure regulations and the courts required to resolve such challenges in the position of second-guessing the political branches of government on matters of foreign affairs. The substitution of the judgment of companies bent on maximization of profits and courts inexperienced in international relations for the wisdom of the political branches to which such questions have been constitutionally committed is unwise and contrary to the historical deference given to the decisions of such branches in this area. A far preferable outcome is the recognition that the interests of the federal government with respect to the conduct of foreign affairs are substantial and often compelling.

B. Disclosure Regulations and the Reasonable Relationship Test: The Limits of Zauderer

Strict scrutiny's polar opposite, the reasonable relationship test set forth in *Zauderer,* has been asserted by the government as the standard by which to sustain disclosure regulations in numerous instances including those concerning disclosure of payments to foreign governments, conflict minerals, and the posting of employee rights pursuant to the National Labor Relations Act. These arguments are also misguided and fail to recognize the limits of *Zauderer's* holding.

There is a legitimate question as to whether *Zauderer* is limited to instances of consumer deception. It is plausible to interpret the opinion as merely holding that the government's interest in protecting consumers from potentially deceptive practices is sufficient to support relaxed constitutional scrutiny rather than necessary. The plausibility of application of *Zauderer* beyond regulations designed to address actual or potential consumer deception has resulted in a split amongst circuit courts. The First, Second, Sixth, and Ninth Circuits have applied *Zauderer* to regulations designed to address issues beyond consumer deception to regulations concerning disclosure of finances and business practices, labeling of restaurant menus and tobacco products, and the environmental impacts of storm-water discharge and improper waste disposal. Conversely, other circuits, most notably the District of Columbia Circuit, have limited the holding in *Zauderer* to instances of potential or past deception.

The approach taken by those circuits limiting the application of *Zauderer* to instances of actual or potential consumer deception is better reasoned. The U.S. Supreme Court's own language in *Zauderer* limits its reach to cases in which the required disclosures are "reasonably related to the State's interest in preventing deception of consumers" (*Zauderer v. Office of Disciplinary Counsel*, p. 651, 1985). The Court has had subsequent opportunities to extend *Zauderer's* reach and has declined to do so on every occasion. For example, in *Ibanez v. Florida Department of Business and Professional Regulation* (1994), the Court held *Zauderer* applicable only when there was an affirmative government showing of threatened deception of consumers. *Zauderer* was inapplicable as the state could only demonstrate "purely hypothetical harm" from the inclusion of a certified financial planner designation in an advertisement for accounting services (*Ibanez v. Florida Department of Business and Professional Regulation*, p. 146, 1994). Seven years later, the Court distinguished *Zauderer* on the basis that the generic advertising requirement at issue was not "necessary to make voluntary advertisements non-misleading for consumers" (*United States v. United Foods, Inc.*, p. 416, 2001). The facts of the Court's only recent application of the reasonable relationship test to a disclosure requirement in *Milavetz, Gallop & Milavetz, P.A. v. United States* (2010) mirrored the circumstances at issue in *Zauderer.*

Zauderer's own language and these bypassed opportunities to expand its reach establish that use of the reasonable relationship standard "is only appropriate if the government shows that, absent a warning, there is a self-evident – or at least 'potentially real'– danger that an advertisement will mislead consumers" (*R.J. Reynolds Tobacco Company v. FDA*, p. 1214, 2012). Evidence of such actual or potential danger must include remedial justifications for the disclosure expressed in the legislative or rulemaking history, the existence of false or misleading claims, and the likelihood of deception in the absence of disclosure. First Amendment values and the Court's precedent require that the further a compelled disclosure strays from these limitations, "the more searching the scrutiny to which it should be subject" (Stern and Stern, p. 13, 2011).

Despite these limitations, the majority of disclosure regulations would be subject to analysis utilizing *Zauderer.* An example in this regard may be found in *Spirit Airlines, Inc. v. U.S. Department of Transportation* (2012). In this case, the U.S. Court of Appeals for the District of Columbia Circuit rejected a challenge to a rule requiring the most prominent figure displayed on print advertisements and websites to be the total price of a ticket inclusive of taxes. Airlines were permitted to continue to provide itemized breakdowns of base fare, taxes and other charges but were prohibited from displaying such price components in a more prominent place or manner than the total price (Enhancing Airline Passenger Protections, 76 Federal Register 23,110, 2011). The court applied the *Zauderer* standard to what it concluded was speech proposing a commercial transaction, referring to a specific product and having an underlying economic motivation. The court rejected the airlines' contention that their existing advertisements were political speech directed at criticizing the "huge tax burden" imposed by the federal government and thus merited strict scrutiny. Heightened scrutiny was inapplicable as Transportation's rule merely governed one aspect of advertising and did not prohibit or unduly burden the speaker's ability to provide additional information or critiques of government policies to consumers. Having determined that *Zauderer* provided the applicable standard of review, the court determined that Transportation's rule was reasonably related to its interest in preventing consumer deception.

There are literally thousands of similar disclosure requirements contained in federal and state regulations dealing with a myriad of topics such as environmental and consumer protection, public health, workplace safety and securities regulation. These regulations do not justify the application of extensive First Amendment scrutiny. Application of more searching standards endangers the existence of such regimes or, at the very least, subjects administrators to costly and drawn-out defenses of every circumstance where information is required to be provided to the government. The existence of alternatives is problematic for regulators "since some alternative option to any proposed regulation will likely always exist … [and] [t]he question remains unclear on how effective an alternative must be to be considered a valid alternative" (Pomeranz, p. 430, 2012). The result may very well be the reduction of the use of disclosure as a regulatory tool. A significant impairment to the use of disclosure will hinder the government's ability to protect citizens from a wide variety of hazards. Businesses and consumers also may find it more difficult to protect themselves from risk in the absence of information. Enhanced judicial scrutiny also threatens to substitute opinions of unelected judges for democratic decision-making in matters of ordinary economic regulation. Justice Breyer has described such a result as "reawaken[ing] *Lochner's* pre-New Deal threat of substituting judicial for democratic decision-making" in the realm of economic regulation (*Sorrell v. IMS Health, Inc.*, p. 2685, 2011). The effect would to be to transform the First Amendment into "a deregulatory bludgeon" potentially impairing even the most innocuous and mundane of disclosure requirements (Hethcoat, p. 200, 2012). Such a result is not wise or effective policy-making and is not constitutionally required.

C. Disclosure Regulations and Intermediate Scrutiny: The Default Standard

A question remains regarding the status of *Central Hudson's* intermediate scrutiny standard. One possible role is to serve as a default standard in those instances where commercial disclosures fall outside of the boundaries of *Zauderer.* These boundaries are the requirements of actual or potential consumer deception and a purely factual or "uncontroversial" subject matter. Two recent decisions serve as models for the future use of *Central Hudson* as a default standard.

The opinion in *R.J. Reynolds Tobacco Company v. FDA* (2012) is an example of proper application of intermediate scrutiny when the required disclosures are not purely factual or uncontroversial. The graphic images were not intended for literal interpretation but rather to symbolize the accompanying textual warnings and provide additional context. The images varied in terms of the clarity of the message purportedly conveyed but all were nonfactual, subject to misinterpretation, and "unabashed attempts to evoke emotion (and perhaps embarrassment) and browbeat consumers into quitting" (*R.J. Reynolds Tobacco Company v. FDA*, p. 1216, 2012). The images did not impart "purely factual, accurate, or uncontroversial information" to consumers, were outside the ambit of *Zauderer,* and were thus subject to analysis utilizing intermediate scrutiny (*R.J. Reynolds Tobacco Company v. FDA*, p. 1216, 2012).

The district court's opinion in *National Association of Manufacturers v. SEC* is an example of proper application of intermediate scrutiny when the required disclosures are not essential to prevent or remedy potential or actual consumer deception. The information to be disclosed regarding the use of conflict minerals was commercial, factual and uncontroversial. However, the disclosures were not intended to prevent or remedy existing or potential misleading or deceptive speech. The absence of actual or potential consumer deception led the court to apply *Central Hudson* rather than *Zauderer.*

The district court upheld the statute and regulations utilizing *Central Hudson*. The district court found the federal government's asserted interest, the promotion of peace and security in the DRC, was directly and materially advanced by the statute and regulations. In so holding, the court did not require empirical evidence to sustain the government's burden. Rather, the disclosures could be upheld "by references to studies and anecdotes … history, consensus, and simple common sense" (*National Association of Manufacturers v. SEC,* pp. 78–79, 2013). Deference to the U.S. Congress' determinations was particularly appropriate given that the law and regulations were "at the intersection of national security, foreign policy, and administrative law" (*National Association of Manufacturers v. SEC,* p. 79, 2013). Congress also considered substantial amounts of evidence including reports prepared by the U.N. and the U.S. State Department in reaching its conclusions. Furthermore, the act and regulations were consistent with previous congressional policy statements such as the Democratic Republic of the Congo Relief, Security, and Democracy Protection Act of 2006 which provided that U.S. policy was to be guided by efforts to ensure responsible and transparent management of natural resources.

The district court also addressed *Central Hudson's* "reasonable fit" prong. The court concluded this prong did not require application of a "least restrictive means" standard, a "perfect means-ends fit," or the "best conceivable option" (*National Association of Manufacturers v. SEC,* p. 79, 2013). Rather, the disclosures were a reasonable fit to accomplish Congress' objective of promoting peace and security in the DRC. The law and regulations avoided unwarranted stigmatization that may have occurred if the disclosures were required to be separately and conspicuously published, or companies were prohibited from providing additional clarifications or explanations. Stigmatization was also avoided through the requirement of identifying minerals of indeterminate origin as "not been found to be DRC conflict free" rather than "not DRC conflict free" and the two- to four-year phase-in requirement which permitted companies additional time to research their supply chains while simultaneously disclosing minerals from indeterminate sources as "DRC conflict undeterminable." Given these limitations, the SEC satisfied the "reasonable fit" prong of *Central Hudson* and was entitled to summary judgment in its favor.

The use of intermediate scrutiny as a default standard in the absence of actual or potential consumer deception or a purely factual or "uncontroversial" subject matter is a preferable approach. The application of intermediate scrutiny to regulations outside *Zauderer's* reach preserves judicial deference to the exercise of administrative discretion in the rulemaking process. Intermediate scrutiny also is consistent with increased convergence of constitutional protection for commercial and non-commercial speech. The distinction between non-commercial and commercial speech is "often thin and artificial," and the theory that non-commercial speech is more important than commercial speech is "deeply flawed" as society's interest in the free flow of commercial information may at times be "keener by far than [its] interest in the day's most urgent political debate" (Stern and Stern, pp. 18–19, 2011). The government's burden should be heightened when it dictates non-factual messages for reasons unrelated to potential or actual consumer deception (Stern and Stern, p. 12, 2011). Intermediate scrutiny provides such a heightened burden without imposing the insurmountable obstacle of strict scrutiny.

Drawing clear boundaries would clarify the distinctions between the three possible standards of constitutional review, identify the specific instances to which each of these standards is applicable, and provide much-needed guidance to regulators and affected businesses. Such an approach could allow legislators and regulators to carefully tailor legislation and rules mandating disclosure with a clear view of the level of constitutional scrutiny they would undergo should they be challenged. It would also better permit affected businesses to anticipate the likelihood of success of any judicial challenge and, perhaps, deter a significant portion of such challenges.

Despite its preferable status, the intermediate scrutiny standard as presently elucidated requires two modifications. The first modification concerns *Central Hudson's* requirement that the speech-related measure directly and materially advance the government's stated interest. One court addressing this prong has required the government to produce substantial empirical evidence that the disclosures directly advanced its interests to a material degree (*R.J. Reynolds Tobacco Company v. FDA*, p. 1218, 2012). The *Reynolds* court raised the bar too high by requiring such evidence of the benefits of specific disclosure regimes. The empirical evidence requirement risks substituting judicial opinion for the considered judgment of more knowledgeable and experienced legislators and regulators who have long studied problems sought to be remedied by disclosure and crafted what they believed to be an appropriate solution.

A better approach may be found in *Fleminger, Inc. v. U.S. Department of Health and Human Services* (2012). In upholding the addition of an FDA disclaimer to the petitioner's claim that daily consumption of epigallocatechin gallate contained in green tea was effective in reducing the risk of breast and prostate cancers pursuant to the Nutrition Labeling and Education Act of 1990, the court refused to interpret Supreme Court precedent to obligate the government to conduct an empirical analysis to prove the petitioner's claims were misleading. According to the court, the U.S. Supreme Court's opinions in *Ibanez v. Florida Department of Business and Professional Regulation* and *Edenfield v. Fane* permitted the government to demonstrate that a speech-related measure alleviated a real harm to a material degree through empirical or anecdotal evidence. Empirical evidence was only necessary if the government banned a proposed health claim rather than modified the claim through preparation of "short, succinct and accurate disclaimers as to the level of scientific support for a qualified health claim" (*Fleminger, Inc. v. U.S. Department of Health and Human Services*, p. 216, 2012). It was only necessary for the government to provide "some actual or real validation" that the speech restriction did in fact advance its interests. (*Fleminger, Inc. v. U.S. Department of Health and Human Services*, p. 215, 2012). The government met its burden through the FDA's expert analysis and assessment of the scientific evidence thoroughly articulated in a detailed report. The court properly deferred to the FDA's assessment of the strength of the scientific data supporting and debunking the proposed health claim and the potential impact of the disclaimer upon consumers.

A second example of judicial deference may be found in *National Association of Manufacturers v. SEC* (2013). The court refused to require the government to provide empirical evidence to support its conclusion that the conflict minerals disclosure requirement directly and materially advanced Congress' interest in peace and security in central Africa in general and the DRC in particular. The imposition of an empirical evidence requirement in such circumstances ignored the foreign relations context in which the disclosure requirement was adopted. Specifically, the "changeable and explosive nature of contemporary international relations" required Congress to "paint with a broader brush than that it customarily wields in domestic areas" (*National Association of Manufacturers v. SEC*, p. 79, 2013). The less specific nature of government goals in the foreign affairs arena made particularized empirical evidence less available and necessary. Although the mere presence of national security and foreign affairs concerns did not warrant abdication of judicial scrutiny, especially in the context of the First Amendment, the court nevertheless noted that judicial review is deferential in these areas. This deference recognized the judiciary's marked lack of competence in collecting evidence and drawing inferences in these areas. Unlike *R.J. Reynolds Tobacco*, the court also did not dismiss congressional reliance upon studies by the U.N., the U.S. State Department, and other international sources. The conclusion that the disclosure requirements would in fact advance U.S. interests in promoting peace and security could be based upon "informed judgment rather than concrete evidence" (*National Association of Manufacturers v. SEC*, p. 79, 2013).

In addition to judicial deference to disclosures requiring scientific analyses or touching and concerning foreign affairs, there is one final modification to intermediate scrutiny which has been recognized by courts but not incorporated in many recent disclosure regulations. This modification concerns disclosures made exclusively to the government as opposed to the general public. Three different courts, including the U.S. Supreme Court, discussing two different levels of constitutional analysis, strict scrutiny and the rational relationship test, have concluded compelled speech concerns may be minimized or eliminated through exclusive disclosure of the requested information to the government with or without subsequent republication. In *Riley v. National Federation of the Blind of North Carolina, Inc.*, the U.S. Supreme Court held that one of the methods the state could have adopted to reduce donor misperceptions without unconstitutionally burdening professional fundraisers' speech rights was disclosure of the requested information to the government and subsequent government republication. The Court described this option as "benign," "narrowly tailored" and "in keeping with the First Amendment directive that government not dictate the content of the speech absent compelling necessity" (*Riley v. National Federation of the Blind of North Carolina, Inc.*, p. 800, 1988).

Two lower courts have reached similar conclusions. In *Full Value Advisors, LLC v. SEC,* the U.S. Court of Appeals for the District of Columbia Circuit upheld disclosure requirements applicable to institutional investment managers holding at least $100 million in securities utilizing the reasonable relationship test. These disclosures were "indistinguishable from other underlying and oft unnoticed forms of disclosure the Government requires for its essential operations" (*Full Value Advisors, LLC v. SEC,* p. 1109, 2011). The SEC was the sole audience for disclosures which were intended to regulate the securities markets, inspire confidence in such markets, and protect proprietary information. Compelled disclosure to the SEC was a rational means by which to accomplish these purposes and did not raise First Amendment concerns.

This approach was most recently followed in the context of strict scrutiny in *American Petroleum Institute v. SEC*. Although the court vacated the SEC's rule on non-constitutional grounds, the court nevertheless noted that "[d]ifferent analytical approaches" may be required for rules compelling disclosure to the government with or without subsequent republication and those compelling direct public disclosure from industry members (*American Petroleum Institute v. SEC*, p. 23, 2013). The court cited with approval the opinions in *Riley* and *Full Value Advisors* in support of this conclusion. However, selection of the appropriate approach was premature as the SEC would be required to rewrite the challenged rules and had yet to determine the method of disclosure. Despite this reticence, the court's opinion sent a clear signal that future rules in this area should focus on disclosure to the SEC with or without subsequent republication.

Any constitutional standard applicable to compelled commercial speech should include a different analysis, if not outright exception, for instances when disclosure is required solely to the government. Different analytical approaches are necessary as compelled commercial disclosures solely to the government tread lightly, if at all, on underlying First Amendment values. Suppression of information, manipulation of public debate or requiring private industry to serve as a billboard for government messages are absent from such disclosures. Disclosure under these circumstances is ordinary, routine and necessary for efficient and effective government operations.

First Amendment analysis in instances of compelled commercial disclosure solely to the government may take one of two forms. Disclosures may be deemed within a First Amendment safe harbor shielding the legislation or regulation from constitutional scrutiny utilizing the compelled speech doctrine. Support for this approach may be found in *Riley* in which the Court held that government compilation and republication of information was narrowly tailored to meet a compelling state interest. If disclosure in this form satisfies the strict scrutiny test, it should also satisfy the less rigorous intermediate scrutiny and reasonable relationship standards.

Alternatively, a government disclosure requirement could become a means by which to satisfy specific requirements within each of the three constitutional standards. The Court's opinion in *Riley* has already established that disclosure to the government may be a narrowly tailored means by which to serve a compelling state interest. Similarly, disclosure to the government is relevant to the fourth prong of *Central Hudson* by demonstrating the regulation is not more extensive than necessary to serve the government's interest. Exclusive disclosure to the government is undoubtedly relevant to the determination of a reasonable fit between the government's ends and the means chosen to accomplish those ends and whether the government could achieve its interests in a manner that does not restrict speech or restricts less speech. Finally, exclusivity is persuasive evidence that the disclosure is not unjustified or unduly burdensome as required by the final prong of the *Zauderer* standard. Of course, exclusive disclosures will place additional burdens on government especially if the underlying rule contains a republication requirement. However, First Amendment rights are adequately protected when the government is the speaker and any burdens associated with such speech fall upon it rather than private individuals and businesses.

IV. CONCLUSION

Regulatory schemes based upon disclosure have generated numerous industry challenges in recent years, challenges which will undoubtedly continue in the absence of future U.S. Supreme Court guidance. Any disclosure requirement mandated by a federal, state or local government could conceivably be called into question and subjected to rigorous constitutional scrutiny. In so doing, judges would be in a position of second-guessing policy determinations made by agencies and individuals with far greater knowledge of the underlying factual circumstances warranting regulation. It is unlikely that it is the intent of a majority of the present Court to return to the jurisprudence of the early-twentieth century in which judges assumed extensive control over a vast array of economic regulations. Nevertheless, avenues of attack remain available absent further clarification of the boundaries between permissible disclosure requirements and unconstitutional compelled speech. This chapter has drawn distinctions, identified factors important to these determinations and suggested an alternative approach to compelled speech jurisprudence in the commercial context.

REFERENCES

American Petroleum Institute v. Securities and Exchange Commission, 953 F. Supp.2d 5 (D.D.C. 2013).

Bankruptcy Abuse Prevention and Consumer Protection Act, Pub. L. No. 109-8, 119 Stat. 23-217 (2005).

Bolger v. Youngs Drug Products Corporation, 463 U.S. 60 (1983).
Central Hudson Gas & Electric Corporation v. Public Service Commission, 447 U.S. 557 (1980).
Dodd-Frank Wall Street Reform and Consumer Protection Act, Pub. L. No. 111-203, 124 Stat. 1376-2223 (2010).
Edenfield v. Fane, 507 U.S. 761 (1993).
First National Bank v. Bellotti, 435 U.S. 765 (1978).
Fleminger, Inc. v. U.S. Department of Health and Human Services, 854 F. Supp.2d 192 (D. Conn. 2012).
Full Value Advisors, LLC v. SEC, 633 F.3d 1101 (D.C. Cir. 2011).
Hethcoat, G. (2012) "Regulating pharmaceutical marketing after *Sorrell v. IMS Health, Inc.*", *Quinnipiac Health Law Journal*, 15(1), 187–208.
Hurley v. Irish-American Gay, Lesbian and Bisexual Group of Boston, Inc. 515 U.S. 557 (1995).
Ibanez v. Florida Department of Business and Professional Regulation, 512 U.S. 136 (1994).
Lorillard Tobacco Co. v. Reilly, 533 U.S. 525 (2001).
Memorandum of Points and Authorities in Support of Plaintiffs' Motion for Summary Judgment, *American Petroleum Institute v. SEC,* 953 F. Supp.2d 5 (D.D.C. 2013).
Milavetz, Gallop & Milavetz, P.A. v. United States, 559 U.S. 229 (2010).
National Association of Manufacturers v. SEC, 956 F. Supp.2d 43 (D.D.C. 2013).
Pharmaceutical Care Management Association v. Rowe, 429 F.3d 294 (1st Cir. 2005).
Pomeranz, J. (2009) "Compelled speech under the commercial speech doctrine: The case of menu label laws", *Journal of Health Care Law & Policy,* 12(2), 159–94.
Pomeranz, J. (2012) "No need to break new ground: A response to the Supreme Court's threat to overhaul the commercial speech doctrine", *Loyola Los Angeles Law Review,* 45(2), 389–433.
Riley v. National Federation of the Blind of North Carolina, Inc., 487 U.S. 781 (1988).
R.J. Reynolds Tobacco Company v. FDA, 696 F.3d 1205 (D.C. Cir. 2012).
Royal, D. (2012) "Resolving the compelled-commercial speech conundrum", *Virginia Journal of Social Policy & Law,* 19(2), 205–51.
Sorrell v. IMS Health, Inc., 131 S. Ct. 2653 (2011).
Spirit Airlines, Inc. v. U.S. Department of Transportation, 687 F.3d 403 (D.C. Cir. 2012).
Stern, N. and Stern, M.J. (2011) "Advancing an adaptive standard of strict scrutiny for content-based commercial speech regulation", retrieved from http://ssrn.com/abstract=2157511.html, pp. 1–20.
Turner Broadcasting System, Inc. v. FCC, 520 U.S. 180 (1997).
U.S. Constitution, amendment I.
United States v. United Foods, Inc., 533 U.S. 405 (2001).
U.S. Department of Transportation, Enhancing Airline Passenger Protections, 76 Fed. Reg. 23, 110–167 (Apr. 25, 2011).

U.S. Securities and Exchange Commission, Conflict Minerals, 77 Fed. Reg. 56,274–365 (Sept. 12, 2012).
U.S. Securities and Exchange Commission, Disclosure of Payments by Resource Extraction Issuers, 77 Fed. Reg. 56,365–419 (Sept. 12, 2012).
Wooley v. Maynard, 430 U.S. 705 (1977).
Zauderer v. Office of Disciplinary Counsel, 471 U.S. 626 (1985).

5. A co-opetition approach to business, human rights organizations and due diligence

Janine S. Hiller and Shannon S. Hiller

The Framework for Business and Human Rights adopted by the United Nations Human Rights Council in 2008 (Framework), led by John Ruggie, created a three-pillar "Protect, Respect and Remedy" standard to address the relationship of businesses and human rights. States have a duty to protect human rights, businesses have a responsibility to respect human rights, and each has a duty to provide a remedy for violations of human rights (U.N. Special Representative of the Secretary-General, 2011). Implementation of the framework is further developed in the Guiding Principles for Business and Human Rights of 2011, also adopted by the United Nations Human Rights Council (U.N. Office of the High Commissioner for Human Rights, 2011). The implementation of the Framework requires businesses to undertake due diligence to identify and prevent harm, and remediate violations of individuals' human rights occurring as a result of business operations. The proactive application of this process could make a significant impact on the prevention of human rights harms. There is much work to be done as the private sector grapples with incorporating the fundamental principles of due diligence into business enterprise management. In addition, and perhaps less recognized, the business responsibility to implement respect for human rights has the potential for creating new, two-way, dynamics between business and the human rights community. This chapter explores the possible impacts that the due diligence responsibility could have on the business–human rights organization relationship, and suggests a conceptual framework for understanding the dynamics.

Under the Framework for Business and Human Rights, a multinational corporation should undertake due diligence to assess the risk of violating human rights in its business practices in the differing environments in which it operates. Information gathering and potential partnership with third parties, non-governmental organizations (NGOs) in particular,[1] operating in the country could be an invaluable source in this regard. John Ruggie recognized the opportunity, stating that NGOs provide important information through research and advocacy, and that certain NGOs "have acquired the capacity to be helpful in structuring certain processes like community engagement strategies … local grievance mechanisms, and … can be brought in as partners or as collaborators" with companies (IBA, 2010).

Recently, Unilever illustrated one way that a multinational corporation (MNC) might engage with an NGO to execute an aspect of due diligence in a developing country. Unilever asked Oxfam to investigate and evaluate human rights at its Vietnamese factories during 2011–12. Oxfam had unprecedented access to the structure and operations of both a Unilever factory and a supplier, together employing 1,500 workers. The results were not what Unilever had hoped, revealing that wages were too low (although above national standards), codes of conduct were unclear and sometimes only provided in English, workers were too intimidated to file complaints, and suppliers did not meet pay and overtime standards. The Unilever factory had a mechanism for workers to file complaints, however there was fear that management would fire any employee making a claim, or that the union, which was state-run, would retaliate if complaints were filed. Oxfam's review revealed the lack of trust in a system that the company assumed, from its standpoint, would effectively address human rights complaints (Slavin, 2013; Smedley, 2013). Unilever stated its commitment to addressing the Oxfam recommendations with regards to its Vietnam presence, and to involving Oxfam in a review of progress in two years. Unilever described the immediate steps it is taking to address the issues; it is organizing workshops with stakeholders to provide training on human rights best practices, targeting its top 80 suppliers for compliance, and reviewing worker grievance procedures for all workers (Wilshaw et al., 2013). More broadly, Unilever reaffirmed its commitment to working with industry, NGOs, the UN Global Compact, and others to "mainstream the integration of human and labour rights by business" (Wilshaw et al., 2013, p. 95).

The Unilever/Oxfam collaboration is an example of a company undertaking due diligence with the assistance of a human rights NGO. It was initiated based on a long-term relationship between the two parties, an acceptance of outcomes by the business, and willingness by the NGO to accept less than perfect results and to defer more intense confrontational steps. It suggests a collaborative relationship between a company and NGO that still contains the potential for confrontation in the future should promises for improvement not be forthcoming. Yet, learning would not have occurred if, based on trust, the two entities did not work together to gather evidence and to undertake due diligence. Oxfam could communicate with and collect information from the affected individuals in ways that Unilever could not. While Oxfam lessened its confrontational approach to a certain degree, it publicly announced the results and held Unilever accountable, thus illustrating the dual nature of its relationship with the company.

Despite such attempts, tension and conflict between businesses and human rights organizations persist, perhaps as the norm, fueled at least in part by the tactics used by human rights organizations to derive their power and influence over private sector entities by means of a "name and shame" approach that utilizes the media and public opinion to identify and then pressure a company into taking remedial actions. As a result, consultation and cooperation often clash with a system of promoting human rights by publicity and confrontation, traditionally some of the most powerful advocacy strategies available to NGOs. Despite increasing opportunities to access new sources of funding from corporations interested in cooperative partnerships, many human rights scholars and practitioners worry that extensive cooperation with MNCs may co-opt their legitimacy in the eyes of the general population while also reducing their overall effectiveness to call attention to harmful MNC actions.

In comparison, the rapidly changing global business environment provides economic incentive for companies to cooperate with their marketplace competitors. From joint ventures to supplier relationships, companies are engaging in cooperation with competitors to gain mutually beneficial advantages. Competition persists at the same time as cooperation, as both basic antitrust principles and market forces mandate that companies who cooperate maintain their competitive postures. Researchers call the relationship co-opetition.

In order to explore the nature of the business and NGO relationship, we begin by reviewing the due diligence responsibility of business, as we propose that this is the venue where the two may be mutually supportive. Recognizing the challenges of this approach, we examine the risk for NGO co-optation, defined as the alignment of NGO interests with corporations through sponsorship, labeling, personal relationships, and related activities (Baur and Schmitz, 2012), and the potential theoretical response in co-opetition. We discuss this conceptualization of the relationship between NGOs and business entities, a potential dynamic that may evolve as the private sector reacts to meet its responsibilities under the Business and Human Rights Framework.

I. THE FRAMEWORK FOR BUSINESS AND HUMAN RIGHTS: DUE DILIGENCE

Formalized in the final report to the Human Rights Council on implementing the Business and Human Rights framework, respect for human rights is operationalized by businesses in three ways: (1) adoption of a high level human rights policy, (2) performance of due diligence, and (3) creating processes for enabling the remediation of adverse impacts caused or contributed by the firm (U.N. Special Representative of the Secretary-General, 2011). The due diligence process is the focus of this article. In Principle 15(b) of the final report, due diligence is described as actions taken to "identify, prevent, mitigate, and account for how [a company] address[es] [its] impacts on human rights." Principle 17 provides further that company human rights due diligence "should include assessing actual and potential human rights impacts, integrating and acting upon the findings, tracking responses, and communicating how impacts are addressed."

The assessment of potential impacts should take place as soon as possible, and should be ongoing, as reflected in the dynamic nature of business and human rights. Rather than wait for problems to arise, execution of due diligence incorporates a proactive approach to identifying and avoiding negative impacts on human rights. Assessment of company impacts will include both direct impacts and those stemming from business relationships, such as supplier relationships. Ruggie stated that he "sought equally to expand the preventative side of the equation directly" through the Framework (Ruggie, 2013, p. xiv).

Principle 18(a) states that the due diligence "process should … [d]raw on internal and/or independent external human rights expertise." The commentary explains that a firm should consider the effects of its actions on individuals under specific circumstances, and whether the actions will negatively impact human rights. Discussing potential harm with affected individuals is important. However, because of language or other barriers this may not be possible, and the firm "should consider reasonable alternatives such as consulting credible, independent expert resources, including human rights defenders and others from civil society" (U.N. Special Representative of the Secretary-General, 2011).

Furthermore, the Interpretive Guide to the corporate responsibility to respect human rights explains that in addition to internal processes for assessment, that media reports, NGO campaigns, and other sources can aid the process. In addition, it could be "reasonable and necessary" to engage third-party, external, participation to "help to bridge cultural gaps" between business and local parties (U.N. Office of the High Commissioner for Human Rights, 2012, p. 35). The Unilever/Oxfam labor case is an example of a business engaging a third party to bridge the cultural gap between a multinational and a local labor force.

In a complex, global world, it is important that a business not only respond to and mitigate harm to human rights, but that it also provides follow-up assessments and remedies or mitigation strategies if necessary. In this regard, Principle 20(b) of the final report states that the business should utilize both internal and external resources. Finally, under Principle 21, the business should report on the actions that they take to address human rights impacts. The report should, in most cases, be made accessible to the public, for purposes of transparency. In addition, the commentary notes that "[i]ndependent verification of human rights reporting can strengthen its content and credibility" (U.N. Special Representative of the Secretary-General, 2011, p. 20).

It is clear that implementing due diligence envisioned by the Framework requires a new, higher level of business involvement with human rights in order to both proactively assess the risks of operations and potential impacts on human rights and to take measures to avoid and mitigate those impacts. A corollary result not specifically addressed, however, is how increased business due diligence will affect the environment for civil society actors, specifically NGOs that operate in the same space. As business due diligence evolves in sophistication, one would expect that a market (in broad terms) for information would also evolve. Both businesses and NGOs will aggressively seek to obtain the best and most current information about the risks to human rights caused by operations. Yet, there is no guarantee that they will agree about the approach. How will these two different sides interact? How can the relationship be conceptualized so that they may assist each other in the common goal of protecting human rights?

The potential exists for business and NGOs to cooperate in the pursuit of proactive due diligence. If the sides can manage their complex relationship, then a dynamic force for the protection of human rights could be harnessed. It is necessary, then, to examine the actors and the potential tensions and conflicts between them that could impede that cooperation.

II. THE ACTORS: NGOS AND MNCS

The actors included in a business's human rights due diligence include nation states, affected persons, and civil society organizations. The state responsibility to protect human rights can be seen in legal obligations for companies; for example, employment discrimination statutes or privacy laws that protect individual rights. Clearly, these are an important part of the framework and will undoubtedly and significantly spur corporate due diligence about the impact of actions on human rights. It is important to note that the business responsibility to respect human rights exists, however, independent of the state duty to protect. This is particularly relevant in weak or failing states. Thus, while recognizing that the state is an essential actor, this discussion focuses on the relationship between business and non-governmental actors in the pursuit of protecting individual human rights.

The complexity of social problems, and the inability of governments to tackle these problems alone, has led to the proliferation of many NGOs (Brown and Timmer, 2006). Indeed, recent studies show that NGOs are more trusted than corporations, media, or governments, so that this growth is not surprising (Burgos, 2013). The increased number and power of NGOs has been called "one of the most significant developments in international affairs over the past 20 years" (Doh and Guay, 2006, p. 51).

The number of NGOs is difficult to pinpoint. Estimates are that from 6,000 to 30,000 national organizations exist within developing countries (Weiss, 2006). If the pool is expanded to community-based organizations (CBOs) then numbers, in the hundreds of thousands, are even more difficult to estimate (Weiss, 2006). Likewise, an exact definition of such an organization is hard to find. However, NGOs are commonly described as non-profit, civil society entities (van Tuijl, 1999). Another way to view the NGO is that it seeks to "serve particular societal interests by focusing advocacy and/or operational efforts on social political and economic goals, including equity, education, health, environmental protection and human rights" (Teegen, Doh and Vachani, 2004, p. 466).

NGOs may be divided into the categories of "operational" or "advocacy." An operational NGO focuses on providing services to individuals while an advocacy NGO focuses on making institutional change such as impacting laws and regulations. The Red Cross is an international, operational NGO, as it delivers disaster aid, for example, across the world (Teegen, Doh and Vachani, 2004). These categories are often unhelpful, however, as NGOs find themselves acting in both functional areas (van Tuijl, 2004). NGOs frequently integrate operational and advocacy functions and may be called a hybrid organization (Teegen, Doh and Vachani, 2004).

NGOs can furthermore be viewed as international or national in scope; CBOs operate at a local, community level but The World Bank has noted a historical change in the type of organization with which it deals. It describes the CBO as primarily a membership organization that is involved in grassroots issues and notes that the international or national NGO often acts as an intermediary between the World Bank and CBO (Weiss, 2006). In addition, each of these types of organizations has found it beneficial to join together in networks in order to broaden their impact around the world. NGOs increasingly see the need to organize their work not in isolation, but rather as a broader movement in coordination with others (van Tuijl, 1999).

Human rights NGOs can be viewed as a specific subset of the NGO community, with distinct goals and purposes. The general goals of a human rights organization are to identify and substantiate abuses, prevent recurrences, and obtain a remedy for the victims from those responsible for injuries (Sonnenberg and Cavallaro, 2012). When human rights NGOs have no formal legal power to achieve these goals, they rely instead on soft power to exert pressure, through public exposure aimed at the violator in order to mobilize change. A key approach is the public "naming and shaming" of a business, using public pressure to spur corrective action (Deitelhoff and Wolf, 2013). Electronic communications that are inexpensive, accessible, and virtually immediate, have bolstered the power of NGOs to name and shame international businesses and to use public opinion to exert pressure for remediation. For example, the Robert Kennedy Center for Justice and Human Rights trains activists to use electronic communications to effectively bring attention to human rights violations (Coughlan, 2012). Businesses, being cognizant of the long-lasting reputational harm that bad publicity can cause, are often responsive to this NGO strategy (Argenti, 2004).

At another level, NGOs serve a broader function as they "engage actively [in] international law-making processes and intergovernmental rule-making" by influencing policy and regulation (Buhmann, 2012, p. 92). Advocacy, education, and public debate can affect laws and the promotion and protection of human rights. The influence of these actions can also result in the creation of a different type of "soft institutionalization," that creates expectations for behavior beyond the letter of the law. In the context of business and human rights and the Guiding Principles, soft law is reflected in the fact that "businesses are seen to have some social responsibility and responsibility for human rights, but without being subjected to legally binding requirements" (Buhmann, 2012, p. 91).

Legitimacy is an essential attribute for NGOs that cannot be over emphasized (Slim, 2002). Historically, human rights organizations derive a great deal of their legitimacy from moral sources:

> An organisational mission to challenge and end human rights violations is derived explicitly from a moral case based on the values of human equality, dignity, impartiality, justice, freedom and personal and collective responsibility. This moral case gives human rights organisations and NGOs an ethical legitimacy that resonates with the moral reasonableness of people across the world. (Slim, 2002, p. 6)

As international human rights norms became more robust, human rights NGOs drew upon broader sources of legal legitimacy. NGOs can point to a wide range of UN treaties with near-universal state signatories, domestic human rights bodies with institutionalized roles for civil society, and the UN Universal Periodic Review to show their role and legitimate place in governance at different levels.

Yet beyond these increasingly institutionalized roles and accepted norms, an individual human rights NGO also needs to establish legitimacy in order to be an effective actor. This may be tangible financial support, relationships, expertise, or successful performance. It may also be the intangible currency of "trust, integrity, and reputation" (Slim, 2002). Not unlike product or brand loyalty, human rights NGOs may establish legitimacy through careful cultivation of this intangible image.

Thus working with MNCs can create a dilemma for human rights NGOs seeking to advance human rights and to maintain legitimacy in the eyes of their key constituents. Having engaged in successful naming, shaming campaigns and building an image as champions of human rights, NGOs may risk delegitimization if they are then perceived as being too soft on a particular company as a result of a beneficial partnership or in exchange for funding. Moreover, this perception plays out on both national and international levels where constituents' goals may be at odds.

The second actor, the corporation, may theoretically be considered from at least two different viewpoints; as either a strictly economic actor that serves shareholder interests, or as a social actor that by its membership in society owes duties to stakeholders outside the shareholder paradigm. While it is beyond the scope of this chapter to discuss the extensive literature on this debate, it is still important to briefly acknowledge that these concepts exist, and that they can be relevant to the due diligence process.

From the shareholder and profit maximization viewpoint, Cragg, for example, argues that the costs of implementing the framework will need to be "justified to the boards and then to the shareholders for whose investments they are stewards" (Cragg, 2012, p. 11). He reasons that since there is no legal requirement that human rights be proactively respected, an appeal to the profit motive would be necessary to convince shareholders of the wisdom of this action. He describes due diligence within this paradigm as a "strategic paradox" because corporations should, under the framework, "respect the human rights interests of their stakeholders whether or not doing so will bring material benefits to the company" (Cragg, 2012, p. 25). Management would need to show either that the benefits of implementation outweigh the costs, or that the actions will result in a strategic advantage in the marketplace (Cragg, 2012).[2]

There is conflict between shareholder profit and stakeholder theories of the corporation, the latter of which includes corporate social responsibility (Bradford, 2012; Muchlinski, 2012). Corporate social responsibility (CSR) theories would require the firm, at least in part, to voluntarily consider the broader interests of stakeholders in the community rather than simply shareholder interests. One approach identifies three categories for corporate responsibility; philanthropy, integration, and innovation (Kourula and Halme, 2008). Philanthropy includes financial support for the NGO, integration is an internalization of corporate responsibility within the firm, and innovation includes a corporate investment to solve social or environmental issues (Kourula and Halme, 2008). The broad and extensive CSR literature speaks to the ways that CSR and particularly stakeholder theory is related to the responsibility to respect human rights (Bradford, 2012; Mares, 2008).

Although corporations may have different approaches to their social responsibility, they will nonetheless search for efficient ways to incorporate due diligence into their procedures, and will look towards those organizations that possess needed information about human rights risks in order to meet their responsibilities. Likewise, NGOs may see corporations as violators or potential partners, and will weigh the risks of different engagement tactics against their underlying legitimacy. Thus, understanding the complex business and NGO relationship becomes particularly important.

III. THE BUSINESS–NGO NEXUS

In the recent past, the business–NGO relationship tended to be fractious and confrontational (Arenas, Lozano and Albareda, 2009; Kourula and Halme, 2008). In contrast, emerging partnerships between business and non-profit organizations tend to be less confrontational overall, and more collaborative (Berger, Cunningham and Drumwright, 2004; Sakarya et al., 2012). As Ban Ki-Moon stated, "[t]hrough partnerships and alliances, and by pooling comparative advantages, we increase our chances [of] success" (U.N. Office for Partnerships).

The increasingly common NGO and business collaboration has been categorized across a continuum, as the degree of involvement and depth of commitment vary enormously. Collaborations have often taken place within the environmental field, and researchers have identified multiple stages of increasingly significant commitment to relationships with NGOs. One methodology suggests the increasingly collaborative categories of sponsorship, single-issue consultation, research cooperation, employee training/volunteering, certification, systemic dialogue, common projects, and strategic partnerships (Kourula and Halme, 2008). Another approach identifies increasingly relational categories of arms-length, interactive (including certification), and intensive environmental alliances for particular projects (Rondinelli and London, 2003). These relationships move from low intensity to high intensity, while the objectives of both the corporation and NGO move correspondingly. Lower intensity relationships such as corporate support (i.e., employee release time) for employee participation in NGO activities are more common while high intensity joint environmental projects are less frequently observed (Rondinelli and London, 2003).

Another relationship that may be useful for comparison is the business alliance, generally adopted for reasons of efficiency, legitimacy, or to provide for stability when the environment is unpredictable. Such an alliance can also prove beneficial for information gathering and learning (Rondinelli and London, 2003). Within the environmental area, an alliance with an NGO can also offer answers for stakeholders, and can lead to new opportunities for products and services. In particular, an alliance with an NGO is sometimes the only way for a firm to access relevant information because otherwise it would be too costly or time consuming to obtain (Rondinelli and London, 2003). Access to information, and sharing information among interested parties, is an important part of the ongoing and dynamic human rights due diligence duty of businesses, especially in the particularly thorny environment of conflict or post-conflict societies.

New types of business and NGO relationships may develop as businesses incorporate due diligence into enterprise management; therefore these relationships will likely exhibit different categories than previously identified. MNCs may identify situations when NGOs are most helpful for certain types of due diligence, as NGOs may find that they are able to work with companies with particular expectations and areas of collaboration. Through this collaboration closer relationships may emerge over time.

Despite the potential benefits of an NGO and MNC relationship to perform due diligence, persistent tensions could make interaction difficult. A 2011 study by the Institute for Human Rights and Business surveying the status and implementation of due diligence by business hardly mentioned the role of NGOs (Danish Institute for Human Rights, 2011). It would seem that businesses are not only slow in their implementation of due diligence for human rights, they are also not taking advantage of the resources and unique position of NGOs to provide input about the risks to human rights.[3]

In many cases, NGOs can be uniquely situated to provide accurate information about the human rights risks and impacts of a company's operations, especially in conflict areas with little or no government stability (Kolk and Lenfant, 2012). In particular, "companies are more likely to take additional meaningful steps … if vibrant local networks exist and offer specific services … including encouraging dialogue across the civil society-business divide" (Mwangi, Rieth and Schmitz, 2013, p. 215). The Danish Institute for Human Rights confirms: "Companies are encouraged to work with independent human rights organizations when undertaking decisions in the field" (Danish Institute of Human Rights, 2011, p. 4). Depending on the circumstances and unlike an MNC or outsourcing company, NGOs are often physically present in a country and may be active monitors of situations that threaten human rights. NGOs are often trusted by local populations and subsequently provided with information that would not be shared with a representative from a large corporation. And NGOs may have expertise in spotting potential cultural or political trouble spots, expertise that may not be within a businesses core competency. The UNDP (United Nations Development Programme) Nordic Office has noted that "open channels of communication are particularly useful for situations where companies 'need tools they cannot develop on their own'" (Mwangi, Rieth and Schmitz, 2013, p. 218). For these reasons, access to knowledge, specialized expertise, and trust of the local community (Allerd and Martinez, 2008) the NGO community could contribute significantly to an MNC's due diligence and at the same time contribute significantly to the fundamental protection of individuals' human rights.

As the business responsibility for human rights develops in practice, NGOs may find it necessary to examine the most efficacious tactics for inducing action. The assumption that public exposure will produce results may be erroneous in a new environment; rather it may be that NGOs "can neither assume that any particular norm target is socially vulnerable, nor that the application of social pressure (e.g., naming and shaming) will have a favorable and unidirectional impact" (Risse and Ropp, 2013,

p. 21). The engagement of business and NGOs during due diligence could be a more effective approach to "solving a joint problem" (Mwangi, Rieth and Schmitz, 2013, p. 208).

In addition, businesses are likely to have resources beyond those of NGOs. The capability of private entities to survey and assess the environment for potential human rights risks is fundamental to the Framework, and will evolve to be an internal business function over time. It is reasonable to assume that even at the present time that there will be occasions when a business possesses information that a NGO would find helpful for proactively protecting human rights. In the future, as the vision of the Framework is achieved, businesses may more often have information that is helpful for the broader NGO community.

IV. CHALLENGES AND A THEORY

Studies of firm behavior have shown the mutual benefits of collaboration between non-profits and corporations, as non-profits gain access to resources while corporations gain reputational capital by being associated with positive non-profit, community, activities and associated entities. Beyond mutual benefit, it has been argued that business should play a role in helping to solve social problems, while still being profit oriented (Porter and Kramer, 2011). However, "[t]he complementarities of NGOs and corporations yielding the benefits of alliances and partnerships are unfortunately often accompanied by differences that make these relationships especially contentious and risky" (Burgos, 2013).

The risk to NGOs may be that they stand to lose their own soft power and legitimacy by being too closely allied with commercial interests. The goals of the business partner can become too intertwined with those of the NGO. As one author explains, "their focus on developing a working relationship with a stronger corporation may distract from pursuing their missions and it may limit their willingness to use protest and other disruptive strategies, even if such strategies would be more effective for goal attainment" (Baur and Schmitz 2012, p. 11).

As noted earlier, co-optation is defined as "the process of aligning NGO interests with those of corporations," through sponsorships, labeling and personal relationships (Baur and Schmitz, 2012, p. 10). The potential for co-optation has been noted for decades in the literature from sociology, critical social theory, cultural studies and management, among others (Baur and Schmitz, 2012). The theories challenge the benefit of close relationships between non-profits and businesses and suggest that the more powerful corporation can co-opt, or undermine, non-profit goals. Even direct engagement with government human rights bodies, for example, has resulted in NGOs becoming less critical, even though the institutions were falling short of their mandate. "This is perhaps because NGOs have developed a working relationship with the [national human rights commission] that they did not enjoy in the early days and therefore feel less able to be vocal and public in their criticisms" (ICHR, 2004, p. 64). Co-optation poses particular risks for advocacy and monitoring NGOs, whose validity and power depend on their independent voice. Thus, it is essential that the NGO maintain an independent and potentially adversarial position with regard to a business and its interactions, even though it may collaborate on another level. On the other side, a business that engages with an NGO with this dual nature may develop mistrust and fail to recognize the advantages of the complex relationship.

Corporations sometimes express frustration surrounding their interactions with human rights NGOs. The antagonistic nature of NGO interactions, and the seemingly unpredictable fluctuation between collaboration on the one hand and public criticism on the other, can affect the willingness of businesses to establish long-term relationships with NGOs. The tension between activists and MNCs stems, at least in part, from those legitimization factors for NGOs; the use of soft power or even economic campaigns to effect change, and maintaining a trust relationship with citizens.

The perception of NGOs by business, and sometimes other stakeholders, can also be frustrating, in large part because of the misunderstanding of the dual nature of collaboration and confrontation, or monitoring. When NGOs also seek funding from business, it increases complicated perceptions. Companies may feel betrayed by an NGO that collaborates or accepts money and then aggressively challenges a company's actions shortly thereafter. However, an NGO must be comfortable with these divergent roles. NGOs may not understand the distrust by businesses and their resulting reluctance to be transparent (Arenas, Lozano and Albareda, 2009).

While collaboration and partnerships may provide significant opportunities for businesses and NGOs to create social and corporate value, businesses anticipate that an ongoing match between fundamental interests and a lessening of antagonistic interactions will control against opportunism. Within the context of failed government protection of human rights in particular, the stature and legitimacy needs of the NGO require that they remain able to challenge business actions, even though cooperation may aid the MNC to engage and protect human rights and provide benefits for the population. This schizophrenic existence is problematic for the business–NGO relationship. Thus, it is proposed that the management literature on the theory of firm co-opetition may inform and provide a basis for conceptualizing this dual collaborative/antagonistic relationship.

Management research has sought to understand the manner in which companies in the same industry can join together in collaborations such as joint ventures while simultaneously engaging in fierce competition in the marketplace. The relationship seems counterintuitive, because the partners are creating value together, yet also vying for a greater appropriation of that value (Gnyawali and Park, 2011). Such relationship, when firms engage in a "simultaneous pursuit of collaboration and competition" (Gnyawali and Park, 2011), is called co-opetition. Co-opetition is further delineated as cooperation between competitors that increases opportunities for both parties. Furthermore, "[c]oopetition creates value through cooperation between competing organizations, aligning different interests toward a common objective and helping to create opportunities for competitive advantage by removing external obstacles and neutralizing threats" (Chin, Chan and Lam, 2008, p. 438). The controlling purpose of the relationship is to "create mutually beneficial exchanges and added values" (Chin, Chan and Lam, 2008, p. 438).

Co-opetition between firms happens most often when product lives are short (generally high technology industries), multiple technologies are involved, and the business activity is research and cost intensive (Gnyawali and Park, 2011). In addition, the business environment is usually characterized by swiftly changing market conditions and consumer demand, and complex production technologies. The result is a common interest in setting mutual standards for the future of the shared technology and the benefit of co-investing in research and development to address "common challenges" (Gnyawali and Park, 2011, p. 652).

Co-opetition relationships, however, must be explicitly understood and managed in order to achieve a successful outcome. Heightened tensions occur between co-opetition partners because of; 1) inherent competitive conflicts, 2) clashes based on the same goal of becoming market leader, and 3) opportunities for misuse of the relationship for private gain. In order to manage these tensions, firms must be capable of "pursu[ing] a win-win approach, manag[ing] the tension, and balance[ing] the relationships" (Gnyawali and Park, 2011, p. 652).

Three broad areas influence the success rate of co-opetition between firms: management commitment; relationship development; and communication management. Of these three, management commitment is the most important, but relationship development is similarly key to success because it supports trust between the entities (Chin, Chan and Lam, 2008). Trust subsequently facilitates information sharing.

In the business–NGO relationship, competition may not be directly observed, as in a business-to-business cooperative relationship, however the use of the media to name and shame, reputational risk, and associated harms can be viewed in the same negative light as competition. Future informational competition may be more risky for both parties; as business becomes more invested in and integrative of human rights due diligence, there is no guarantee that they will approach remedies and mitigation the same way as NGOs. Since there are multiple ways of addressing human rights due diligence, a sense of competition between business and NGOs may emerge.

The Bangladesh factory safety programs illustrate the potential competition for acceptance. Following the tragic collapse of a factory in Bangladesh that killed over 1,000 workers, many retailers signed an Accord on Fire and Building Safety in Bangladesh, designed by the ILO and other NGOs, in which they committed to a five-year, legally enforceable, factory-improvement plan. American retailers, however, declined to join the group and designed their own plan to loan factories over $100 million dollars for improvements and donated $42 million dollars for worker safety programs. Each side remains critical of the other's approach (Ahad, 2013). Importantly, improvement of critical factory safety and the resulting protection of workers lives may hinge, however, on communication and information sharing between these opposing sides. Recognition of a co-opetition relationship could assist the difficult task.

Cooperation between market entities can be viewed in parallel with a business and NGO relationship. Cooperation between competitors occurs, as noted, when there is an innovative, fast-moving marketplace where competitors will cooperate in order to reduce costs for common goals. Competitors both gain by sharing resources and information. The same dynamic nature exists within the human rights arena, especially within a weak state where there is inherent unpredictability about, or risk to, human rights. On one level, the uncertainty is similar to the high volatility in a high-tech marketplace. Cooperating to perform due diligence gives both sides a benefit and reduces that uncertainty. Costs of performing due diligence are reduced in the common goal of identification of potential human rights impacts. Thus, the business and NGO are cooperating in a relationship in order to create the benefit of increased protection of human rights.

Although co-opetition theory has much to offer the firm–NGO relationship, the importance of the confrontation element cannot be discounted. An adaptation of the co-opetition theory in the business–NGO relationship is necessary in order to recognize the continued importance of potential confrontation. Despite an increased emphasis and perhaps a priority for collaboration during due diligence, NGOs will need to rely on the power of confrontation for several reasons. Confrontation serves to legitimize the organization for individuals, can spur businesses to respond positively in order to preserve reputational capital, may aid in monitoring, and could shield NGOs from co-optation. It has been argued that the value of confrontational aspects of NGOs may be undervalued, and that care should be taken that it not be suppressed (Laasonen, Fougére and Kourula, 2012).

Businesses, too, recognize the value of the monitoring function of NGOs and the importance of their independence. Shell Oil commented about Amnesty International that "we don't want to get too pally with Amnesty because that would undermine their very value in the first place" (Baur and Schmitz, 2012, p. 17). Lastly, under some circumstances confrontation can achieve results more effectively than collaboration (Van Huijstee and Glasbergen, 2010). Therefore, confrontation between businesses and NGOs is a fundamental institutional factor.

From the perspective of human rights NGOs, there is precedent for adaption to changing relationships; they were able to adjust their tactics and realize broader sources of legitimacy as human rights became increasingly codified in international law. New cooperative relationships with businesses to perform due diligence would allow civil society actors to "bring essential knowledge and expertise to global problem-solving and, by relying on their global networks and communication strategies they are able to amplify local voices, spotlight problems and spread awareness in ways scarcely imaginable a generation ago" (Melish and Meidinger, 2012, p. 318). The same shift could be considered in response to the increasing recognition of human rights norms within the business community today. In this vein, it has been suggested that:

> [t]he human rights movement has at times been too committed to a small subset of tactics such as naming and shaming – tactics that worked well in initial campaigns but may be less well suited when applied to other issues and in other settings. The tactics and mechanisms should be designed with an eye to taking the full range of relevant scope conditions into account. (Risse and Sikkink, 2013, p. 295)

Thus one could also understand the predicted shift by businesses and the concomitant shift in tactics by considering Risse and Sikkink's "spiral model" of human rights change in nation states as applied to corporations. First applied to human rights organizations' pressures to change repressive nation states, the model describes a process of a state change in response to intense public criticism, which over time moves on a spectrum towards consistently acceptable behavior as a government internalizes compliance with international human rights standards. The first stage is described as a tactical response to criticism, followed by a prescriptive phase, when nations adopt international treaties to protect human rights and lastly, the compliance stage where there is consistent conformity and implementation of human rights principles. The spiral concept reflects that movement may not be linear, but rather a matter of socialization over time in response to additional pressures (Risse and Sikkink, 1999). Continued involvement is required to move a nation across the continuum (Davis, Murdie and Steinmetz, 2012).

Currently, certain corporations could be considered between the tactical concession and prescriptive stage of human rights acceptance (Mwangi, Rieth and Schmitz, 2013). While Risse and Sikkink identify shaming as an effective strategy in the tactical concession phase, they identify increased communication and creation of applicable institutions as additional tools once a state has entered the prescriptive stage (Risse and Sikkink, 1999). More recently, Deitelhoff and Wolf specifically applied the spiral model to the private sector noting that "companies go through a similar process [as states] of denial, tactical concessions, norm acceptance and institutionalization" (Deitelhoff and Wolf, 2013, p. 236). Keeping this "spiral model" in mind can be instructive to human rights NGOs exploring the most effective strategy in engaging corporations. Rather than viewing corporations only as profit-driven violators in need of perpetual shaming, human rights NGOs can assess and appropriately address corporations at each of the stages as they move towards fully institutionalized human rights norms (Deitelhoff and Wolff, 2013). Within the business literature, this process could be described as organizational learning (Dashwood, 2012).

Some have argued that the Framework should have a fourth pillar that would recognize and give credibility to the civil society, NGOs, as they have powers of "persuasion, coercion and acculturation-based strategies" (Melish and Meidinger, 2012, p. 329). We suggest that the use of a co-opetition strategy can accomplish a similar result under the present Framework, and could spur change that may be more innovative and quicker paced, depending on the country location, risks, and relative position of the firm with regards to respect for human rights. The co-opetition model is particularly promising for business and NGOs in the assessment of human rights impacts.

V. CONCLUSION: OPPORTUNITIES FOR A CO-OPETITION APPROACH

To date, MNCs have had some success using outside consultants with specific experience to conduct initial and periodic HR assessments. However, these are most effective as one-time documents and are often conducted as comprehensive, yet expensive and temporally limited, site visits. In fact, companies surveyed in 2011 identified reliable, relevant, and affordable HR assessment as a critical need:

> Some existing human rights risks mapping tools aimed at the business market demand heavy fees and are incomplete and sometimes even misleading, according to companies in this research. Furthermore, investment risk reports by consulting firms do not have information on human rights, and freely-available reports of human rights organizations are state-centric and do not provide the information that businesses require. (Danish Institute for Human Rights, 2011)

In light of this need, we suggest that the flexibility of an ongoing co-opetition arrangement with NGOs could fill the gap. The core mission of many NGOs involves extensive stakeholder engagement, either as a direct part of programming or through re-granting and coordinating functions in the case of larger organizations. In addition, NGOs can benefit from increased perspective on business operations and complaint mechanisms, as well as potentially secure additional sources of funding. The challenge remains to tap into this existing role and expertise in a way that preserves legitimacy.

While further research is necessary to identify operational requirements for creating a co-opetition institutional relationship, several considerations may be noted. First, relationships that are founded as ongoing cooperative partnerships are likely to be the most successful. Both sides must view the relationship not only as a source of information, as already occurs in some alliances, but also as a valuable and ongoing partnership in achieving the common goal of preventing human rights violations. In co-opetition terms, the common good between the two competing players is the creation of more open, reliable, and timely channels of information in order to allow both players to act proactively in the absence of functioning government safeguards. Within this communication structure, it will be valuable to bolster the ability of MNCs and NGOs to communicate warnings about potential human rights risks in real time. In addition to the well-established function of providing initial assessments and advice, the partnership should seek to implement the proactive, preventive approach of the Framework through due diligence. This could include frequent informal reporting, both from the MNC (and related business partners) and NGO, on recent workplace complaints or abuses. It could, for example, include training exchanges for reporting officers from both parties, with the goal of building personal relationships that can enhance the trust necessary for more efficient exchange of information and the institution of feedback loops throughout the process.

Second, creating individual co-opetition arrangements, related to size and complexity for example, rather than applying a single overarching formula, will encourage MNCs and NGOs to negotiate appropriate terms for each individual context. This is particularly critical in negotiating fair compensation and sufficient resources to the NGO, if the nature of the relationship dictates, while still creating open channels and serving to address the MNC's main risk. It should be remembered that cooperation must explicitly allow for competition, or confrontation, which is an essential element of a co-opetition approach to future business and human rights organizations' relationships.

The proposed co-opetition approach to understanding the business and NGO relationship deserves further study, and many questions remain for future research. What categories of NGOs are most able to translate the co-opetition into practice? Which elements of due diligence are best suited for information sharing between partners? Are corporations able to see the value of co-opetition? What kinds of on-the-ground situations are best for the multi-dimensional nature of a co-opetition relationship? Can human rights organizations evolve, when appropriate, in order to participate with business in the proactive protection of human rights and the prevention of abuses? Can NGOs be transparent in the dual relationships with businesses?

Much work is to be done to align business responsibility with human rights in practice, a new concept in relative terms. Despite many challenges, businesses and human rights organizations can create relationships that are not counter to their core interests, and which effectively contribute to implementing the responsibility of business to respect human rights.

NOTES

1. For consistency, we refer throughout the chapter to "NGOs" as a broad range of organizations that encompass local, national, and international civil society. In our discussion of the "naming and shaming" tactic, human rights advocacy and monitoring NGOs are the most relevant. In our later discussion of opportunities within the due diligence framework, we suggest many different types of NGOs may be relevant,

including both advocacy and operational organizations depending on the context. See Section III for an elaboration of these categories and the Conclusion for a brief discussion of areas for future research based on this distinction.

2. Cragg argues instead that a moral and ethical foundation for the framework should be recognized since he believes that a strategic one cannot be made (Cragg, 2012).
3. Although not the subject of this chapter, it is interesting to note that the report advises that businesses are generally not using the language of human rights in their policies and assessments; this is an additional area in which the HRNGO could be helpful.

REFERENCES

Ahad, A.M. (2013, July 11) "U.S. retailers offer plan for safety at factories", *New York Times,* p. B1.

Allard, G. and Martinez, C.A. (2008, March 27–28) "The influence of government policy and NGOs on capturing private investment", OECD Global Forum IV on International Investment" retrieved from www.oecd.org/investment/globalforum/40400836.pdf.

Arenas, D., Lozano J.J. and Albareda, L. (2009) "The role of NGOs in CSR: Mutual perceptions among stakeholders", *Journal of Business Ethics,* 88(1), 175–97.

Argenti, P.A. (2004) "Collaborating with activists: How Starbucks works with NGOs", *California Management Review,* 47(1) 91–116.

Backer, L.C. (2012) "From institutional misalignments to socially sustainable governance: The guiding principles for the implementation for the United Nations' 'Protect, Respect and Remedy' and the construction of inter-systemic global governance", *Pacific McGeorge Global Business & Development Law Journal,* 25(1), 69–171.

Baur, D. and Schmitz, H.B. (2012) "Corporations and NGOs: When accountability leads to co-optation", *Journal of Business Ethics,* 106(1), 9–21.

Berger, I.E., Cunningham, P.H. and Drumwright, M.E. (2004) "Social alliances: Company/nonprofit collaboration", *California Management Review,* 47(1), 58–90.

Bradford, W. (2012) "Beyond good and evil: The commensurability of corporate profits and human rights", *Notre Dame Journal of Law, Ethics, & Public Policy,* 26(1), 141–280.

Brown, L.D. and Timmer, V. (2006) "Civil society actors as catalysts for transnational social learning", *International Journal of Voluntary and Nonprofit Organizations,* 17(1), 1–16.

Buhmann, K. (2012) "Business and human rights: Analysing discursive articulation of stakeholder interests to explain the consensus-based construction of the *'Protect, Respect, Remedy'* UN Framework", *International Law Research* 1(1), 88–101.

Burgos, S. (2013) "Corporations and social responsibility: NGOs in the ascendancy", *Journal of Business Strategy,* 34(1), 21–9.

Chin, K., Chan, B.L. and Lam., P. (2008) "Identifying and prioritizing critical success factors for coopetition strategy", *Industrial Management & Data Systems,* 108(4), 437–54.

Coughlan, S. (2012, November 5) "Human rights activists taught online tactics", *BBC* retrieved from http://www.bbc.co.uk/news/business-20085559.

Cragg, W. (2012) "Ethics, enlightened self-interest, and the corporate responsibility to respect human rights: A critical look at the justificatory foundations of the UN Framework", *Business Ethics Quarterly,* 22(1), 9–36.

Danish Institute for Human Rights (2010) *Doing Business in High-Risk Human Rights Environments*. Copenhagen, Denmark.

Danish Institute for Human Rights (2011) *The "State of Play" of Human Rights Due Diligence*. Copenhagen, Denmark.

Dashwood, H.S. (2012) "CSR norms and organizational learning in the mining sector", *Corporate Governance,* 12(1), 118–38.

Davis, D.R., Murdie, A. and Steinmetz, C.G. (2012) "'Makers and Shapers': Human rights INGOs and public opinion", *Human Rights Quarterly*, 34(1), 199–224.

Deitelhoff, N. and Wolf, K.D. (2013) "Business and human rights: how corporate norm violators become norm entrepreneurs", in Risse, T., Ropp, S.C. and Sikkink, K. (eds) *Persistent Power of Human Rights: From Commitment to Compliance*, pp. 222–38, Cambridge, UK: Cambridge University Press.

Doh, J.P. and Guay, T.R. (2006) "Corporate social responsibility, public policy, and NGO activism in Europe and the United States: An institutional-stakeholder perspective", *Journal of Management Studies,* 43(1), 47–73.

Gnyawali, D.R. and Park, B. (2011) "Co-opetition between giants: Collaboration with competitors for technological innovation", *Research Policy,* 40, 650–63.

International Bar Association (2010) "Interview with Professor John Ruggie, Special Representative of the UN Secretary-General on Business and human rights-transcript", http://www.ibanet.org/Article/Detail.aspx?ArticleUid=4b5233cb-f4b9-4fcd-9779-77e7e85e4d83

International Council on Human Rights Policy (2004) "Performance and Legitimacy: National human rights institutions", http://www.ichrp.org/files/reports/17/102_report_en.pdf.

Kolk, A. and Lenfant, F. (2012) "Business – NGO collaboration in conflict setting: Partnership activities in the democratic Republic of Congo", *Business & Society* 51(3) 478–511.

Kourula, A. and Halme, M. (2008) "Types of corporate responsibility and engagement with NGOs: an exploration of business and societal outcomes", *Corporate Governance,* 8(4), 557–70.

Laasonen, S., Fougére, M. and Kourula, A. (2012) "Dominant articulations in academic Business and society discourse on NGO-Business relations: A critical assessment", *Journal of Business Ethics,* 109(4), 521–45.

Mares, R. (2008) *The Dynamics of Corporate Social Responsibility*, Leiden, Netherlands: Martinus Nijhoff.

Melish, T.J. and Meidinger, E. (2012) "Protect, Respect, Remedy *and Participate*: 'New Governance' lessons for the Ruggie Framework", in Mares, R. (ed.), *The UN Guiding Principles on Business and Human Rights: Foundations and Implementations*, pp. 303–36. Leiden, Netherlands: Brill.

Mena, S., Leede, M., Baumann. D., Black, N., Lindeman, S. and McShane, L. (2010) "Advancing the business and human rights agenda: Dialogue, empowerment, and constructive engagement", *Journal of Business Ethics,* 93(1), 161–88.

Muchlinski, P. (2012) "Implementing the new UN Corporate Human Rights Framework: Implications for corporate law, governance, and regulation", *Business Ethics Quarterly,* 22(1), 145–77.

Mwangi, W., Rieth, L. and Schmitz, H.P. (2013) "Encouraging greater compliance: local networks and the United Nations Global Compact", in Risse, T., Ropp, S.C. and Sikkink, K. (eds) *Persistent Power of Human Rights: From Commitment to Compliance*, pp. 203–21. Cambridge, UK: Cambridge University Press.

Porter, M.E. and Kramer, M.R. (2011) "Creating shared value", *Harvard Business Review,* 89 (1/2), 62–77.

Risse, T. and Ropp, S.C. (2013) "Introduction and Overview", in Risse, T., Ropp, S.C. and Sikkink, K. (eds) *Persistent Power of Human Rights: From Commitment to Compliance*, pp. 222–38. Cambridge, UK: Cambridge University Press.

Risse, T. and Sikkink, K. (1999) "The socialization of international human rights norms into domestic practices: Introduction", in Risse, T., Ropp, S.C. and Sikkink, K. (eds) *The Power of Human Rights: International Norms and Domestic Change*, pp. 1–38. Cambridge, UK: Cambridge University Press

Risse, T. and Sikkink, K. (2013) "Conclusions", in Risse, T., Ropp, S.C. and Sikkink, K. (eds.) *Persistent Power of Human Rights: From Commitment to Compliance*, pp. 275–9. Cambridge, UK: Cambridge University Press.

Rondinelli, D.A. and London, T. (2003) "How corporations and environmental groups cooperate: Assessing cross-sector alliances and collaborations", *Journal of Management Executive,* 17(1), 61–76.

Ruggie, J. G. (2013) *Just Business: Multinational Corporations and Human Rights*, New York, NY: W.W. Norton & Co.

Sakarya, S., Bodur, M. Yildirim-Öktem, Ö. and Selekler-Göksen, N. (2012) "Social alliances: Business and social enterprise collaboration for social transformation", *Journal of Business Research,* 65, 1710–20.

Seitanidi, M.M., Koufopoulos, D.N. and Palmer, P. (2010) "Partnership formation for change: Indicators for transformative potential in cross-sector social partnerships", *Journal of Business Ethics,* 94(1 Supp.), 139–61.

Slavin, T. (2013, February 7) "Unilever's labour practices in Vietnam found wanting by Oxfam report", *Guardian*, retrieved from http://www.theguardian.com/sustainable-business/blog/unilever-labour-practices-vietnam-oxfam-report.

Smedley, T. (2013, March 28) "UN guidance on the business approach to human rights", *Guardian,* retrieved from http://www.theguardian.com/sustainable-business/business-cohesive-approach-human-rights.

Slim, H. (2002) "By what authority? The legitimacy and accountability of non-governmental organization", *The International Council on Human Rights Policy: International Meeting on Global Trends and Human Rights – Before and After September 11*, retrieved from http://www.gdrc.org/ngo/accountability/by-what-authority.html.

Sonnenberg, S. and Cavallaro, J.L. (2012) "Name, shame, and then build consensus? Bringing conflict resolution skills to human rights", *Washington University Journal of Law and Policy,* 39, 257–308.

Teegen, H., Doh, J.P. and Vachani, S. (2004) "The importance of nongovernmental organizations (NGOs) in global governance and value creation: an international business research agenda", *Journal of International Business Studies,* 35(6), 463–83.

U.N. Office for Partnerships (*quoting* Ki-Moon, Ban). Retrieved from http://www.un.org/partnerships/unfip_byNumbers.html.

U.N. Office of the High Commissioner for Human Rights (2011) "Guiding principles on business and human rights", U.N. Document HR/PUB/11/04, retrieved from http://www.ohchr.org/Documents/Publications/GuidingPrinciplesBusinessHR_EN.pdf.

U.N. Office of the High Commissioner for Human Rights (2012) "The corporate responsibility to respect human rights: An interpretative guide", U.N. Document HR/PUB/12/02, retrieved from http://www.ohchr.org/Documents/Publications/HR.PUB.12.2_En.pdf

U.N. Special Representative of the Secretary-General (2011, March 21) "Guiding principles on business and human rights: Implementing the United Nations 'protect, respect and remedy' framework", U.N. Document A/HRC/17/31.

Van Huijstee, M. and Glasbergen, P. (2010) "Business-NGO Interactions in a multi-stakeholder context", *Business & Society Review,* 115(3), 249–84.

van Tuijl, P. (1999) "NGOs and human rights: Sources of justice and democracy", *Journal of International Affairs*. 52(2), 493–512.

Weiss, M.A. (July 5–7, 2006) "Cities and participatory democracy", *USAID Training*, retrieved from http://www.globalurban.org/USAID_Training_PARTICIPATORY_DEMOCRACY.pdf.

Wilshaw, R., Unger L, Chi, D.Q. and Thuy, P.T. (2013) "Labour rights in Unilever"s supply chain: From compliance towards best practice", Oxfam, retrieved from http://www.oxfam.org/sites/www.oxfam.org/files/rr-unilever-supply-chain-labor-rights-vietnam-310113-en.pdf.

PART II

THE HUMAN RIGHTS OF AFFECTED STAKEHOLDERS

6. Labor rights are human rights: Sustainability initiatives and trade policy

Marisa Anne Pagnattaro*

An important aspect of the growing movement for more accountability in global business is that of recognizing that labor rights are human rights. International organizations, nongovernmental organizations, and consumers are calling on companies to take affirmative steps to promote the fair treatment of workers. However, companies struggling in a tight economy to remain competitive and viable may be resistant to undertaking steps that create better conditions for their global workforce, especially when those changes have a detrimental effect on profits. Some executives, however, are realizing that corporate responsibility is tied to sustainability and innovation and that a long-term strategic vision should take into account the need for a consistent workforce.

Despite this fact, immediate economic realities drive many companies to seek out the cheapest possible labor, often working under the worst possible conditions. This has led the United Nations to champion and advance the idea that business and human rights must be considered together to effectuate any meaningful change for millions of workers. This proposition is not a simple one to see to fruition. As John Ruggie observes, "The idea of human rights is both simple and powerful. The operation of the global human rights regime is neither" (Ruggie, 2013a, xxviii). If labor rights are, indeed, human rights, it is important to discuss how and why this cause should be advanced by business, as well as ways in which trade laws can be used to further reinforce this message. This chapter begins with the backdrop of global initiatives designed to promote labor rights as human rights. The next section then analyzes the on-going challenges for the garment industry in Bangladesh and the worker-related problems confronted by Apple, Inc. in China.

Based on lessons learned from these difficult labor situations, the chapter then establishes a variety of reasons why corporations should adopt and enforce voluntary labor standards as a long-term sustainability strategy. The final section reviews how the current labor protections required by U.S. trade agreements and Section 301 of the Trade Act of 1974 can be used to reinforce the call for higher labor standards and to block goods from being imported into the U.S. This section also recommends enhanced provisions that should be included in future trade agreements as incentives for corporations to protect workers. The ultimate conclusion is that, despite the short-run challenge of competing with corporate entities that do not endeavor to protect workers, this is outweighed by the importance of corporate labor-related initiatives as a strategy to maintain a sustainable and productive global workforce. Moreover, trade agreements and laws can be used to provide incentives for corporate responsibility toward workers for both domestic companies and other companies importing goods into the U.S. Ultimately, however, the recognition of and meaningful enforcement of labor rights as human rights will require direct collective action by a variety of stakeholders (Ostrom, 2000).

I. GLOBAL INITIATIVES TO PROMOTE LABOR RIGHTS AS HUMAN RIGHTS

Proponents of human rights believe that international agreements recognize – but did not create – these rights. Based on this mindset, following World War II, the U.N. set out to "reaffirm faith in fundamental human rights" (U.N. Charter, preamble). As an extension of that general goal, a range of global initiatives were developed to establish and promote labor rights as human rights. The foundation for this movement rested on the Universal Declaration of Human Rights adopted by the UN General Assembly. Fundamental to the Universal Declaration is Article 25, which states that "[e]veryone has the right to a standard of living adequate for the health and well-being of himself and of his family" (U.N. General Assembly, 1948, art. 25). Two additional articles specifically articulate certain conditions of work to be fundamental human rights:

Article 23

(1) Everyone has the right to work, to free choice of employment, to just and favorable conditions of work and to protection against unemployment.
(2) Everyone, without discrimination, has the right to equal pay for equal work.

(3) Everyone who works has the right to just and favorable remuneration ensuring for himself and his family an existence worthy of human dignity, and supplemented, if necessary, by other means of social protection.
(4) Everyone has the right to form and join trade unions for the protection of his interests.

Article 24

Everyone has the right to rest and leisure, including reasonable limitation of working hours and periodic holidays with pay (U.N. General Assembly, 1948, arts. 23, 24).

The Universal Declaration is unequivocal in its linkage of human dignity to the importance of just working conditions. Accordingly, it calls on all Member States to honor their pledge to realize these fundamental human rights. The U.N. International Covenant on Economic, Social and Cultural Rights (ICESCR) further reinforced the significance of work and human rights in 1966. Part III includes the "right of everyone to the enjoyment of just and favourable conditions of work," including fair wages and equal remuneration for equal work; safe and healthy working conditions; equal opportunity; and reasonable limitation of working hours. Additionally, states that are parties to the ICESCR affirm their responsibility to ensure that everyone has the right to form and join trade unions, as well as to strike (U.N. General Assembly, 1966).

The obligations set forth in both the Universal Declaration and the ICESCR, however, are intended to be binding on governments, not corporations. It was not until the 1970s that the U.N. attempted to establish binding rules to regulate the activities of global businesses. This was initially unsuccessful and the movement languished until it was reinvigorated by voluntary initiatives. The so-called "soft-law" approach garnered more appeal in the 1970s as many businesses expanded their international reach, generating concerns about the potential negative effect of corporations on developing nations. The subsequent international movement seeks to hold corporations to labor and employment standards that may be more rigorous than those established by national laws. Both the Organisation for Economic Co-operation and Development (OECD) and the International Labour Organization (ILO) adopted measures aimed at greater accountability for businesses during this decade, then revised the documents in 2000. First, the OECD adopted the Guidelines for Multinational Enterprises, which specifically set forth a framework for how businesses should address employment and industrial relations issues. Significantly, the OECD calls on businesses to respect the right of employees to be represented by unions, to be protected from discrimination, to work in a safe workplace, and for them to negotiate fairly with employees. In the commentary to the guidelines, the OECD specifically refers to the ILO as the competent body to articulate and promote fundamental labor standards and worker rights (OECD, 2000).

Shortly thereafter, the ILO adopted the Tripartite Declaration of Principles Concerning Multinational Enterprises, which sets forth key principles designed to protect workers at the most fundamental level. The Tripartite Declaration invites a range of stakeholders, most notably, multinational enterprises, to observe its principles regarding employment, including equal opportunity and security; training; conditions of work and life; and industrial relations, specifically freedom of association, the right to organize, and the right to engage in collective bargaining (ILO, 2000). This is consistent with the earlier ILO Declaration of Fundamental Principles and Rights at Work (1998), which sets out the four core conventions:

(a) freedom of association and the effective recognition of the right to collective bargaining;
(b) the elimination of all forms of forced or compulsory labour;
(c) the effective abolition of child labour; and
(d) the elimination of discrimination in respect of employment and occupation.

Importantly, also in 2000, the U.N. introduced the Global Compact, a voluntary initiative, which now has over 10,000 participants, including over 7,000 businesses in 145 countries. The first two principles of the Global Compact clearly request businesses to support and respect the protection of human rights, including ensuring that they are not complicit in human rights abuses. The next four principles deal specifically with labor, tracking the ILO core principles:

> Principle 3: Businesses should uphold the freedom of association and the effective recognition of the right to collective bargaining;
>
> Principle 4: the elimination of all forms of forced and compulsory labour;
>
> Principle 5: the effective abolition of child labour; and
>
> Principle 6: the elimination of discrimination in respect to employment and occupation (U.N. Global Compact, n.d.).

Additionally, the final principle, addressing corruption, is also relevant to labor as there can be corruption issues in connection with the enforcement of labor and employment laws, including issues related to workplace inspections. In addition to its Global Compact, the U.N. also adopted its Millennium Declaration in 2000, again reiterating its commitment to human rights, including its resolution to uphold the Universal Declaration of Human Rights (U.N. General Assembly, 2000, para. 25). Similarly, the ILO Declaration on Social Justice for a Fair Globalization (2008) notes that it is "a renewed statement of faith in the ILO."

Each of these international documents is central to establishing the link between human rights and labor rights. This, coupled with concerns about the negative effects of global businesses on human rights, prompted the 2003 U.N. initiative, the Norms on Responsibilities of Transnational Corporations and Other Business Enterprises with Regard to Human Rights. This initiative unsuccessfully sought to create an obligation under international law for businesses to have the same duties as countries to "have the obligation to promote, secure the fulfillment of, respect, ensure respect of, and protect human rights recognized in international as well as national law" (U.N. Commission on Human Rights, 2003, para. 1). The draft was not embraced by the business community and also lacked any significant government support.

It was against this backdrop that the U.N. Secretary-General appointed John Ruggie as Special Representative on the issue of human rights and business in 2005. Part of his mandate was to "identify and clarify standards of corporate responsibility and accountability for transnational corporations and other business enterprises with regard to human rights" (Ruggie, 2006, p. 3). One of the driving forces behind this inquiry was the belief that the inadequate labor standards of some companies and industries generated demands for greater corporate responsibility and accountability. Ruggie undertook this task with what he called "principled pragmatism," defined as "an unflinching commitment to the principle of strengthening the promotion and protection of human rights as it relates to business, coupled with a pragmatic attachment to what works best in creating change where it matters most – in the daily lives of people" (Ruggie, 2006, p. 20).

From 2005 to 2011, Ruggie undertook these responsibilities, ultimately culminating with the Guiding Principles on Business and Human Rights (Guiding Principles). Three pillars form the foundation for the Guiding Principles: "states must protect; companies must respect; and those who are harmed must have redress" (Ruggie, 2013a, p. xxi). With regard to corporate responsibility for human rights, the report is unequivocal that it is the responsibility of business enterprises to respect internationally recognized human rights, including those related to labor and expressed in the Universal Declaration, the ICESCR and the ILO Fundamental Principles. The Commentary to the Guiding Principles states that this responsibility "exists independently" of any government obligations and "it exists over and above compliance with national laws and regulations protecting human rights" (U.N. Human Rights Council, 2011, p. 13). According to the U.N., the Guiding Principles do not, however, create any new legal obligations; instead, they are a "clarification and elaboration of existing standards" under international law (U.N. Human Rights Council, 2012). This seems to be a significant jurisprudential shift, however, as those international obligations historically have been viewed as applying to states, not private entities. In any event, the Guiding Principles call on business enterprises to take action in three specific ways:

(1) to adopt a policy commitment to meet their responsibility to respect human rights;
(2) to have a human rights due diligence process to identify, prevent, mitigate, and account for how they address their impacts on human rights; and
(3) to have processes in place to enable the remediation of any adverse human rights impacts they cause or to which they contribute. (U.N. Human Rights Council, 2011, p. 15)

The operational principles stipulate that all business enterprises should have in place publicly available policies and processes expressing their commitment to respecting human rights. In the labor context, this means that enterprises should have clear labor and employment policies in place regarding the terms and conditions of employment, as well as the treatment of workers consistent with ILO principles and other international obligations. Business enterprises should also carry out due diligence and take reasonable steps in connection with supply chains to avoid any involvement with human rights abuses. In practical terms, this requires businesses to use leverage over vendors and suppliers, which may include termination of the relationship. Moreover, business enterprises should have tracking procedures in place to demonstrate that policies are being implemented and enforced. To ensure transparency and accountability, the data collected should then be communicated to the relevant stakeholders and businesses should be prepared to publish the information externally.

The Guiding Principles are central to the resolution adopted by the U.N. Human Rights Council in July 2011, which emphasizes that transnational corporations and other business entities "*have a responsibility to protect human rights*" (U.N. Human Rights Council, 2011). The Human Rights Council's unanimous endorsement established the Guiding Principles as the international touchstone for all considerations of the nexus between business and human rights. A year later, the Human Rights Council revisited the Guiding Principles, reporting on the status of its business and human rights agenda (U.N. Human Rights Council, 2012). One major concern is the risk of problems with the implementation of the Guiding Principles due to a lack of a coordinated effort to ensure consistency. Given the scale and complexity of the issue, one recommendation is that the U.N. should engage in a coordinated strategic effort to support implementation. The actual logistics of such a plan, however, are not articulated. Because of the lack of any enforcement mechanism, progress on implementation of the Guiding Principles is, at best, tentative. Moreover, there is criticism that there are no real incentives for businesses to integrate the required due diligence into their core activities (Taylor, 2012).

Similar concerns were raised at the first Annual Forum on Business and Human Rights in December 2012. One particular challenge addressed violations in global supply chains; monitoring of these is especially difficult as most companies are rarely in full control of the processes. According to the head of the Fair Labor Association (FLA), who participated in the discussion, he was attempting to discuss the problems and devise practical solutions in a "safe space" for stakeholders, which avoided "naming and shaming" exposure (Ruggie, 2013b, p. 7). Other practical issues raised in the Forum included: the fact that "human rights implementation may be outside of the comfort zone of some companies," the need for training and risk assessment with companies and the "challenge of 'translation' of human rights in various cultural contexts" (Ruggie, 2013b, p. 7). Although the Guiding Principles are a groundbreaking attempt to require business enterprises to promote and protect human rights, especially global labor rights, much work is needed to integrate these concerns into business operations.

The Guiding Principles are at the mercy of governments and corporations to take the initiative. Although the first pillar of the Guiding Principles requires states to "respect, protect and fulfil the human rights of individuals within their territory and/or jurisdiction" (U.N. Human Rights Council, 2011, p. 6), it is the exception, not the rule, for countries to require reporting problems uncovered by a company's due diligence. On the other hand, one of the explicit goals of EU trade policy is promoting human rights. Interestingly, at least one study concludes that mandatory reporting requirements on corporate social responsibility affect management practices, leading to more sustainable development and employee training, as well as a decrease in corruption issues and an increase in managerial credibility (Ioannou and Serefeim, 2011).

Especially in light of the precarious financial state of the global economy since 2008, many governments have not made a priority of introducing any additional laws and requirements focused on promoting human rights for fear that such regulation could fetter already fragile economies. Even worse, enforcement is often lacking because resources are used for more pressing concerns or because corruption hinders it. For many reasons, the movement is now focusing on the sensibility of investors, calling on them to undertake the cause to "diminish their risks and enhance the rights of others" (Institute for Human Rights, 2013, p. 57). The hope is that investor pressure can help bridge the problematic gap between the Guiding Principles and the need for effective enforcement.

II. PROBLEMATIC CASES

As the garment industry in Bangladesh and Apple's experience in China illustrate, the lack of effective policies has a detrimental effect on corporate reputations and makes companies targets for criticism. More often than not, companies wait until a public relations issue arises before they address fundamental labor issues. This is particularly evident when assessing both the ongoing challenges for the garment industry in Bangladesh and Apple's labor-related issues over the last few years. In both cases, extreme labor conditions and subsequent deaths led to widespread calls for change, prompting industry action.

A. Garment Industry in Bangladesh

Manufacturing in Bangladesh has long been problematic because of corruption issues and a widespread lack of protections for workers. Imports from Bangladesh's ready-made garment (RMG) sector have increased substantially over the last decade. The U.S. Department of Labor (2013b) estimates that there are about five thousand RMG factories in Bangladesh, employing over four million workers. In 2007, the American Federation of Labor and Congress of Industrial Organizations (AFL-CIO, 2007) petitioned to remove Bangladesh from the list of beneficiary countries under the Generalized System of Preferences (GSP), alleging a variety of violations of workers' rights in the garment industry (GSP Petition). The Office of the U.S. Trade Representative

(USTR) accepted the petition for review and placed Bangladesh under continuing review to monitor the progress of the Bangladesh Government towards a set of benchmarks in a 2008 demarche.

But although Bangladesh's RMG industry is growing rapidly, worker protections are not keeping pace with this progress. For this reason, the AFL-CIO filed an update in 2011 of its GSP Petition, alleging that conditions in the RMG sector had gotten progressively worse (AFL-CIO, 2011). The AFL-CIO renewed its call for the U.S. to suspend Bangladesh's GSP trade preferences, unless the Government of Bangladesh agreed to a binding plan to improve labor conditions and took immediate steps toward implementation. Unfortunately, no substantial changes were implemented, and the RMG labor situation was then marked by tragedy in November 2012. Over a hundred workers died in a factory fire at Tazreen fashions, which was manufacturing for a number of well-known global companies, including Wal-Mart. Public scrutiny was directed immediately at Wal-Mart, as documents found at the Tazreen apparel factory showed that five of the factory's 14 production lines were devoted to manufacturing apparel for Wal-Mart and its Sam's Club subsidiary (Yardley, 2012).

Just as the furor over the Tazreen fire was starting to wane, a multi-story garment factory collapsed in Bangladesh in April 2013, killing over a thousand workers. Yet again, Wal-Mart was in the spotlight, along with a number of other American and European companies. Days later, another fire at a Bangladeshi garment factory killed eight workers. Taken together, these tragedies reignited the debate about who should be responsible and how safety issues should be resolved. Importantly, the discussion about labor rights as human rights also gained traction, as companies were criticized for seeking rock-bottom labor standards; consumers were criticized for wanting fast, cheap fashion; and the Government of Bangladesh was criticized for corruption and failing to protect its citizens (Hazan, 2013).

Acknowledging that audits alone were insufficient to improve worker safety, firms questioned whether they should pull out of Bangladesh or stay and work for effective change. The result was three different, important and significant actions: a binding agreement among mostly European firms; a separate agreement crafted by American firms; and a decision by the U.S. to end GSP status for Bangladesh. First, on May 13, 2013, European retailers led an initiative resulting in an Accord in which the parties agreed to establish a fire and building safety program in Bangladesh for five years. The signatories to the Accord agreed to a number of key provisions, including:

- requiring suppliers to accept inspections and implement remediation measures;
- appointing a Steering Committee with equal representation chosen by the trade union signatories and the company signatories and a representative chosen from the ILO as a neutral chair;
- resolving disputes pursuant to binding arbitration, enforceable in a court of law in the domicile of the signatory against whom enforcement was sought;
- undertaking credible inspections by an independent qualified safety inspector with fire and safety expertise and impeccable credentials;
- taking prompt, remedial corrective action where warranted, including taking reasonable efforts to protect workers;
- establishing an extensive fire and building safety training program;
- making information about suppliers and inspection reports publicly available to ensure transparency;
- terminating agreements with suppliers who did not participate fully in the program; and
- providing financial support to fund the implementation of the program. (*Accord on Fire and Building Safety*, 2013)

The Accord is legally binding on the 70 signatory retailers, which are primarily European except for two American companies: Abercrombie & Fitch and PVH. The legally binding nature of the Accord, as well as its involvement of multiple stakeholders, indicates a substantial commitment to workplace safety, which has not previously been seen in Bangladesh.

In contrast, most major American retailers, including Wal-Mart, opposed the Accord, citing concerns about legal liability. The binding nature of the Accord does create legal liability, and many U.S. companies were unsure about how that may translate into litigation in the U.S. With pressure mounting from consumer and labor groups, a group of U.S. retailers (including Wal-Mart, Gap, JC Penney, Sears, and Target) worked with the nonprofit group Bipartisan Policy Center to develop their own plan aimed at addressing safety concerns in Bangladesh. In July 2013, they announced their proposal for an Alliance for Bangladesh Worker Safety (Alliance), which would, within the following 12 months, inspect an estimated 500 Bangladesh factories used by the companies, ensure all workers were trained, and develop plans to fix any substantial safety problems (Mitchell and Snowe, 2013). Central to the Alliance plan was the agreement to make a five-year commitment, involving direct funding of at least $42 million, plus $100 million in access, to low-cost capital funding for factory improvements (Mitchell and Snowe, 2013). The plan is not as comprehensive as the Accord and also currently lacks participation by unions; yet, it is an important step towards improving workplace safety in Bangladesh.

Another important aspect of effecting a change in fire and safety conditions, as well as other protections for Bangladeshi workers, is the extent to which foreign governments should take action. With continuing pressure from unions, including the AFL-CIO, the U.S. moved to suspend benefits to Bangladesh under the GSP. (Pursuant to Section 502(b)(2)(G) of the Trade Act of 1974 (2006), the President will not designate any country a beneficiary developing country under the GSP if the country has not taken or is not taking steps to afford internationally recognized worker rights in the country.) The suspension of Bangladesh's GSP benefits became effective 60 days after publication of the proclamation in the Federal Register (White House, 2013). Since the initial AFL-CIO petition in 2007, the U.S. Department of Labor has provided technical assistance to improve the labor framework in Bangladesh, including building fire and safety standards (U.S. Department of Labor, 2013a). The position of USTR was that this action has been taken in connection with initiating new discussions with the Government of Bangladesh regarding steps to improve the "worker rights environment," so that GSP benefits can be restored (Office of the USTR, 2013b).

The suspension of GSP was largely symbolic, as garments were not covered by that scheme. Subsequent action by the USTR, however, illustrates the commitment to worker rights and safety in Bangladesh. To that end, the USTR outlined specific steps to be taken to improve labor rights and worker safety in its Bangladesh Action Plan 2013. The action plan sets forth specific steps to be taken, including increasing the number of inspectors and improving their training. It also contains the threat of increased fines and other sanctions such as loss of import and export licenses if future violations of fire and general safety standards occur (U.S. Department of Labor, 2013b). The European Union is also considering taking action through its Generalized System of Preferences to incentivize responsible management of supply chains if Bangladesh does not act to ensure that factories comply with international labor standards, including ILO conventions (Spiegel and Wilson, 2013).

In the wake of intense international pressure from a wide array of stakeholders, Bangladesh passed the Bangladesh Labour (Amendment) Bill 2013 (Labor Act). The Bangladeshi Secretary of Labor claims that 87 sections of the 2006 labor law have been amended and that all obstacles to freedom of association have been removed (Al-Mahmood, 2013). According to Human Rights Watch, however, even though Bangladesh has ratified most of the core ILO standards, important sections of the Labor Act still do not meet ILO standards. With regard to factory safety, one key feature of the new law is that all factories that sell products within Bangladesh must set aside five percent of net profits in a welfare fund, yet the subjective exemption for export-oriented factories undercuts its effectiveness, as many factories will likely seek exemption (Greenhouse, 2013). Moreover, the Labor Act requires prior approval from the Bangladeshi Labor and Employment Ministry before trade unions or employer organizations can receive technical, technological, health, safety, and financial support from international sources (Human Rights Watch, 2013). Although Bangladesh is touting the new Labor Act as ensuring that labor rights are strengthened, its shortcomings are readily apparent for those who seek meaningful change for Bangladeshi workers, and there is no assurance that there will be effective enforcement of pro-worker provisions.

B. Apple in China

Conditions in electronics factories are now facing similar criticisms to those which face the international garment industry sector. As one of the fastest growing global industries, sustainability issues are being raised in the electronics sector, including workplace labor practices. Apple has been a highly respected company, yet its prominence has been tarnished by revelations about the treatment of the workers who manufacture its products. Worker suicides, large amounts of overtime, and difficult working conditions caused the mainstream media to start scrutinizing Apple's practices, particularly at the Foxconn manufacturing facility.

Ruggie (2013a) points out, however, that what is most surprising is that Apple managed to avoid close scrutiny for both its apparent failures to address the problems at Foxconn, as well as for contributing to the problem through its demands for what Apple praised as supply chain "speed and flexibility." Apple's manufacturing capacity is impressive, yet it comes at an enormous human cost. One of the most telling examples is when Apple demanded that its Chinese factory overhaul its assembly line to accommodate a new screen for the iPhone in 2007, pressing 8,000 sleeping workers into service for a 12-hour shift fitting glass screens into beveled frames (Duhigg and Brasher, 2012). This kind of just-in-time manufacturing can push suppliers to drive workers beyond what is reasonable or within the law, as well as in violation of a company's own standards.

Despite Apple's Supplier Code of Conduct containing specific protections for workers, there has been a lapse between that Code of Conduct and its enforcement. Apple's 2011 Supplier Responsibility Progress Report addresses its audit results for 2010, and its compliance program revealed a number of repeat and first-time violations. The report also specifically addresses the suicides at the Foxconn manufacturing facility, noting Apple's subsequent investigation and quick response action, including hiring psychological counselors, establishing a 24-hour care center and attaching large nets to the factory buildings to prevent impulsive suicides. The latter step immediately subjected Apple to ridicule, as photos of the enormous nets around Foxconn circulated (Emerson, 2012). Instead of addressing the root of the problems – the working and living conditions – leading to the suicides, Foxconn was merely establishing triage measures.

Subject to scrutiny, Apple continued its monitoring program focusing on the five core areas in its Supplier Code of Conduct (labor and human rights; worker health and safety; environmental impact; ethics; and management systems), ultimately reporting the findings in its Supplier Responsibility 2012 Progress Report (Apple, 2012). At the behest of labor rights groups, journalists and academics who were seeking more transparency, Apple also published a list of its leading suppliers – the 156 companies which manufacture more than 97 percent of what Apple pays to suppliers to manufacture products – on its Supplier Responsibility website. In the 2012 Progress Report, Apple reports that it conducted 229 audits (60 percent more than the previous year) and that it found fewer core violations. Problems with excessive working hours continued to persist, in violation of Apple's Code of Conduct. To address this issue, Apple began weekly tracking of working hours, required facilities to make changes to their work shifts and hiring, and hired a consultant to provide additional training to facilities on factory planning to avoid the excessive hours problem (Apple, 2012).

Because Apple's monitoring and compliance was not as effective as it could be, there was ongoing criticism about the treatment of workers in Apple's supply chain. Undoubtedly, this prompted Apple to take several proactive steps. First, it joined the FLA, agreeing to align its compliance program with FLA obligations within two years. Apple also announced that it would work with Verite, a nonprofit group to help improve the working conditions at the factories manufacturing its products. Lastly, Apple joined the IDH electronics program, a public–private consortium of electronics brands, suppliers, NGOs, international donors, and governments working together to improve the sustainable performance of the suppliers in the electronics industry. Apple finally realized that it must engage in a dialogue with multiple stakeholders to develop a sustainable supply chain and workforce to be more competitive (Krosinsky, 2012); instead of focusing on policies, it needed to listen to workers' complaints and the recommendations from advocacy groups. The company, therefore, tripled its corporate responsibility staff, reevaluated how it works with manufacturers, and asked competitors to curb overtime in China (Bradshir and Duhigg, 2012).

Instead of moving their manufacturing from Bangladesh and China, causing thousands to be unemployed, the signatories to the Accord and Alliance and Apple took action to show their true commitment to corporate social responsibility for labor practices. As these cases illustrate, codes of conduct and monitoring working conditions were not sufficient (Locke, Qin and Brause, 2007). In both situations, companies were caught in a defensive mode, trying to engage in brand damage control, while also addressing the root causes of the problem. They show that the success of voluntary, multistakeholder governance programs that monitor labor standards in global supply chains varies significantly depending on the depth of the monitoring (Anner, 2012). Research demonstrates that a commitment-oriented approach to improving labor standards aimed at root-cause problem solving, coupled with transparency, will gradually lead to a "ratcheting up" of labor standards (Locke, Amengual and Mangla, 2009, p. 324). Hopefully, agreements such as the Accord and the Alliance, as well as the kind of action taken by Apple, will lead to more of such substantial changes in working conditions.

III. THE IMPORTANCE OF A STRATEGY OF SUSTAINABILITY

Although there is an international framework clearly establishing labor rights as human rights, there is no framework for any meaningful enforcement. Why then, would any business enterprise adopt and enforce voluntary labor standards that exceed those required by national laws? The answer is that business enterprises should incorporate fair labor and employment practices as part of a long-term sustainability strategy.

This argument is contrary to some dominant twentieth-century economists who argued that social (and environmental) policies could undermine the profitability of a company (Eccles, Ioannou and Serafeim, 2011). This position was epitomized by Milton Friedman who proclaimed that "there is one and only one social responsibility of business – to use its resources and engage in activities designed to increase its profits, so long as it stays within the rules of the game, which is to say, engages in open and free competition without deception or fraud" (Friedman, 1970, p. 122). In Friedman's view any concept of corporate social responsibility is an anathema; he does not acknowledge that social responsibility can lead to increased profits. Similarly, it has been argued that companies will not grant workers basic rights to organize or change the "sweatshop structure" of industry, because there is a limited ability to raise prices for goods manufactured under better – usually more costly – working conditions (Levinson, 2001). Moreover, despite the fact that an overwhelming number of global chief executives believe that corporate social responsibility creates shareholder value, one study observes that the connection between virtuous firms and profitability is, at best, "inconclusive" (Vogel, 2005, p. 29).

The current wisdom is that a strategic approach is "increasingly important to the competitiveness of enterprises" (European Commission, 2011, p. 3). Businesses are making a commitment to respecting labor rights because it is in their long-term interest on many fronts, including risk management, customer relationships, human resource management, and innovation capacity. There is currently research underway to shed more light on the relationship between social responsibility, including labor rights and profitability (Locke, 2013). The belief is that addressing social responsibility can develop "long-term employee, customer and citizen trust as a basis for sustainable business models," that will ultimately foster the kind of productive environment in which "enterprises can innovate and grow" (European Commission, 2011, p. 3).

Corporate success and social welfare are not pitted in a zero-sum game. On the contrary, the concept of shared value is emerging as a way to conceptualize this issue. Defined as "policies and operating practices that enhance the competitiveness of a company, while simultaneously advancing the economic and social conditions in the communities in which it operates," shared value creation focuses on "identifying and expanding the connections between societal and economic progress" (Porter and Kramer, 2011, p. 66). Approaching societal issues from a value perspective, as opposed to seeing them as peripheral matters, is an important re-conceptualization of the debate. This is particularly important as job satisfaction and commitment are important for long-term stability and lead to sustainable human resource management policies.

This fact was demonstrated by a recent study that compared 90 companies that adopted a substantial number of social and environmental policies (high-sustainability companies) with 90 comparable companies that adopted almost none of the policies (low-sustainability companies). Researchers found that over an 18-year period, the high-sustainability companies substantially outperformed low-sustainability companies both in the stock market as well as in accounting performance. The authors are championing the study as "convincing evidence that sustainability pays off," debunking the critics who ague that sustainability destroys shareholder value (Eccles, Ioannou and Serafeim, 2012). This study marks an important milestone in research being conducted to determine the value of social policies, such as the protection of workers' rights. There is still work to be done to determine the cost of mistreating workers, such as how this affects the bottom line, and how the lack of worker protections affects consumer choices and perceptions of the company.

Companies need to determine what strategies are effective to link social progress to business success. To determine how to track the impact of social policies or to ascertain the "shared value measurement," companies need to take four steps: (1) identify the social issues to target; (2) make the business case for how the social improvement will directly improve business performance; (3) track the progress of the targets; and (4) measure the results and use the insights gained to unlock new value (Porter and Kramer, 2011). The hope is that this kind of shared value measurement will also make the business attractive to investors, who will be able to see direct evidence of the economic value resulting from the company's social policies.

Investors who are interested in "responsible investment" are those who favor an approach that is "founded on the view that the effective management of environmental, social and governance (ESG) issues is not only the right thing to do, but is also fundamental to creating value" (PwC, 2012b, p. 1). Social issues are defined to include human rights and labor conditions, which encompass treatment of employees, health and safety, and supply chains. A recent PwC survey of its clients in the private equity (PE) industry revealed that 94 percent "believe that ESG activities can create value," yet only about 40 percent are attempting to measure the value of these activities (PwC, 2012b, p. 3). Interestingly, PwC found geographic differences: U.S.-headquartered PE firms are focusing on environmental concerns, whereas EU-headquartered PE firms also take into account social issues. In fact several E.U. firms "described how they're working with their portfolio companies to improve the way they manage 'social' issues like labour issues in supply chains, health and safety, and employee management" (PwC, 2012b, p. 14). Better practices regarding labor issues in supply chains, as well as health and safety improvements, are leading to a range of benefits that may be difficult to quantify, but are significant, such as "decreasing turnover and attrition, boosting morale to increase productivity and retention, attracting new customers, and enhancing reputation and brand" (PwC, 2012b, p. 14; Torelli, Monga and Kaikati, 2012).

The question is how best to assess the economic value of these social and labor policies. During the mid-1990s, there was a movement to use what became known as the *triple bottom line* (TBL) to measure performance in terms of sustainability. The TBL is defined as "an accounting framework that incorporates three dimensions of performance: social, environmental and financial" (Slaper and Hall, 2011, p. 4). Although this is not a new concept, there is no real consensus on the best way to determine the value of sustainability practices. Some more progressive companies are producing sustainability reports. It is expected that as more companies learn how to produce "an integrated view of economic, environmental, and social performance," there will be increased interest from investors "in different forms of corporate reporting that combine ESG and financial metrics" (PwC, 2012a, p. 5). Moreover, to the extent that financial institutions are forming sustainability research departments and a number of companies are creating tools making it easier for investors to analyze sustainability data, there should be new research forthcoming about the long-term strategic benefits of sustainability strategies. In any event, it is clear that consumers are becoming more conscious about the origins of what they buy and how the products are produced. Responding to this demand, the Sustainable Apparel Coalition (n.d.) has been testing a measure called the Higg Index to understand and quantify sustainability impacts of apparel and footwear products.

IV. TRADE AGREEMENTS AND LAWS TO PROMOTE WORKER RIGHTS

While Apple and other companies, particularly in the E.U., focusing on long-term sustainable labor practices are making advances, there is some question about whether they can survive in the short run competing against companies who are able to gain a competitive edge because they take advantage of cheaper manufacturing costs. Apple, for example, is competing directly with Samsung, yet despite allegations about illegal labor practices, Samsung does not participate in the IDH Electronics Program and any remediation efforts are not transparent. There are limits to ethical consumerism and less scrupulous companies could gain enough market share to force out companies with a longer term vision (Levinson, 2001). As such, companies seeking to recognize and promote labor rights as human rights could be at a short-term disadvantage.

Accordingly, trade policy should be used to reinforce the call for labor standards consistent with human rights and level the playing field for companies who want to sell their products in the U.S. This section reviews ways to enforce core labor standards by using current labor protections required by U.S. trade agreements and other trade laws, including the power to block goods from being imported into the U.S. This section also recommends enhanced provisions that should be included in future trade agreements that would function as incentives to corporations that respect labor rights in their international supply chains.

Trade agreements are an extension of foreign policy goals. The U.S. State Department has been guided by former Secretary of State Clinton's vision of what has been termed "economic statecraft," thinking about national security through diplomacy, development, and defense. This philosophy was inspired by the Quadrennial Diplomacy and Development Report, which explains how diplomacy can promote American prosperity by expanding "diplomatic engagement around trade and commercial issues" (U.S. Department of State and USAID, 2010, p. 39). This policy also serves long-term U.S. foreign policy goals about spreading democratic values. The essential idea is to use a range of tools to support reform-minded individuals as they work toward democratic societies that protect the rights of all citizens. The promotion of security and democracy is seen as critical to the achievement of decent global work standards (U.S. Department of State and USAID, 2010).

Trade agreements promoting and enforcing labor rights as human rights advance this democratic agenda. Stated another way, by "making trade conditional on respect for human beings' right to dignity, a few economically powerful countries are changing the politics of trade and the politics of repression" (Hafner-Burton, 2009, p. 4). Trade agreements that promote workers' rights and prevent goods in violation of the agreement from being imported to the U.S. help to enforce the global initiatives detailed in Part I. When incentives are not effective, conditioning entry into the U.S. market on enforcement of labor rights is a powerful way to get the attention of manufacturers.

The labor provisions in the free trade agreement between the U.S. and Jordan (U.S.–Jordan FTA) were seen as holding great promise for elevating working conditions in Jordan. In this agreement, the labor provisions are incorporated into the body of the agreement (as opposed to in a side agreement), which is particularly important, as it means that the dispute resolution procedures are the same for labor disputes as they are for commercial disputes. Accordingly, if a dispute cannot be resolved, the affected party "shall be entitled to take any appropriate and commensurate measure," and are not relegated to some alternative less effective measures (U.S.–Jordan FTA, 2001, art. 17, at para. 2(b)). The U.S.–Jordan FTA also specifically reaffirms the parties' obligations as members of the ILO requiring them to strive to ensure that internationally recognized labor rights are protected by national law. Despite the provisions, however, a lack of enforcement of the labor provisions has allowed working conditions in violation of these labor rights to persist in Jordan. If an agreement is to be more than just words on paper, the U.S. must take steps to enforce labor provisions, such as this one, to fully realize its promise.

Another example of an agreement with groundbreaking labor provisions is the Cambodia Bilateral Textile Agreement (Cambodia Agreement; Wells, 2006). The Cambodia Agreement expressly acknowledged that the United States and Cambodia were seeking to:

> ensure that labor laws and regulations provide for high quality and productive workplaces; and seek to foster transparency in the administration of labor law, promote compliance with, and effective enforcement of, existing labor law, and promote the general labor rights embodied in the Cambodian labor code. (*Cambodia Bilateral Textile Agreement*, 1999, p. 4)

A key aspect of the Cambodia Agreement was the government's agreement that it would "support implementation of a program to improve working conditions in the textile and apparel sector, including internationally recognized core labor standards, through the application of Cambodian labor law" (*Cambodia Bilateral Textile Agreement*, 1999, p. 4). The U.S. and Cambodia agreed to have at least two consultations each year to discuss labor standards, specific benchmarks and the implementation of the program. If, as a result of those consultations, the U.S. makes a positive determination that working conditions substantially comply with labor law and standards, then additional textiles and apparel from Cambodia could be imported into the U.S.. If, however, a significant change in working conditions occurs that is not positive, then any increased amounts of imports would be withdrawn.

This concept of increasing imports based on positive changes for workers in the textile and garment industry has been very successful with the help of the ILO, which started Better Factories Cambodia (BFC). The ILO established this project in 2001 to help the garment industry make and maintain improvements in working conditions for Cambodian workers. Pursuant to the program, monitors make unannounced visits to factories to assess working conditions, including compliance with the law and ILO standards. Twice a year, the monitors check for issues related to child labor, freedom of association, employee contracts, wages, working hours, workplace facilities, noise control and machine safety. In 2002, based on Cambodia's progress in reforming labor conditions in textile factories, the Cambodia Agreement was extended through the end of 2004 and the quota for textile exports from Cambodia increased. Regrettably, the BFC's most recent report that assessed 130 garment and six footwear factories, revealed backsliding on a number of compliance issues, particularly relating to safety and health. These issues may have been precipitated by growth in the garment (11 percent) and footwear (12 percent) industries, which put pressure on both workers and factory managers. During the first ten months of 2012, BFC registered 65 new factories, which employ over 25,500 workers (Better Factories Cambodia, 2013). This rapid growth is straining the ability of the BFC to monitor compliance and underscores the need for labor protection in the new bilateral trade agreement with Cambodia. Moreover, this increase in compliance violations, corresponding with the spike in manufacturing, further underscores the reason why workers need labor protections that are reinforced by trade. Despite the recent strain on the BFC and compliance issues, there is still much to praise about the incentive-based compliance promoted by the Cambodia Agreement. Thus far, this carrot – as opposed to stick – approach is a relative success (Leary, 2010).

Unfortunately, the incentive model of the Cambodia Agreement was not replicated in subsequent agreements. In the U.S.–Dominican Republic Central American Free Trade Agreement (CAFTA-DR), for example, the parties agree to "strive to ensure" that the principles in the ILO Declaration on Fundamental Principles and Rights at Work and its Follow-up and other internationally recognized labor rights are recognized and protected by law, but this is not mandatory. Because the parties retain "the right to exercise discretion" with respect to investigating, prosecuting, regulating, and complying with "other labor matters determined to have higher priorities," it makes it difficult to take action against a party. If a party believes that a violation of the Labor Chapter (Chapter 16) exists, it may request "consultations" by submitting a written request containing "information that is specific and sufficient" to enable the alleged offending party to respond. The parties are then to make "every attempt to arrive at a mutually satisfactory resolution" within 60 days of the request. If the parties are unable to resolve the matter, then either party "may request that the Council be convened to consider the matter." At such a proceeding, the Council may consult with "outside experts." Failure by a party to enforce its own labor laws can subject the party to binding dispute settlement and, ultimately, fines or sanctions. The maximum fine is set at $15 million per year, per violation. The fines, however, are not paid to the injured party – instead they may be directed towards remedying the labor violation. Although the labor provisions are arguably more robust than earlier free trade agreements, they do not require full incorporation of ILO standards (CAFTA-DR).

These provisions have been put to the test in connection with a CAFTA-DR request by the U.S. for consultations with Guatemala regarding labor rights violations. In July 2010, the Obama Administration responded to a 2008 submission by the AFL-CIO by requesting, pursuant to CAFTA-DR, consultations with the Guatemalan Government to address workers' rights violations (Kirk and Solis, letter to Echeverria and Rodriguez, July 30, 2010). This is the first labor case brought by the U.S. to a dispute settlement under a trade agreement. The act signaled that the U.S. was finally sending a strong message that it will not tolerate labor violations under its trade agreements and it will enforce rights agreed to under those agreements. The action received support from the AFL-CIO, as well as labor groups in Guatemala (AFL-CIO, 2010; U.S. Labor in the Americas Project, 2010). After negotiations for several years, the U.S. and Guatemala announced that they had reached a landmark 18-point plan including concrete actions and time frames that Guatemala agreed to implement within six months to improve labor law enforcement. Under the Enforcement Plan, Guatemala agreed to strengthen labor inspections, expedite and streamline the process of sanctioning employers, order remediation of labor violations, increase labor law compliance by exporting companies, improve the monitoring and enforcement of labor court orders, publish labor law enforcement information, and establish mechanisms to ensure that workers are paid what they are owed when factories close (Office of the USTR, 2013a). Although there is no agreement to limit imports if the terms are not met, the agreement is a positive step to demonstrate that the U.S. will enforce labor obligations pursuant to its trade agreements.

In addition to remedies under trade agreements, another tool that could be used to enforce labor rights is Section 301 of the Trade Act of 1974. Section 301 provides the U.S. with the authority to enforce trade agreements and to resolve trade disputes. Overall, it is the principal authority that the U.S. may use to impose trade sanctions on foreign countries that violate trade agreements or engage in other unfair trade practices. Under Section 301, if negotiations regarding the practice at issue fail, the U.S. may take action to raise import duties on the country's products as a way of rebalancing trade (Trade Act of 1974, 2006). The AFL-CIO made two unsuccessful attempts to use the law during the Bush administration (Blustein, 2004). The first workers' rights petition was brought in 2004, against the Chinese Government, contending that exploitation of Chinese workers was an unfair trade practice that created unfair competition. Six weeks later, the Bush Administration cabinet members rejected the petition (AFL-CIO, 2004). With problematic labor conditions continuing in China, the AFL-CIO submitted a new petition to the White House in 2006, alleging violations of workers' rights by suppressing strikes, banning independent unions, and permitting factories to violate minimum wage and child labor laws: The White House also rejected the second petition (AFL-CIO, 2006) and although no other petitions have been filed under Section 301 for violations of labor rights, the statute presents another avenue for potential recourse.

The U.S. has the opportunity to include effective and comprehensive labor provisions in future trade agreements, such as the Trans-Pacific Partnership, that could improve labor conditions and give meaning to labor rights with all of its trading partners. The following proposal includes provisions that could be included in future trade agreements to help promote and protect labor rights, as well as encourage businesses to develop sustainable practices with regard to the workers who manufacture their products. Several components are crucial to that goal. First, all labor provisions should be part of the main text of the trade agreement. At a minimum, trading partners should agree to reaffirm their obligations as members of the ILO and their commitments under the ILO Declaration and also to strengthen domestic law to be consistent with core ILO labor standards. Second, any failure to comply with the labor provisions should be subject to the same dispute resolution procedures used to resolve any disagreement under the agreement, including the right of any party to the agreement to bring an action against another party in open, transparent proceedings. Dispute resolution should not be limited to a party's failure to enforce its own labor laws. Third, trade sanctions should be available for disputes regarding any provision of the labor article as they are for a commercial dispute, in the form of suspension of tariff benefits and/or payment of penalties or fines. Importantly, goods manufactured in violation of a member's labor laws should not be allowed to be imported into the U.S. Lastly, the agreement should contain a specific provision for adequate funding to ensure that the goals of improving labor laws and enforcement can be met.

V. CONCLUSION

Ultimately, this chapter concludes that although it may be a challenge to compete with corporate entities that do not endeavor to protect workers, that challenge is outweighed by the importance of corporate, labor-related initiatives as a strategy to maintain a sustainable and productive global workforce. Strategic trade policy can be used to further incentivize corporate responsibility toward workers for both domestic companies and other companies importing goods into the U.S. The U.S. should seize the opportunity to improve the labor standards of its trading partners and hold countries and companies accountable to internationally recognized labor standards. Over 50 years of work by the ILO and other international groups to promote core international labor standards could move toward full realization if the U.S. required its trading partners to respect core labor rights. Access to U.S. markets should be an incentive for countries to enforce fundamental and internationally recognized labor standards. The U.S. should not allow its trading partners and companies doing business in those countries to violate the human rights of their workers.

NOTE

* The author gratefully acknowledges funding for this project from a University of Georgia Terry-Sanford research grant. The author is also indebted to Shareen Hertel for her invaluable insights.

REFERENCES

Abed, F.H. (2013, April 3), "Op-Ed., Bangladesh needs strong unions, not outside pressure". *New York Times,* retrieved from http://www.nytimes.com/2013/04/30/opinion/bangladesh-needs-strong-unions-not-outside-pressure.html?pagewanted=all.

Accord on Fire and Building Safety in Bangladesh (2013, May 13), retrieved from http://www.laborrights.org/sites/default/files/publications-and-resources/Accord_on_Fire_and_Building_Safety_in_Bangladesh_2013-05-13.pdf.

American Federation of Labor and Congress of Industrial Organizations (AFL-CIO) (2004), "Bush administration officially rejects AFL-CIO section 301 trade petition" (Press Release), retrieved from http://www.aflcio.org/Press-Room/Press-Releases/Bush-Administration-Officially-Rejects-AFL-CIO-Sec.

AFL-CIO (2006), Statement by AFL-CIO Secretary-Treasurer Trumka on Bush administration's rejection of 301 petition against Chinese government [Press Release], retrieved from http://www.aflcio.org/Press-Room/Press-Releases/Statement-by-AFL-CIO-Secretary-Treasurer-Trumka-on.

AFL-CIO (2007, June 22) "Petition to remove Bangladesh from the list of eligible beneficiary developing countries pursuant to 19 U.S.C. 2462(d) of the generalized system of preferences", retrieved from http://www.aflcio.org/content/download/721/6570/2007+AFL-CIO+petition+on+Worker+Rights+in+Bangladesh.pdf.

AFL-CIO (2010), "Statement by AFL-CIO president Richard Trumka on announcement of Guatemala labor rights case" [Press Release], retrieved from http://www.aflcio.org/index.php/Press-Room/Press-Releases/Statement-by-AFL-CIO-President-Richard-Trumka-on-A.

AFL-CIO, (2011, April), "2011 update of the AFL-CIO's 2007 petition to remove Bangladesh from the list of eligible beneficiary developing countries under the generalized system of preferences (GSP)", retrieved from http://www.aflcio.org/content/download/720/6567/2011+upd.

Al-Mahmood, S.Z. (2013, July 15), "Bangladesh passes new labor law", *Wall Street Journal*, retrieved from http://online.wsj.com/article/SB10001424127887323664204578607814136238372.html.

Anner, M. (2012), "Corporate social responsibility and freedom of association rights: The precarious quest for legitimacy and control in global supply chains". *Politics & Society*, *40*(4), 609–44.

Apple Supplier Responsibility 2012 Progress Report (2012), retrieved from http://www.apple.com/supplierresponsibility/pdf/Apple_SR_2012_Progress_Report.pdf.

Better Factories Cambodia (2013), "Twenty Ninth synthesis report on working conditions in Cambodia's garment sector", retrieved from http://betterwork.com/cambodia/wp-content/uploads/2013/04/Synthesis-Report-29th-EN-Final.pdf.

Blustein, P. (2004, Sept. 10), "Labor seeks pressure on China", *Washington Post*, p. E03.

Bradsher, K. and Duhigg, C. (2012, Dec. 27), "Signs of changes taking hold in electronics factories in China", *New York Times*, p. A1, retrieved from http://www.nytimes.com/2012/12/27/business/signs-of-changes-taking-hold-in-electronics-factories-in-china.html.

Cambodia Bilateral Textile Agreement. (1999), retrieved from http://khmer.cambodia.usembassy.gov/media2/pdf/uskh_texttile.pdf.

Duhigg, C. and Brasher, K. (2012, Jan. 22), "How the U.S. lost out on iPhone work", *New York Times*, p. A1, retrieved from http://www.nytimes.com/2012/01/22/business/apple-america-and-a-squeezed-middle-class.html?pagewanted=all.

Eccles, R. G., Ioannou, I. and Serafeim, G. (2011), "The impact of corporate sustainability on organizational processes and performance", (HBS Working Paper No. 12-035), retrieved from Social Science Research Network: http://papers.ssrn.com/sol3/papers.cfm?abstract_id=1964011.

Eccles, R. G., Ioannou, I., and Serafeim, G. (2012, Jan. 6), "Is sustainability now the key to corporate success?" *The Guardian*, retrieved from http://www.theguardian.com/sustainable-business/sustainability-key-corporate-success.

Emerson, R. (2012), "John Stewart argues with Siri over Foxconn", *Huffington Post*, retrieved from http://www.huffingtonpost.com/2012/01/17/jon-stewart-foxconn-siri-the-daily-show-video_n_1210556.html.

European Commission (2011, Oct. 25), "Communication from the Commission to the European Parliament, the Council, the European Economic and Social Committee and the Committee of the Regions", COM (2011) 681 final, available at http://eur-lex.europa.eu/LexUriServ/LexUriServ.do?uri=COM:2011:0681:FIN:EN:PDF.

Friedman, M. (1970, Sept. 13), "The social responsibility of business is to increase its profits", *New York Times Magazine*, pp. SM17, 122.

Greenhouse, S. (2013, July 17), "Under pressure, Bangladesh adopts new labor law", *New York Times*, p. A6, retrieved from http://www.nytimes.com/2013/07/17/world/asia/under-pressure-bangladesh-adopts-new-labor-law.html?emc=eta1&_r=0.

Hafner-Burton, E. M. (2009). *Forced to be Good: Why Trade Agreements Boost Human Rights*. Ithaca, NY: Cornell University Press.

Fazle Hasan Abed (2013, Apr. 29), "Bangladesh needs strong unions, not outside pressure", *New York Times*, http://www.nytimes.com/2013/04/30/opinion/bangladesh-needs-strong-unions-not-outside-pressure.html?pagewanted=all.

Human Rights Watch (2013), "Bangladesh: Amended labor law falls short", retrieved from http://www.hrw.org/news/2013/07/15/bangladesh-amended-labor-law-falls-short.

International Labour Organization (ILO) (2008, Aug. 13), "ILO declaration on social justice for a fair globalization", retrieved from http://www.ilo.org/global/resources/WCMS_099766/lang–en/index.htm.

ILO (1998, June 18), "ILO declaration of fundamental principles and rights at work", retrieved from http://www.ilo.org/declaration/thedeclaration/text declaration/lang–en/index.htm.

ILO (2000, Nov.), "Tripartite Declaration of Principles Concerning Multinational Enterprises and Social Policy", *ILO Office Bulletin*, *83*(3), retrieved from http://www.ilo.org/dyn/normlex/en/f?p=1000:62:3061440463449594::NO:62:P62_LIST_ENTRIE_ID:2453910:NO.

Institute for Human Rights (2013), "Investing the rights way; A guide for investors on business and human rights", retrieved from http://www.ihrb.org/pdf/Investing-the-Rights-Way/Investing-the-Rights-Way.pdf.

Ioannou, I. and Serefeim, G. (2011), "The consequences of mandatory corporate sustainability reporting" (HBS Working Paper Series, No. 11-100), retrieved from Social Science Research Network: http://papers.ssrn.com/sol3/papers.cfm?abstract_id=1799589.

Kirk, R. and Solis, H.L. (2010, July 30), "Letter to E.C.H. Echeverria & E.A. Rodriguez", retrieved from http://www.ustr.gov/webfm_send/2114.

Krosinsky, C. (2012, June 13), "Is Apple the model of a sustainable company?" *Bloomberg Sustainability: The Grid*, retrieved from http://www.bloom berg.com/news/2012-06-13/is-apple-the-model-of-a-sustainable-company-.html.

Leary, V. (2010), "Labor standards and extraterritoriality: Cambodian textile exports and the International Labour Organization", in S. Skogly and M. Gibney (eds.), *Universal Human Rights and Extraterritorial Obligations* (pp. 157–65), Philadelphia, P.A.: University of Pennsylvania Press.

Levinson, M. (2001), "Wishful thinking", in A. Fung, D. O'Rourke, and C. Sabel (eds.) *Can We Put an End to Sweatshops?* (pp. 54–8), Boston, MA: Beacon Press.

Locke, R. (2013), *The Promise and Limits of Private Power: Promoting Labor Standards in a Global economy*, Cambridge: Cambridge University Press.

Locke, R., Amengual, M., and Mangla, A. (2009), "Virtue out of necessity? Compliance, commitment and the improvement of labor conditions in global supply chains", *Politics & Society*, *37*(3), 319–51.

Locke, R., Qin, F., and Brause, A. (2007), "Does monitoring improve labor standards?: Lessons from Nike", *Industrial and Labor Relations Review*, *61*(1), 3–31.

Mitchell, G. and Snowe, O. (2013, July 10), "A shared responsibility: North American alliance of retailers and brands reach agreement on a Bangladesh worker safety program", *Huffington Post*, retrieved from http://www.huffingtonpost.com/george-mitchell/bangladesh-worker-safety-program_b_3573861.html.

Office of the U.S. Trade Representative (2013a), "Acting U.S. Trade Representative Marantis and Acting Labor Secretary Harris announce groundbreaking labor rights enforcement agreement with Guat", [Press release], retrieved from http://www.ustr.gov/about-us/press-office/press-releases/2013/april/marantis-harris-labor-enforcement-guatemala.

Office of the U.S. Trade Representative (2013b), "U.S. Trade Representative Michael Froman comments on President's decision to suspend GSP benefits for Bangladesh", [Press release], retrieved from http://www.ustr.gov/about-us/press-office/press-releases/2013/june/michael-froman-gsp-bangladesh.

Organisation for Economic Co-operation and Development (OECD) (2000), "Guidelines for Multinational Enterprises: Text, Commentary and Clarifications", OCED Doc. DAFFE/IME/WPG (2000) 15/FINAL at 18–25, retrieved from http://search.oecd.org/officialdocuments/displaydocumentpdf/?doclanguage=en&cote=daffe/ime/wpg(2000)15/final.

Ostrom, E. (2000), "Collective action and the evolution of social norms", *Journal of Economic Perspectives*, *14*(3), 137–58.

Porter, M. E. and Kramer, M. R. (2006), "Strategy and society: The link between competitive advantage and corporate social responsibility", *Harvard Business Review*, *84*(12), 78–92.

Porter, M. E. and Kramer, M. R. (2011), "Creating shared value: How to reinvent capitalism – and unleash a wave of innovation and growth", *Harvard Business Review*, *89*(1/2), 62–77.

PwC (2012a, March), "*Do investors care about sustainability? Seven trends provide clues*", retrieved from http://www.pwc.com/en_US/us/corporate-sustainability-climate-change/assets/investors-and-sustainability.pdf.

PwC (2012b, March), "*Responsible investment: Creating value from environmental, social and governance issues*", retrieved from http://www.pwc.com/en_GX/gx/sustainability/research-insights/assets/private-equity-survey-sustainability.pdf.

Ruggie, J. G. (2006), "Interim Report of the Special Representative of the Secretary-General on the Issue of Human Rights and Transnational Corporations and Other Business Enterprises", U.N. Doc. E/CN.4/2006/97, retrieved from http://daccess-dds-ny.un.org/doc/UNDOC/GEN/G06/110/27/PDF/G0611027.pdf

Ruggie, J. G. (2013a). *Just Business: Multinational Corporations and Human Rights*, New York, NY: W.W. Norton & Co.

Ruggie, J. G. (2013b, Jan. 23), "Summary of discussions of the forum on business and human rights, prepared by the chairperson, John Ruggie", U.N. Document A/HRC/FBHR/2012/4.

Slaper, T. F. and Hall, T. J. (2011), "The triple bottom line: What is it and how does it work*?" Indiana Business Review 86*(1), 4–8, retrieved from http://www.ibrc.indiana.edu/ibr/2011/spring/pdfs/article2.pdf.

Spiegel, P. and Wilson, J. (2013), "EU considers trade limits on Bangladesh", *Financial Times*, retrieved from http://www.ft.com/intl/cms/s/0/7f6d9cb0-b24d-11e2-8540-00144feabdc0.html#slide0.

Sustainable Apparel Coalition. (n.d.), *Higg Index*, retrieved from http://www.apparelcoalition.org/higgindex.

Taylor, M. (2012, June 18), "A glass filling up – Reflections on the first year anniversary of the UN Guiding Principles on Business and Human Rights", *Institute for Human Rights and Business*, retrieved from http://www.ihrb.org/commentary/guest/a-glass-filling-up.html.

Torelli, C. J., Monga, A., and Kaikati, A. M. (2012), "Doing poorly by doing good: Corporate social responsibility and brand concepts", *Journal of Consumer Research*. *38*(5), 948–63.

Trade Act of 1974, 19 U.S.C. § 2411 (2006).

U.N. Charter, preamble.

U.N. Commission on Human Rights, Sub-Commission on the Promotion and Protection of Human Rights (2003, Aug. 23), "Norms on responsibilities of transnational corporations and other business enterprises with regard to human rights", U.N. Document E/CN.4/Sub.2/2003.

U.N. General Assembly (2000, Sept. 18), "United Nations millennium declaration", G.A. Res. 55/2, U.N. Document A/Res/55/2.

U.N. General Assembly (1966, Dec. 16), *"International covenant on economic, social and cultural rights"*, G.A. Res. 2200A(XXI), U.N. Document A/6316 (entered into force Jan. 3, 1976).

U.N. General Assembly (1948), "Universal Declaration of Human Rights", G.A. Res. 217 (III), U.N. Document A/810, retrieved from http://www.un.org/en/documents/udhr/index.shtml.

U.N. Global Compact (n.d.), "The Ten Principles", retrieved from http://www.unglobalcompact.org/AboutTheGC/TheTenPrinciples/index.html.

U.N. Human Rights Council (2011, March 21), "Guiding principles on business and human rights: Implementing the United Nations "'Protect, Respect and Remedy' framework"*:* Report of the Special Representative of the Secretary-General on the issue of human rights and transnational corporations and other business enterprises, John Ruggie, U.N. Document A/HRC/17/31, retrieved from http://www.ohchr.org/documents/issues/business/A.HRC.17.31.pdf.

U.N. Human Rights Council (2012, July 2), "Contribution of the United Nations system as a whole to the advancement of the business and human rights agenda and the dissemination and implementation of the Guiding Principles on Business and Human Rights: Report of the Secretary-General", U.N. Document A/HRC/21/21, retrieved from http://www.ohchr.org/Documents/Issues/Business/A.HRC.21.21_AEV.pdf.

U.N. Human Rights Council (2011, July 6), *Human rights and transnational corporations and other business enterprises*. HRC Res. 17/4, U.N. Document A/HRC/RES/17/4, retrieved from http://daccess-dds-ny.un.org/doc/RESOLUTION/GEN/G11/144/71/PDF/G1114471.pdf?OpenElement

U.S. Department of Labor (2013a), "Improving fire and general building safety in Bangladesh" [Funding announcement], retrieved from http://www.dol.gov/dol/grants/SGA-13-08.pdf.

U.S. Department of Labor (2013b), "Statement on labor rights and factory safety in Bangladesh" [Press release], retrieved from http://www.dol.gov/opa/media/press/ilab/ILAB20131494.htm.

U.S. Department of State and U.S. Agency for International Development [USAID]. (2010), "Leading through civilian power: The first quadrennial diplomacy and development review", retrieved from http://www.state.gov/documents/organization/153108.pdf.

U.S. Labor in the Americas Project (2010, Summer), "Four years after CAFTA-DR: A coup and incessant violence against workers", *U.S. Leap*, *2010*(2), pp. 4–5.

United States-Dominican Republic-Central American Free Trade Agreement (2004, Aug. 5), retrieved from http://www.ustr.gov/trade-agreements/free-trade-agreements/cafta-dr-dominican-republic-central-america-fta/final-text.

United States-Jordan Free Trade Agreement (2001), retrieved from http://www.ustr.gov/sites/default/files/Jordan%20FTA.pdf.

Vogel, D. (2005), *The Market for Virtue: The Potential and Limits of Corporate Social Responsibility*, Washington, DC: Brookings Institution Press.

Wells, D. (2006), "'Best practice' in the regulation of international labor standards: Lessons of the U.S.-Cambodia textile agreement", *Comparative Labor Law & Policy Journal*, *27*(2), 357–6.

White House, Office of the Press Secretary (2013), "Technical trade proclamation to Congress regarding Bangladesh" [Press Release], retrieved from http://www.whitehouse.gov/the-press-office/2013/06/27/technical-trade-proclamation-congress-regarding-bangladesh.

Yardley, J. (2012), "Recalling fire's horror and exposing global brands' safety gap", *N.Y. Times*, retrieved from http://www.nytimes.com/2012/12/07/world/asia/bangladesh-fire-exposes-safety-gap-in-supply-chain.html?pagewanted=all.

7. The human rights-related aspects of indigenous knowledge in the context of common law equitable doctrines and the Kiobel decision

David Orozco, Kevin McGarry and Lydie Pierre-Louis

The San people are indigenous hunter-gatherer groups from South Africa. They have used the Hoodia cactus plant along with traditional knowledge about the plant to suppress their appetite during long hunting expeditions. A South African research organization patented the molecule and then sold the commercialization rights to Pfizer for $21 million. The San people had no knowledge of the transaction and did not receive any benefit until international social action led to a modest benefit-sharing program many years later (Bratspies, 2007).

A significant portion of the world's biodiversity and genetic material exists within indigenous lands and a race is currently underway to exploit indigenous peoples' traditional knowledge, land and resources (Bratspies, 2007). Access to these resources has been propertized under western intellectual property (IP) regimes to generate significant wealth. Under the current international IP law framework, however, indigenous knowledge is typically relegated to the commons and at its worst the system legitimizes the transfer of exclusive ownership of biological resources and traditional knowledge from indigenous peoples to western individuals and corporations without offering any recognition, reward or protection to indigenous communities (Bratspies, 2007). These practices have engendered a heated debate that draws parallels to past instances of neocolonialism and exploitation.

As illustrated in the above example, corporations sometimes commercially exploit indigenous knowledge and in the process ignore the interests and rights of indigenous communities. Indigenous communities are among the world's most vulnerable groups, and the disregard for indigenous rights, which formerly concerned mainly land, now extends into the realm of knowledge (Bratspies, 2007). Under established human rights law, however, the appropriation of indigenous knowledge without consent or benefit-sharing violates the right to self-determination, culture, religious practice, and the right to participate in cultural life, the benefits of scientific progress, and protection of authorial interests (Ruggie, 2013).

To date, however, businesses have faced few legal consequences when they engage in bio-piracy[1] or the unsanctioned appropriation of indigenous knowledge. Any remedial measures taken to uphold and vindicate indigenous knowledge rights are largely initiated by stakeholders in a non-market context. For example, various non-governmental organizations (NGOs) actively pursue cases of indigenous knowledge misappropriation and work with indigenous communities to prevent bio-piracy and cultural appropriation (Shiva, 2000). In general, these groups achieve the greatest results through the use of public discourse techniques that can severely impact a business's reputation and, therefore, require managerial attention at the highest levels of the firm (Orozco and Poonamallee, 2013).

The recently developed U.N. Guiding Principles on Business and Human Rights provide a potentially useful framework for making corporations legally responsible for indigenous knowledge appropriations that violate their human rights. The case has been made for businesses to respect indigenous knowledge from an ethical and practical standpoint (Orozco and Poonamallee, 2013). However, this chapter goes one step further and proposes the integration of indigenous knowledge within the Guiding Principles to clarify: (1) businesses' responsibility to protect indigenous knowledge[2] and (2) the United States' duty to protect indigenous knowledge more specifically. The approach taken here is unique since it applies equitable U.S. contract and tort law principles to protect the human rights of indigenous communities, which are arguably based on deontological Lockean and Hegelian theories of property.

The use of equitable contract and tort law doctrines may serve as a grievance mechanism within the Guiding Principles (Ruggie, 2013). The framework established under the Guiding Principles affirms that states "must ensure access to effective judicial remedy for human rights abuses committed within their territory and/or jurisdiction … " (p. 102) Alternatively, U.S. equitable doctrines of contract and tort law may be used to achieve human rights goals independent of whether courts wish to uphold the state's duty to protect human rights under international law. From this perspective, U.S. equitable doctrines of contract and tort law principles may indirectly serve as an instrument to achieve greater "normative compatibility" with international human rights law (Ruggie, 2013).

The need to utilize these legal doctrines to provide a human-rights compatible remedy for violations of indigenous knowledge misappropriation has never been more necessary given the recent trend in American jurisprudence to reject human rights doctrines outright. Until recently, international human rights cases have been successfully addressed by U.S. federal courts under the Alien Tort Statute (ATS) also known as the Alien Tort Claims Act, which permits federal courts to have original "jurisdiction of any civil action by an alien for a tort committed in violation of the law of nations or a treaty of the United States" (Judiciary Act of 1789, 2006). However, in 2013, the U.S. Supreme Court substantially closed that door. It found in *Kiobel v. Royal Dutch Petroleum* that the ATS did not confer subject-matter jurisdiction when a defendant has engaged in tortious conduct (including human rights violations) in a foreign country unless some aspect of "the relevant conduct" of the foreign defendant's misconduct would "touch and concern" the territory of the U.S. (2013).

I. INDIGENOUS KNOWLEDGE, INTELLECTUAL PROPERTY AND HUMAN RIGHTS

Indigenous knowledge is defined as knowledge that is held and used by a people who identify themselves as indigenous of a place based on a combination of cultural distinctiveness and priori territorial occupancy relative to a more recently arrived population with its own distinct and subsequently dominant culture (Orozco and Poonamallee, 2013). As stated by Orozco and Ponamallee (2013, p. 3):

> In its present usage, [indigenous knowledge] conveys misguided and incomplete notions of property and ethical norms shared among societies with vastly diverse cultural and socio-political realities. [Indigenous knowledge] has strong ecological ties, and assumes symbolic and cultural significance and, therefore, in that important cultural sense, [indigenous knowledge] extends beyond the established Western notions of intellectual capital.

As a type of knowledge that is distinct from Western notions of property and intellectual capital, indigenous knowledge has been largely unrecognized by Western knowledge systems and international legal frameworks. Instead, the Western, developed world places a priority on knowledge that is economically productive, explicit, and subject to legal ownership by an individual or juridical person such as a corporation (Orozco and

Poonamallee, 2013). In contrast, indigenous groups regard ownership of their traditional knowledge as being inextricably linked to their ecology, sovereignty, cultural identity and survival (Bratspies, 2007). Consequently, Western legal regimes try to compartmentalize indigenous resources into property definitions that are external to the indigenous culture, and exclude important items such as traditional knowledge, folklore and traditions.

The emphasis on the property aspects of IP and its productive economic uses has caused a great deal of concern in the developing world since a significant amount of knowledge in these areas is produced, maintained, and governed by indigenous peoples who regard their stocks of indigenous knowledge in a much different light (Whiteman and Cooper, 2000). These concerns and tensions between Western and indigenous systems have been recognized in discussions of U.S. domestic patent reform legislation impacting pharmaceutical R&D and international public health (McGarry, 2008).

The underlying epistemological difference has real world implications. For example, the issue of biopiracy has drawn considerable attention and scrutiny among activists. According to one estimate, at least $50 million dollars of sales are obtained every year in the U.S. through the sale of crops developed by indigenous knowledge and techniques (Roht-Arriaza, 1996). As a result, activists are increasingly using legal and nonmarket strategies to deter the unethical appropriation of this knowledge and its commercial exploitation (Orozco and Poonamallee, 2013).

To examine the relationship between indigenous knowledge and human rights, it is helpful to take a step back and examine the relationship between IP rights and human rights. Intellectual property rights are a relatively new topic within human rights discourse, and they have been largely discussed in light of some of the contentious aspects of the most relevant international treaty, the Trade-Related Aspects of Intellectual Property Treaty (TRIPS) (Yu, 2007). In the debate concerning the relationship between IP and human rights, there are two general approaches that are adopted by intergovernmental organizations, policymakers, and scholars: the coexistence approach and the conflict approach (Yu, 2007). Helfer (2003, p. 48) summarizes these two approaches as follows:

> The first approach views human rights and intellectual property as being in fundamental conflict. This framing sees strong intellectual property protection as undermining – and therefore as incompatible with – a broad spectrum of human rights obligations, especially in the area of economic, social, and

> cultural rights. The prescription that proponents of this approach advocate for resolving this conflict is to recognize the normative primacy of human rights law over intellectual property law in areas where specific treaty obligations conflict.
>
> The second approach to the intersection of human rights and intellectual property sees both areas of law as concerned with the same fundamental question: defining the appropriate scope of private monopoly power that gives authors and inventors a sufficient incentive to create and innovate, while ensuring that the consuming public has adequate access to the fruits of their efforts. This school views human rights law and intellectual property law as essentially compatible, although often disagreeing over where to strike the balance between incentives on the one hand and access on the other.

The approach advocated in this chapter with respect to indigenous knowledge fits largely within the coexistence approach since it provides an avenue for protecting the rights of the indigenous community while recognizing that a company may obtain access to the rights under certain circumstances that yield fair results. Demarcating that line is a difficult but necessary policy objective.

Intellectual property rights are not specifically protected by existing human rights instruments. Both the Universal Declaration of Human rights (UDHR, 1948) and the International Covenant on Economic, Social and Cultural rights (ICESCR, 1966), however, do recognize "the right to the protection of the moral and material interests resulting from any scientific, literary or artistic production of which he [or she] is the author." As mentioned in the UDHR and the ICESR, and discussed in greater detail in the next section, the right to the protection of interests in intellectual creations extends to both moral and material interests. According to the drafters of the ICESR, the moral interest "safeguards the personal link between authors and their creations and between peoples, communities, or other groups and their collective cultural heritage" (ICESCR). The material interest enables authors to "enjoy an adequate standard of living" (ICESCR).

A human rights and deontological approach towards knowledge-based rights differs from the utilitarian theory that serves as the foundation for many existing domestic and international IP rights systems. For example, many Western societies do not recognize a moral interest in IP and fail to legally enforce what are known as moral rights. The U.S.has one statute that recognizes moral rights in a very limited fashion, which was arguably enacted to comply with the Berne Convention's moral rights provisions (Visual Artists Rights Act, 2012). Also, utilitarian motives justify many IP rights, in contrast to the deontological nature of human rights. For example, the limited lifetime of some IP rights is viewed as a compromise that strikes the appropriate balance between incentives for creation and social welfare, in contrast to a "just desserts" theory of IP which might grant unlimited lifetime rights.

According to the drafters of the ICESR, the right to the protection of the interests in intellectual creations "derives from the inherent dignity and worth of all persons" and this right should be contrasted with "most legal entitlements recognized in intellectual property systems" (ICESCR; Yu, 2007; Helfer, 2007). As human rights, these interests are "fundamental inalienable and universal entitlements belonging to individuals and, under certain circumstances, groups of individuals and communities" (ECOSOC, 2006). From a human rights perspective, any national positive law or international treaty related to IP rights should, therefore, take into account these fundamental and universal interests.

Another important and contentious aspect of indigenous knowledge within the context of human rights is the issue of community rights. It is recognized that community rights exist from a moral perspective (Kymlicka, 1995), not necessarily because of their intrinsic cultural value but because of the harm or benefit that membership in the community bestows upon its individual members (Killmister, 2012). Indigenous knowledge is often a participatory good (Reaume, 1988; Killmister, 2012) since the community participates in its meaning and implementation. Any loss of control outside this deeply symbolic and sacred cultural and communal practice would constitute a harm against a community member. The act of propertizing indigenous knowledge removes the communal knowledge from the shared participatory space and offends other important interests such as self-determination, respect and sacredness.

II. INDIGENOUS KNOWLEDGE AND HUMAN RIGHTS WITHIN INTERNATIONAL ECONOMIC LAW AND THE WTO

Public international law has historically regulated international economic law and states were granted wide discretion with respect to policy and enforcement. Public international law has remained the main source of international economic law, but has been supplemented by other normative standards. For example, major international institutions have obliged states to open their markets and promote liberal economic policies to generate trade efficiency through the World Trade Organization/General Agreement on Tariffs and Trade (WTO/GATT) system. As a consequence of this institutional proliferation, separate normative rules emerged from existing and newly formed institutional frameworks. In the process, the WTO, World Bank, International Monetary Fund (IMF) and the U.N.'s approaches to IP-related issues generated controversy for both failing and succeeding to functionally incorporate and recognize human rights. The recognition and protection of indigenous knowledge remains a significant challenge in human rights and international IP coordination.

Interfaces have slowly developed between the WTO global trade regime, international human rights treaties, and other international treaties associated with the protection of indigenous knowledge. Currently, there are several primary international legal regimes for the protection of traditional knowledge.

A. The UNESCO Conventions on Cultural Intangibles and Expressions

The two binding UNESCO conventions that address IP associated with cultural or traditional knowledge are: the Convention for the Safeguarding of the Intangible Cultural Heritage of 2003 (CSIH) and the Convention on the Protection and Promotion of the Diversity of Cultural Expressions of 2005 (Protection Convention). These Conventions build upon human rights principles in internationally recognized agreements, such as the UDHR and the ICESCR. The CSIH became the first binding international legal instrument to cover intangible cultural heritage and more specifically traditional knowledge associated with indigenous ecological wisdom and uses of local flora and fauna for healing under its Article 2 (UNESCO, 2003). Later, the Protection Convention, which entered into force in 2007, filled in some gaps with a more expansive protection mechanism that covered additional cultural items under its Article 4 (UNESCO, 2005).

In its preambulatory clause, the CSIH refers to three primary international human rights instruments (the UDHR, ICESCR and the International Covenant on Civil and Political Rights (ICCPR) and ties-in the principles expressed in these instruments with the primary purpose of "safeguarding" intangible cultural heritage property identified subsequently in Articles 1 and 2 (UNESCO, 2003). In Articles 11 and 12 the CSIH provides for protection of cultural IP at the national level using an inventory system whereby parties to the CSIH are obligated to compose a list of intangible cultural heritage in their territory and submit this list to the Intergovernmental Committee for the Safeguarding of the Intangible Cultural Heritage (ibid.). At the international level, Articles 16 and 17 respectively provide for a "Representative List" and an "Urgent Safeguarding" list of intangible cultural heritage. In order to have an intangible cultural heritage item included in an Article 16 or 17 list for international safeguarding purposes, the knowledge-based rights must be included in a national inventory list under Articles 11 and 12 (UNESCO, 2009).[3]

The Protection Convention demonstrates movement in a different direction to the CSIH in terms of scope, containing a broader scope of protection inclusive of goods and services derived from cultural expressions. The specific inclusion of terms referring to the production and commercial value of cultural goods and services indicates an intention to relate the Protection Convention's cultural concerns to international trade (UNESCO, 2005). Additionally, the Protection Convention's provisions exhibit greater international legal force than the CSIH due to the non-subordination of its terms to other binding international instruments.

In the final version of the Protection Convention, Article 8 allows parties to take measures to protect threatened cultural expressions within their own territory; however, the article does not obligate them to do so (UNESCO, 2005). On the other hand, Article 17 at least obligates parties to "cooperate" with other parties seeking to utilize Article 8's measures to protect threatened cultural expressions. Article 17 places particular emphasis on an obligation to assist developing country members with Article 8 actions (ibid.). In 2009, four years after the adoption of the Protection Convention, the Conference of Parties approved several "Operational Guidelines" explaining the protection requirements of the parties to the Protection Convention (UNESCO, 2009).

The Operational Guidelines clarify parties' obligations and provide interpretative guidance for the parties to the Protection Convention. The Operational Guidelines explain that threats to cultural expressions giving rise to the "special situations" mentioned in Article 8 can be cultural, physical or economic in nature (UNESCO, 2009, pp. 3–4). Further, the "measures" which a party may enact under Article 8(2) includes both short-term emergency action and long-term protection policies coupled with international cooperation should the requesting party feel such cooperation is necessary for protection efforts to be effective. Lastly, Article 8(3) requires any actions taken by a party under Article 8(2) to be reported to the Intergovernmental Committee.

The legal relationship of the Protection Convention to other binding international treaties is addressed in Articles 20 and 21. Article 20(1)(b) specifically states a mandatory obligation on parties to "foster mutual supportiveness between this Convention and the other treaties to which they are parties" (UNESCO, 2005). It is also made clear that the

Protection Convention signatories may not subordinate their obligations under the treaty to other treaties. To this end, Article 21 addresses the interaction between parties' obligations under the Protection Convention and parties' participation in other international forums, such as the WTO. Currently, there are no operational guidelines for Articles 20 and 21. The lack of operational guidelines for these articles led to conflicting interpretations of Article 21's "international forum" and the working legal relationships between the Protection Convention and other international legal instruments.[4] Wouters and De Meester (2008) discussed the inevitable conflicts that ambiguities in Article 20 would generate, particularly in relation to matters before the WTO. They concluded that such conflicts between the WTO and the rights and obligations of the Protection Convention are unavoidable despite conflict clauses, such as Article 20.

B. ILO Convention 169 and the U.N. Declaration on the Rights of Indigenous Peoples

Aside from the UNESCO Conventions, there are other U.N. treaties that assert the human rights of indigenous people, particularly their self-determination rights with respect to economic, social and cultural rights. The ILO was one of the earlier U.N.-affiliated entities to incorporate binding human rights protection measures for indigenous populations. This provided the groundwork for the eventual adoption of the U.N. Declaration on the Rights of Indigenous Peoples.

In 1957 the ILO adopted Convention 107, also known as the "Indigenous and Tribal Populations Convention", which established a general obligation on behalf of governments to protect the rights of indigenous populations in its Article 2 (ILO). A significant problem with Convention 107 when evaluated today exists in its "integration approach," which provides a backdoor for governments to undermine protection obligations mentioned in the treaty. As a response to these challenges, the ILO adopted the Indigenous and Tribal Peoples Convention 169. The biggest change in Convention 169 is the removal of all integration language, continuous reference to harmonization between governments' obligations to protect indigenous human rights and a dual coordination obligation with national laws and internationally recognized human rights (ILO, 1989). Other modifications specifically recognize governmental obligations to protect the economic, social and cultural rights of indigenous populations within their territories. For example, Article 15 obligates governments to safeguard against exploitation of indigenous peoples' biological and natural resources. Although Convention 169 represents a marked improvement over the earlier Convention 107, only 22 countries have ratified it since it entered into force in 1991.

The Declaration on the Rights of Indigenous Peoples (the "DRIP") is a more recent U.N. foray into comprehensively addressing the rights of indigenous people, particularly traditional knowledge. The U.N. General Assembly adopted the DRIP in September of 2007 with only Australia, Canada, New Zealand, and the U.S. opposing it (UN A/RES/61/295, 2007). Article 31(1) of the DRIP states that indigenous peoples have "the right to maintain, control, protect and develop their intellectual property over such cultural heritage, traditional knowledge" and is followed by the obligation of governments to work with indigenous peoples on these issues (ibid.). Article 32 mentions governments' obligations to protect against unfair or inappropriate commercial exploitation of natural resources on the lands of indigenous peoples (ibid.).

In contrast to ILO Convention 169, the DRIP itself is non-binding standing alone; yet, some of the rights addressed in the DRIP reflect customary international law. The legal nature of the DRIP remains a major area of contention for the U.S., one of the four opposing parties to the adoption of the declaration (U.S. State Dept., 2010).[5] To this end, on the fifth anniversary of the DRIP, the UN General Assembly adopted a resolution encouraging member states to ratify ILO Convention 169 (United Nations, 2012).

C. The WTO, ESCR and the Ruggie Framework

Although the WTO primarily adheres to the comparative advantage economic model and a core principle of non-discrimination, these aspects should not lead one to discount the potential for using the world trade regime to promote and protect human rights. The potential for conflicts in terms of negative and positive rights, however, presents some tension in reconciling the world trade regime with human rights. Negative rights tend to focus on the deregulation aspect generally tied to world trade rules, while positive rights tend to focus on regulation and intervention aspects (Charnovitz, 1999). Charnovitz posited, "International trade law needs to become more like international human rights law in establishing norms for what a State owes its own citizens. International human rights law needs to become more like international trade law in enforcing norms through mandatory dispute settlement and potential penalties for non-compliance."

Economic, social, and cultural rights (ESCR), primarily falling within the category of positive rights, encompass a malleable grouping of human rights that are defined by various international bodies. There is a perception of ESCR as development goals or social policy aspirations rather than as justiciable human rights. Early attempts at modern international recognition of ESCR can be found in agreements such as the Universal Declaration of Human Rights (the UDHR), which was adopted by a majority vote within the U.N.'s General Assembly in 1948. However, although the UDHR included provisions for ESCR, the exact legal status of these rights was and continues to be tenuous. In particular, some believe that only a few of the rights outlined in the UDHR have become customary international law while others feel the document in its entirety, including the ESCR provisions, reflect customary international law (Hannum, 1996). However, as some international human rights scholars point out, increased recognition of the human rights enshrined within the UDHR over time in international case law, international treaties, and by the governments of U.N. member states provides great evidence to support arguments in favor of recognizing human rights as a part of customary international law.

From a practical standpoint, it is perhaps impossible to conceptualize human rights and the world trade regime as falling neatly into one particular grouping. Yet, there is significant room for exploring convergence between both systems. Earlier critics who held steadfast to the belief of the incongruence of the economic or the "Efficiency Model" and the "natural rights … non-utilitarian liberalism of Locke and Kant" failed to perceive the potential for convergence (Garcia, 1999). Garcia initially considered ideas of convergence, but then regressed back to a belief that world trade rules and human rights are indeed at a "fundamental and insolvable tension." Contrary to this belief, the international trade system and protection of human rights can be and are slowly, if painstakingly, becoming intertwined. As Charnovitz (1999) simply stated: "[W]hen they are viewed more abstractly, international trade law and international human rights law grow in resemblance" (p. 113).

The Ruggie Principles, developed from six years of work defining the relationship between business and human rights, added to the growing body of scholarly and multilateral institutional literature addressing human rights concerns of businesses involved in international trade (U.N. Special Representative of the Secretary-General, 2011). Principle 10 of the Ruggie Principles addresses multilateral policy coherence with respect to human rights among multilateral institutions that deal with business-related issues, such as the WTO. The commentary to Principle 10 emphasizes the obligation of states to uphold their human rights commitments in conjunction with their participation in the WTO and other multilateral institutions.

Prior to the Ruggie Principles, interfacing ESCR with development efforts within the world trade system had been accomplished by implementation of measures such as the Doha Development Agenda (WTO, 2001b) and waiver for preferential tariff treatment for least-developed countries (WTO, 1999). Zagel (2005) specifically mentions several suggestions for convergence of international economic law, world trade rules and human rights (p. 10). One tested approach for ESCR application within the WTO involves the use of GATT, Article XX – general exception clause paragraphs for implementing trade-related human rights measures (p. 13). For example, GATT, Article XX may have some application in future cases involving medicinal products derived from stolen traditional knowledge,

Article XX contains four sub-clauses with potential application to enforcing ESC human rights within the WTO system. The four sub-paragraphs are "the public morals exception (para. (a)), the protection of human, animal or plant life or health exception (para. (b)), the prison labor exception (para. (e)) or measures relating to the conservation of exhaustible natural resources (para. (g))" (Zagel, 2005, p. 12). Of greatest relevance to the issue of protection of traditional knowledge and/or biological resources associated with that knowledge may be paragraphs (b) and (g). The GATT Article XX(g) exception is of particular interest for addressing human rights concerns involving protection of indigenous traditional knowledge (ITK) through trade measure protections of the biological materials involved in ITK exploitation or misappropriation. Despite such relevance, until the dominant issue of the relationship between TRIPS Article 27 and the Convention on Biological Diversity is resolved by the WTO membership, attempts at utilizing other WTO provisions en masse for protection of indigenous knowledge will likely prove to be difficult.

D. TRIPS Article 27 and the Biodiversity Debate on Traditional Knowledge Disclosure

Article 27 of the TRIPS Agreement contains rules on what governments must allow and exclude from patentability. Article 27 is, therefore, one of the most contentious articles in the entire TRIPS Agreement. The text of Article 27 clause 2 permits members to:

> [E]xclude from patentability inventions, the prevention within their territory of the commercial exploitation of which is necessary to protect *ordre public* or morality, including protect human, animal or plant life or health or to avoid

serious prejudice to the environment provided that such exclusion is not made merely because the exploitation is prohibited by their law. (TRIPS, 1994)

Disputes involving Article 27 and its clauses are limited. However, the information gleaned from the Panel and Appellate Body reports involving some of the disputes containing Article 27 concerns may be useful in the evolving debate over use of traditional knowledge. One case in particular, *Canada – Pharmaceutical Patents*, discussed overall policy implications of Article 27 on matters of discrimination (WTO, 2000). In its decision, the Panel stated that Article 27 "does not prohibit bona fide exceptions to deal with problems that may exist only in certain product areas" (para. 7.91). The Panel also made note of the European Communities' argument that the TRIPS Agreement envisions non-discriminatory application of exceptions to avoid "limit[ing] exceptions to areas where right holders tend to be foreign producers" (para. 7.92.).

Another significant debate involves the implementation of Article 27 clause 3(b) disclosure requirements for the country of origin where traditional knowledge and genetic resources are used in inventions. Article 27 clause 3(b) is most relevant to the issue of biopiracy and other forms of misappropriation of traditional medicinal knowledge. Much of the efforts undertaken in regard to Article 27 were launched by the Doha Declaration in 2001, paragraph 19 of which instructs the TRIPS Council to examine the relationship between patent exclusions covered in TRIPS Article 27 clause 3(b) and other international instruments, specifically the Convention on Biological Diversity (CBD) and the protection of traditional knowledge and folklore (WTO, 2001b).

In 2011, the Director-General released a report summarizing the various issues and positions of WTO members on the relationship between Article 27 clause 3(b) and the CBD. The report discusses the three primary approaches proposed to connect the CBD with TRIPS: (1) a disclosure requirement (the BIC (Brazil, India and China) proposal); (2) Committee of World Intellectual Property Organization (WIPO) amendments with a database system (the Swiss proposal); and (3) a national contract-based approach (the U.S. proposal) (WTO, 2011a). These three primary approaches have dominated the discussions over the relationship between TRIPS and the CBD.

Shortly before the 2011 report, the BIC countries formed a coalition with several other countries to propose revising the TRIPS Agreement and adding an article titled "Disclosure of Origin of Genetic Resources and/or Associated Traditional Knowledge" (WTO, 2011b). The proposed new article (Article 29*bis*) contains five paragraphs, with the first paragraph incorporating the Convention on Biological Diversity and the

Nagoya Protocol. Paragraph 2 outlines the disclosure requirements in two sub-parts: (1) the country of origin of the traditional knowledge and/or genetic resources or a country that has acquired such resources in compliance with the BD; and (2) the source providing the traditional knowledge or genetic resources contained in Part 1 and evidence that the genetic resources were accessed with prior informed consent and access as well as fair and equitable benefit sharing. The remaining requirements set forth in paragraphs 3–5 relate to procedural aspects associated with the granting and filing of patents containing traditional knowledge and/or genetic resources and non-compliance with paragraph 2.

The earliest of the three major proposals on TRIPS-CBD legal interactivity came from Switzerland. The Swiss proposal involves amending the Patent Cooperation Treaty (the PCT) and Patent Law Treaty (the PLT) to require declaration by patent applicants of the source of genetic resources and/or traditional knowledge (WTO, 2003). The Government of Switzerland stressed its belief that the WIPO is the most effective international forum to handle patents and protection of traditional knowledge. Additionally, the Swiss proposal suggests adoption of one of the largest international administrative undertakings for traditional knowledge in the form of harmonized international standards for traditional knowledge databases to assist in documenting and determining prior-art. The basis of the Swiss database harmonization proposal rests in the principle of building upon existing NGO and local governmental databases for traditional knowledge.

The Swiss proposal represents a middle ground between the BIC and the U.S. proposals. For example, the Swiss and U.S. Governments share the position that the TRIPS Agreement does not need to be modified, but differ as to the level of multilateralism that should be involved in the protection of traditional knowledge. The general thrust of the Swiss Government's stance on the legal interactivity between TRIPS and the CBD is that neither takes precedence over the other, but rather the two agreements are "mutually supportive". Overall, the Swiss Government holds the view that enhancing the mutual supportiveness of the CBD and TRIPS Agreement through external modifications (e.g., the PCT and PLT amendments) is the best approach to strengthen the TRIPS-CBD legal relationship.

Similar to the Swiss Government's position on the legal relationship between TRIPS and the CBD, the U.S. Government believes there is no conflict between TRIPS and the CBD, and, in fact, both agreements are and should be implemented in a "mutually supportive manner" (WTO, 2006, p. 3). Additionally, the U.S. Government supports the development of databases for traditional knowledge and the efforts of WIPO in general; however, it does not go as far as the Swiss Government's stance that WIPO is ultimately the most effective international forum for these issues. In contrast to the Swiss and BIC proposals, the U.S. Government asserted disagreement on "whether it [disclosure] can prevent the grant of mistakenly granted patents," answering this supposition by holding that disclosure cannot prevent the grant of mistakenly granted patents (WTO, 2006, pp. 11–12, para. 21). Further, the U.S. Government reaffirmed its support for the utilization of a national, contract-based system that is international in character (similar to those used in international business transactions) to enforce access and benefit-sharing laws (ibid.). The general philosophy underlying the U.S. Government's national contract position is that "many inventions resulting from research and development of biological resources are a result of independent discovery and are not developed based on previous knowledge" (ibid, p. 18, para. 33).

These three proposals continue to be debated by WTO members with varying interests and perspectives on the cultural, environmental and human rights concerns associated with patentability of traditional knowledge and biological resources. These proposals show a strong divide between the U.S. and the developing world on the best way to handle protecting indigenous IP within the international trade system. Given the long-standing divide between countries over the three major proposals relating to the CBD and TRIPS, perhaps WTO members should consider other more flexible solutions. Two out of the three proposals (the Swiss and BIC proposals) coincide well with Principle 10 of the Ruggie Principles by utilizing multilateral institutions for capacity building and sharing of best practices for handling indigenous traditional knowledge. However, the U.S. proposal, with some modification, can also work well within the Ruggie Framework since the U.S. proposal could support the promotion of consistency through a contract-based system that is international in character. The U.S. Government's national contract-based approach reflects a strong belief in the U.S.' own legal system. The next section of the chapter will discuss a modified U.S. contract law-based approach that fits within this perspective.

III. COMMON LAW EQUITABLE DOCTRINES IN THE CONTEXT OF INDIGENOUS KNOWLEDGE AND IMPLICATIONS OF THE *KIOBEL* DECISION

The opening discussion in this chapter of the San tribe's ordeal highlights a challenge to the existing U.S. legal system. That is that it is difficult, although not impossible, for courts to craft a remedy for parties that have been treated unfairly in a commercial context. The difficulty is two-fold. First, is there a legal basis for a remedy? Second, how should a remedy be crafted – that is, what factors should be considered by the court to arrive at a balanced and equitable outcome? It is true that a wrong can exist without a corresponding remedy in law. An equitable remedy may be available when there is no appropriate legal remedy. However, the availability and applicability of the equitable remedy must be based on a recognized legal harm. As such, the remedy must be grounded in an existing common law.

A. The Nexus of Policy, Law, and the Duty to Protect Human Rights under U.S. Law

The Ruggie framework conceptualizes: (1) a multi-stakeholder duty to protect human rights; (2) corporate social responsibility to respect human rights; and (3) implementation of effective access to remedies (Ruggie, 2013). The Ruggie framework is a laudable construct, and may generate positive results under international human rights law or in civil law countries. Currently, however, outside international legal commitments and very specific domestic law, the U.S. has no affirmative duty to protect human rights. Moreover, corporate social responsibility is a voluntary business guideline, and not law in the U.S. As it currently stands, the Ruggie framework does not provide access to a legal remedy under U.S law. The U.S. legal structure only permits a legal remedy when a legal duty exists.

U.S. federal law, in particular the Civil Rights Act of 1964, rendered illegal discrimination against minorities and women based on racial, ethnic, national and religious beliefs in the workplace and places of public accommodation. U.S. courts, however, do not equate individual civil rights to human rights as defined by international law. In the context of a legal basis for a U.S. court to assert jurisdiction for human rights abuses that occur abroad, the non-extraterritorality of U.S. law prohibits a court from hearing such a case due to lack of jurisdiction.

In theory, U.S. courts would not be prevented from providing monetary awards to indigenous communities in cases where indigenous knowledge has been unfairly appropriated, e.g., in cases involving biopiracy. A difficulty arises, however, in the practical application of the remedy to determine how much of a monetary award should be awarded and to whom should it be awarded, e.g., the leaders of a tribe, a trust, or national government (Orozco and Poonamallee, 2013). An equitable payment would likely take the form of a royalty if the indigenous knowledge has been commercialized. Nevertheless, the practical difficulty of calculation should not preclude a remedy to indigenous communities. From an ethical and human rights perspective, the focus should be to recognize and uphold the knowledge-based rights of indigenous communities and ensure that a remedy is granted in cases where inequitable behavior leads to the commercialization of indigenous knowledge without appropriate consent. There is, however, a sound moral and historical basis to argue that the U.S. Government, and by extension the U.S. courts have a duty to protect human rights.

B. Implications of the *Kiobel* Decision and the Alien Tort Statute as Instrumentalities of Equity

Recently, the U.S. Supreme Court in the *Kiobel v. Royal Dutch Petroleum* decision clarified, and limited, U.S. federal courts' subject-matter jurisdiction over corporate civil tort liability under the ATS when a foreign corporation is the defendant. The ATS was adopted as a part of the Judiciary Act of 1789; historians have not, however, been able to provide a definitive answer as to the purpose of the ATS. What is clear is that Congress adopted the ATS, and provided federal courts with universal jurisdiction to prosecute tortious violations, including human rights violations, wherever they may have occurred in the world under international law when the national authorities of countries affected by the violations failed to act. The particular language that created the ATS has been amended several times over the centuries to solidify the federal court's authority to adjudicate the particular types of cases that arise under the ATS (Bradley, 2002). The original text provided that federal district courts "shall also have cognizance, concurrent with the courts, or the circuit courts as the case may be, of all causes where an alien sues for a tort only in violation in the law of nations or a treaty of the United States …" (Judiciary Act, 1789). The federal courts have interpreted this grant to mean that federal courts have "authorized jurisdiction over suits between non-U.S. citizens for violations of customary international law …" (*Filartiga v. Pena-Irala*, 1980). Traditionally, under the ATS, federal courts may assert *in personam* jurisdiction when the parties are present in the U.S. or operate a business in the U.S.

The Second Circuit's decision in *Filartiga* permitted federal courts to apply the ATS to a wide spectrum of human rights cases arising under international law as U.S. federal law (*Kiobel v. Royal Dutch Petroleum*, 2013). The Supreme Court in the *Sosa* decision upheld the constitutionality of the ATS, in a unanimous decision the court held that "ATS did not create a separate ground for suit for violations of the law of nations.

Instead [ATS] was intended only to give courts jurisdiction over traditional law of nations cases" (*Sosa v. Alvarez-Machain*, 2004). Since the ruling in *Sosa* several international human rights cases have been successfully decided by U.S. federal courts. The international community has heralded ATS as a scarce vehicle for foreign nationals to redress human rights violations.

In the ATS cases that have been successfully brought before the U.S. federal courts the corporate wrongdoers have been American corporations or their agents as well as foreign corporations with operations in the U.S. In the *Kiobel* case, the Supreme Court focused on a legal issue that neither the petitioners nor the respondents had raised with the Court, nor on which the Court had granted certiorari for review, in particular the Court inquired "under what circumstances [does] the Alien Tort Statute allow American courts to litigate tort claims that are based on actions that did not occur within the territory of the United States?" Chief Justice Roberts stated, a presumption against extraterritorial application can be overcome "where the claims touch and concern the territory of the United States," provided that "they do so with sufficient force to displace the presumption … mere corporate presence … will not suffice … [for corporations] to remain on notice they can still be held accountable for their abuses outside the U.S." Therefore, U.S. federal courts do not have subject-matter jurisdiction over foreign corporations who engaged in tortious conduct in a foreign country unless some aspect of "the relevant conduct" of the foreign corporation's misconduct "touch and concern" the territory of the U.S. Commentators have argued that corporate domicile in the U.S. would be sufficient to rebut a presumption against the ATS extraterritoriality application. As such, the ATS claims against American corporations would be sufficient and the ATS claims against foreign corporations whose misconduct in some relevant aspect touch and concern the territory of the U.S. would also suffice to rebut a presumption against the ATS extraterritorial application.

In the *Kiobel* case, the defendant corporations Royal Dutch Petroleum Co., Shell Transport and Trading Company plc are foreign corporations incorporated under the laws of The Netherlands and their operations in the U.S. were deemed by the Supreme Court to be "too tenuous." The *Kiobel* case was decided on a procedural, due-process basis, in particular whether it would be appropriate for a U.S. federal court to assert jurisdiction over a foreign corporation with tenuous connections to the U.S. It is on this procedural question as to whether foreign defendant corporations whose businesses do not "touch and concern" the territory of the U.S. that the Supreme Court affirmed the Second Circuit Court's decision. The decision is analogous to the due process safeguards contained in the Bill of Rights, and has a particular resonance reminiscent to the *International Shoe* decision, wherein the Supreme Court noted:

> due process requires only that in order to subject a defendant to a judgment in personam, if he be not present within the territory or forum, he have certain minimum contacts with it such that the maintenance of that suit does not offend traditional notions of fair play ad substantial justice. (*International Shoe Company v. State of Washington*, 1945)

The Supreme Court affirmed the Second Circuit's decision in *Kiobel* to deny extraterritorial application of the ATS over foreign corporations. The Court determined that the underlying tort of corporate liability is not a discernible norm of customary international law (Kupersmith, 2013). As such, the ATS is inapplicable, as grant of subject-matter jurisdiction to U.S. federal courts because the corporate liability claim was not recognized under customary international law, nor did the foreign corporations' conduct "touch and concern the territory of the United States." The *Kiobel* decision in the Second Circuit and the Supreme Court did not reach the substantive issue as to whether the defendant foreign corporations actually engaged in abusive humans rights violations. Both the Second Circuit and Supreme Court's decisions were decided on procedural grounds.

The Supreme Court's decision in *Kiobel* was not meant to address the underlying issue of corporate liability. The decision merely determined that the ATS could not be used to provide federal courts with jurisdiction in matters that "did not touch and concern the territory of the United States" and in matters that did not fall within the scope of international customary law. Perhaps a more appropriate judicial jurisdiction for the *Kiobel* case would be a court that has greater ties to the underlying tortious conduct or the defendant corporations. In the context of the *Kiobel* case, the court with greater ties to the underlying human rights abuses would be Nigeria, and the court with greater ties to the foreign defendant corporations would be The Netherlands.

C. Equitable Contract Doctrines of Good Faith, Fair Dealing and Unconscionability as Instrumentalities of Equity

Regardless of the lack of explicit statutory remedies, all is not as bleak as it might appear after *Kiobel*. Common law jurisdictions will enforce and provide a remedy for common law violations. However, the difficulty with the application of common law equitable principles in the context of indigenous knowledge is that the principles presume that there is a relationship in existence between the parties. It is the nature of the relationship that is examined by the court to determine whether any of the traditional tenets of contract or tort law have been violated for which a remedy in equity may be available.

The difficulty with the application of equitable contract principles in the context of indigenous knowledge is that the common law equitable principles presume that there is a contract already in existence between the parties. Therefore, doctrinal equitable contract principles such as good faith, fair dealing, and unconscionability all presume that there is a verbal or written understanding between the parties. The underlying presumption is that there is a meeting of the minds whereby the indigenous community has agreed to transfer its knowledge to the multinational corporation. These equitable contract principles where not designed to cover areas where in fact there is no contract. Without the existence of a contract, or pre-contract, negotiation stage, equitable remedies such as good faith, fair dealing, and unconscionability cannot be granted under U.S. law.

American jurisprudence has long recognized the common law doctrines of good faith, fair dealing, and unconscionability as settled principles of contract law (*Commerce International Company v. United States*, 1964). The principles of good faith and fair dealing are embedded in the bargained-for-exchange during the parties' exchange of communication, which may or may not be memorialized in writing. The underlying implied duty of fairness extends to the pre-contact negotiation stage as manifested in the doctrine of unconscionability. The implied duty of fairness exists with every contract (written or unwritten) and its ancient origins are derived from principles of honor, fidelity, and justice.

The doctrine of good faith, fair dealing, and unconscionability extends to the negotiations stage, the performance of the contract, and post-contract performance. If a court determines that at any juncture during the contract a party did not act in accordance with the implied duty of good faith and fair dealing, the contract will be deemed to have been breached (Farnsworth, 1963). At its core, the good faith and fair dealing doctrine may be used to protect a weaker party from a stronger party (Patterson, 1964). The traditional breach of good faith usually involves relatively sophisticated parties that are contracting at arm's length during the contracting process. The difficulty arises when one party realizes that their perceived strength is untrue, and that the stronger party has controlled the contracting process. It is at that juncture wherein the weaker party will seek redress from the courts on an appropriate administrative legal regime. The standard of review that courts apply will seek to answer a single dispositive question – whether the parties have treated each other fairly during the scope of the alleged contract.

D. The Doctrine of Unconscionability

The subject of contract formation will be implicated in cases where parties have not acted in good faith (Summers, 1968; Kessler and Fine, 1964). However, the scope of good faith does not include pre-contract formation such as the negotiation stage. The doctrine of unconscionability governs the pre-contract formation (negotiation) phase, and empowers the court to refuse to enforce any part of, or the entirety of a contract that is not based on a meaningful choice by both parties or when a contract unreasonably favors one party over another party (Uniform Commercial Code-Sales, §2-302, 2002). As such, unconscionability allows the courts broad latitude to review the bargaining exchange of the parties, and to undo the stated intent of the parties in the interest of justice (Ellinghaus, 1969; Burton, 1981).

E. The Courts' Standard of Review of Equitable Contract Doctrines

The good faith doctrine established a standard of contract interpretation for the courts, and a covenant that is implied in every contract irrespective the parties' statements to the contrary or silence regarding good faith (Farnsworth, 1968). Courts have long recognized that express terms of a contract are insufficient to determine a party's good faith and whether parties have treated each other fairly during the scope of the contract. The doctrine of an implied good faith and fair dealing was developed as a standard of review for the courts to effectuate the stated and unstated intention of parties as well as to protect the reasonable expectation of the parties (*Ryder Truck Rental, Inc. v. Central Packing Co.*, 1965).

United States courts have similarly recognized the opposite corollary to good faith and fair dealing – bad faith and unfairness. There are six broadly defined categories of bad faith and unfairness: (1) evasion of the spirit of the deal; (2) lack of diligence; (3) willfully rendering only "substantial" performance; (4) abuse of a power to specify terms; (5) abuse of a power to determine compliance; and (6) interference with or failure to cooperate in the other party's performance (Summers, 1968). The issue of whether a party acted in good faith or in bad faith is a question of fact to be determined at trial. The doctrine of unconscionability requires courts to determine whether a weaker party's weakness altered the substantive fairness of the negotiation, which resulted in the terms of contract creating an unfair advantage for the stronger party (*Williams v. Walker-Thomas Furniture Co.*, 1965; Leff, 1967).

In the context of indigenous knowledge, the query then becomes – can the courts craft a legal remedy in cases where indigenous knowledge rights have been appropriated against their consent? Stated differently, what is the nature of the commercial transference that is in play when multinational corporations engage in commercial activity with vulnerable indigenous communities? It has been true historically, and it remains true, that developing economies offer multinational corporations: (1) cheap physical labor; and (2) the richness of the natural resources of the particular environment. Nevertheless, the legal remedy to be crafted by the courts for the benefit of the indigenous community does not exist in contracts but rather in tort, for the unlawful use of or taking of an individual's property.

F. Lockean and Hegelian Theories of Property as Instrumentalities of Equity

Equitable property principles have been used to define and center the discussion regarding the intersection of genetic commons existing in nature, indigenous knowledge, and equity. The indigenous knowledge that is expressed through the particularized combination of the genetic commons has traditionally been argued as the equitable property principles that arise not from the traditional process of purchase and sale of property. Rather, the equitable property principle arises from the ability to take the basic genetic commons, and transform the property through knowledge (labor) that is placed into the basic genetic commons to create an entirely unique property that is useful and has commercial value. This argument is based primarily in the Lockean and Hegelian theories of property rights.

Locke's labor theory of property has greatly influenced the philosophical framework and the contours of intellectual debates concerning property, labor, value, exploitation, the creation of capital, the creation of wealth, and IP. Locke believed that every individual has a natural right to the fruits of his labor. This natural right is separate and independent from the laws or rights that are established within a society. As such, Locke wrote:

> … [E]very Man has a Property in his own Person. This no Body has any Right to but himself. The Labour of his Body, and the Work of his hands, we say are properly his. Whatsoever then he removes out the State of Nature hath

> provided, and left it in, he hath mixed his Labour with, and joyned to it something that is his own, and thereby makes it his Property. (Locke, 1970 § 27)

Locke's theory of property is a normative and prescriptive theory. It is based on a hypothetical state very early in the political and legal development of what Plato would refer to as an ideal city-state whereby the structural frameworks of political and legal systems are in their infancy stages, and where man must consider the nature and value of justice and the other virtues as they appear both in the structure of society as a whole and in the personality of an individual human being. (Brown, 2011). The political and legal systems that emerge within the society may not, in fact, necessarily recognize the natural right that Locke theorizes exists. Locke's argument is that a developing state should reflect, in the laws that it chooses to recognize and adopt to govern itself, man's natural right to the fruits of his labor. For Locke there should be a set of positive laws that provide man with a natural right to the fruits of his labor. The recognition and incorporation of man's natural right to the fruits of his labor into descriptive law would codify man's right to the fruits of his labor into the rule of law.

Locke is often regarded as the father of liberal democratic theory, in part, because he was the first philosopher to interlink the labor theory of property and the labor theory of value to strengthen his argument that man has a natural right to his labor because what man produces with his labor enhances the inherent value of the property that he used. As such Locke wrote:

> … an Acre of the same Land lying in common, without any Husbandry upon it, and he will find, that the improvement of labour makes the far greater part of the value. I think it will be but a modest Computation to say, that of the Products of the Earth useful to the Life of Man 9/10 are effects of labour, nay, if we will rightly estimate things as the come to our use, and cast up the several Expenses about them, what in them is purely owing to Nature, and what to labour, we shall find, that in most of them 99/100 are wholly to be put on the account of labour. (Locke, 1970 § 40)

Hegel was well versed in Locke's theories and expanded on the underlying premise. Hegel believed in the philosophical hierarchy of human elements; an individual's mental consciousness includes: (1) the will; (2) personality; and (3) freedom of self. Hegel viewed the will as the core of the individual's existence, which is continuously seeking actuality and effectiveness towards expressing the freedom to be his true self in the physical world. As such, Hegel wrote:

> [a] person must translate his freedom into an external sphere in order to exist as an idea ... and ... [p]ersonality is the first, still wholly abstract, determination of the absolute and infinite will ... therefore ... [p]ersonality is that which struggles to lift itself above this restriction and to give itself reality, or in other words to claim that external world as its own. (Hegel, §§172–5, 1962)

It is within this paradigm that Hegel defined property as a means to express the will and "self-actualize" the personality by "objectification" of the will into physical property. The "immediate freed of the self to act on things," which the realized self believes is an expression and extension of the individual in the physical world. Property then is an instrumentality of the individual in physical form. As such, the self is an inferior form of property because freedom permits the will to struggle to create "something new" in the physical world (Hegel, §§176–7). The "something new" that is created in the physical form is an extension of, and belongs to, the individual. They are inseparable. Commentators have defined this struggle of self-actualization as the right of the individual to self-determination (Gordon, 1993).

A right to property in the foundational theory of property means to "protect the personality's struggle to self actualize itself in the physical property, and to create conditions for further free action" (Hegel, §§ 182–5). However, society must acknowledge and approve the individual's moral claim to physical property as an external expression of oneself in the physical object (Hegel, §186). Society's approval of the individual's moral claim on the physical property is the confirmation and recognition of the individual's right in the property (Hegel, §187). The claim to property is, therefore, as much a moral claim as it is a legal claim. The moral claim has no meaning other than between the parties who recognize each other as persons and as equals. An individual's labor is the process by which the will "occupies" (first to possess) and "embodies" property (Hegel, §188). There are three ways in which the will can possess property: (1) seize it; (2) impose a form on it; and (3) mark it (thereby preserving it and making it a permanent part of things enjoyed by the individual) (Hegel, §197–8). It is in the process of laboring and possessing the physical property to make it reflect his will and expression that the individual makes the property his own.

Perhaps there is space within the discussion for another argument to be raised, not as a substitute for equitable property principles as an instrumentality of equity, but rather as a supplement or alternative. The argument would be based on equitable principles of tort law as an instrumentality of equity to protect indigenous knowledge.

G. Equitable Tort Doctrines of Unjust Enrichment, Misappropriation and Estoppel as Instrumentalities of Equity

Unjust enrichment, misappropriation and estoppel were designed to cover factual scenarios where there is no meeting of the minds, and as a result a contract has not been created. The doctrine of unjust enrichment was designed to address precisely the factual scenario where no contract exists in either verbal or written form. However, in cases where there is transference of an economic benefit to one party without a corresponding benefit to the other party, in particular, unjust enrichment occurs when a party receives an economic benefit as a direct result of another party's detriment (Restatement (Third) of Restitution and Unjust Enrichment § 250). This transference of economic benefit from one party to another may happen simply by happenstance, therefore, no intent to transfer is required. Nevertheless, the receiving party's ability to continue to retain the economic benefit without payment for such benefit is deemed socially unfair.

The doctrine of misappropriation is invoked when one party takes another's property and by so doing receives an economic benefit. The misappropriation cannot be accomplished in error, unbeknownst to the one who received the economic benefit. Misappropriation requires the one who receives the economic benefit to knowingly engage in conduct that will result in the commercial transference of another's property without their consent. Misappropriation requires a level of insidious culpability that may range from deception to intent to fraud.

The doctrine of estoppel was developed to prevent a party with superior bargaining power or knowledge from arguing that a contract does not exist. In these cases, a powerful party benefits at the weaker party's expense and fails to offer value. In these cases, the courts prohibit the powerful party from arguing that a contract does not exist especially when the powerful party has benefitted from the weaker party's performance and there is an element of deception, intentionality or fraud. For example, a multinational that knowingly fails to disclose their intent to commercialize indigenous knowledge or knowingly appropriates the knowledge without consent from the indigenous community might justify an estoppel remedy.

H. Equitable Remedies That Can be Crafted by the Courts

The remedy that courts often craft to remove the economic benefit that has unfairly transferred to another party is restitution. The two primary forms of restitutions are: (1) monetary awards to remove the unfair economic benefit; and (2) rescission to undo the transference of the benefit and make the injured party whole as if the transference has never occurred. Whether the remedy is one of monetary award or rescission, the vehicle that the courts will use to effectuate the remedy is to create a quasi-contract, which would provide the indigenous community with contractual rights in the transference of the indigenous knowledge.

A quasi-contract is an *obligationes quasi ex contractu* and was first recognized in Roman law as distinct in character from contract and tort (Corbin, 1912). The Roman usage of the tem *obligationes quasi ex contractu* has been followed in the legal codes of France, Louisiana, Scotland and additional codes derived from Napoleonic Law. English and American judges have long used quasi-contract to conceive of the possibility of a legal obligation neither contractual nor *delictos* in character:

Obligations *ex delicto* are those arising from a tort, an illegal act other than a breach of contract, and are enforced by giving to the obligee compensatory money damages equivalent to the amount of his loss. It is always a secondary and remedial obligation. The primary, antecedent obligation, the breach of which is a tort, is not an obligation *ex delicto*. It is like the obligation not to commit a crime, enforced against sane persons only by threats of punishment, and not by action. It is the correlative of a right *in rem*, not of a right *in personam* (Corbin, 1912).

Roman law separated the obligations *ex delicto* tort into two categories: (1) where the party was actively and knowingly involved in the tort, which has developed into intentional tort; and (2) where the party was mistakenly involved, which has developed into negligence. Quasi-contract developed out of the mistaken tort of negligence. A quasi-contract has the following elements: (1) there is not an agreement; and (2) the remedy is restitution of what has been inappropriately received and is never compensatory damages. The remedy specifically compels the enriched party to restore the value of that by which he was unjustly enriched.

Modern quasi-contract remedy is based on tort law rather than contract law. U.S. courts have historically created a quasi-contract where no formal written contract exists and equity is required to make whole the party who has been unfairly treated. One key instance is when one party takes unfair advantage of another party by deceit, e.g., by knowingly misappropriating the transference of another's property, or knowingly misrepresenting facts on which the deceived party relies to her detriment.

In theory, tort law does provide a legal basis for a U.S. court to craft a remedy that would provide monetary awards to indigenous communities in cases where indigenous knowledge has been misappropriated, or the court may create a quasi-contract in situations where multinationals have been unjustly enriched by their commercialization of indigenous knowledge without consent. However, the challenge is the practical application of who in the indigenous community should receive an equitable award, and how should the damage award be calculated. Nevertheless, the challenge of the practical application should not prevent the ability of a court to provide an equitable remedy to indigenous communities. Ethical principles of tort law recognize and may provide a remedy in cases where inequitable behavior leads to the commercialization of indigenous knowledge without appropriate consent. After all, "this is not the time to falter … this is the time to stand up for what we know to be right" (Blair, 2003).

IV. CONCLUSION

Intellectual property rights and human rights are on the path to becoming inexorably linked. A particularly contentious aspect of this dynamic evolution, however, involves the rights of indigenous communities to traditional knowledge that is misappropriated by businesses. Some of the human rights that are violated when this occurs include the right to: self-determination; culture; religious practice, and the right to participate in cultural life; the benefits of scientific progress; and the protection of authorial interests (Ruggie 2013). This chapter adopted a perspective that recognizes indigenous knowledge as a human right that belongs to a community, and argues that international law has recognized the legitimate status of this right. The chapter discussed the international legal framework that currently applies to indigenous knowledge. Finally, this chapter provided a novel conceptual foundation for applying U.S. equitable remedy law in an instrumental fashion to achieve greater normative compatibility with international human rights law, uphold the state's legal duty to protect human rights and offer judicial remedies as an element within the U.N. Guiding Principles on Human Rights and Business (Ruggie, 2011). This approach would also provide another mechanism to encourage U.S. companies to respect these internationally recognized human rights.

NOTES

1. Biopiracy is the commercial effort undertaken by a firm to establish property rights to the genetic commons existing in nature, often through the appropriation of indigenous knowledge.

2. This chapter primarily deals with traditional knowledge and genetic resources that can be appropriated to develop pharmaceuticals. As indicated by Ruggie, "some rights will be at greater risk than others in particular industries or operating contexts, and thus should be the focus of heightened attention" (Ruggie, 2013).
3. At present, "Chinese Acupuncture and Moxibustion" is the only form of traditional medicine inscribed for protection under the CSIH ("Representative List of the Intangible Cultural Heritage of Humanity", 2010). This sole registration involves both the intangible practice of traditional medicine in terms of procedure and a traditional knowledge use of plant matter for specific, cultural, medicinal purposes; Moxibustion involves the use of medicinal instruments crafted from dried mugwort leaves. An important question is why has only *one* form of traditional medicinal knowledge been inscribed on a CSIH Article 16 or 17 list in the past ten years? A possible answer could be found in the overlap between the CSIH and other binding international agreements. In relation to other international instruments, the CSIH, by its own terms under Article 3(b), takes a subordinate (and therefore non-conflict) position to other treaties or conventions "relating to intellectual property rights or to the use of biological and ecological resources" (UNESCO, 2003).
4. At the third Conference of Parties in 2011, the Protection Convention signatories took action to build a "compendium of cases wherein the Convention is invoked or utilized in other international fora" (UNESCO, "Third Conference of Parties", 2011, p. 6). A second consultation was carried out in 2012 to update this compendium of Article 21 cases ("Promoting the Convention in International Forums", 2012). As of February 2014, there are 39 entries in the Article 21 compendium of cases, 8 of which relate directly to international agreements and 18 to declarations or resolutions ("International Coordination – Documents List", 2014). Only one of the 39 entries in the compendium specifically involves an international trade agreement. It appears, therefore, that despite the existence of protection schemes for cultural expressions, there is little interaction between UNESCO protective measures in the area of international trade. As of June 2013, at the Fourth Conference of Parties, the parties noted that the Protection Convention has been invoked in 2 WTO cases, but that there was a also a wide array of members' definitions for the phrase "international forum." (UNESCO, "Fourth Conference of Parties", 2013, p. 7).
5. The U.S. State Department in 2010 officially announced support for the ideas behind the DRIP, however, the U.S. government held fast to its position that the DRIP is both non-binding and not a current statement of international law (or customary international law) (U.S. Dept. of State, 2011).

REFERENCES

Blair, A.C.L. (2003), "Opening speech at debate on the Iraq crisis in the House of Commons", retrieved from http://www.theguardian.com/politics/2003/mar/18/foreignpolicy.iraq1.

Bratspies, R.M. (2007), "The new discovery doctrine: Some thoughts on property rights and traditional knowledge", *American Indian Law Review*, 31(2), 315–40.

Brown, E. (2011). *Plato's ethics and politics in the republic. The Stanford Encyclopedia of Philosophy,* Edward N. Zalta (ed.), available at http://plato.stanford.edu/archives/win2011/entries/plato-ethics-politics/.

Burton, S.J. (1981), "Breach of contract and the common law duty to perform in good faith", *Harvard Law Review*, 94(2), 369–404.

Charnovitz, S. (1999), "The globalization of economic human rights", *Brooklyn Journal of International Law*, 25(1), 113–24.

Civil Rights Act of 1964, Tit. VII, Pub. L. No. 88-352, 78 Stat. 241 (codified as amended at 42 U.S.C. §§ 2000e–2000e-17 (2013)).

Commerce International Company v. United States, 338 F.2d 81 (Ct. Cl. 1964).

Committee on Econ., Soc. & Cultural Rights (ECOSOC) (2006, Jan. 12). General Comment No. 17: The Right of Everyone to Benefit from the Protection of the Moral and Material Interests Resulting from Any Scientific, Literary or Artistic Production of Which He Is the Author (Article 15, Paragraph 1(c), of the Covenant), ¶ 4, U.N. Doc. E/C.12/GC/17.

Corbin, A.L. (1912), "Quasi-contractual obligations", *Yale Law Journal*, 21(7), 533–54.

Dodge v. Ford Motor Co., 170 N.W. 668 (Mich. 1919).

Ellinghaus, M.P. (1969), "In defense of unconscionability", *Yale Law Journal*, 78(5), 757–815.

Farnsworth, E.A. (1963), "Good faith performance and commercial reasonableness under the Uniform Commercial Code", *University of Chicago Law Review*, 30(4), 666–79.

Farnsworth, E.A. (1968), "Disputes over omission in contracts", *Columbia Law Review*, 68(5), 860–91.

Filartiga v. Pena-Irala, 630 F.2d 876 (2d Cir. 1980).

Friedman, M. (1970, Sept. 13), "The social responsibility of business is to increase its profits", *New York Times Magazine*, 122–6.

Garcia, F.R. (1999), "The global market and human rights: Trading away the human rights principle", *Brooklyn Journal of International Law*, 25(1), 51–97.

General Agreement on Tariffs and Trade (GATT) (1994, Apr. 15), "Marrakesh Agreement Establishing the World Trade Organization", Annex 1A, 33 I.L.M. 1153.

Gordon, W.J. (1993), "A property right in self-expression: Equality and individualism in the natural law of intellectual property", *Yale Law Journal*, 102(7), 1533–609.

Hannum, H. (1996), "The status of the Universal Declaration of Human Rights in national and international law", *The Georgia Journal of International and Comparative Law*, 25(1 and 2), 287–398.

Hegel, G.W.F. (1962), *Philosophy of Right*. (Knox, T.M, ed. and trans.), London, England: Oxford University Press (original work published 1820).

Helfer, L.R. (2003), "Human rights and intellectual property: Conflict or coexistence?" *Minnesota Intellectual Property Review*, 5(1), 47–62.

International Covenant on Civil and Political Rights (ICCPR) (1966, Dec. 16), 999 U.N.T.S. 171, S. Treaty Doc. No. 95-20.

International Covenant on Economic, Social and Cultural Rights (ICESCR) (1966, Dec. 16), 999 U.N.T.S. 3.

International Labour Organization (ILO) (1957, June 26), *The Indigenous and Tribal Populations Convention*, C107, 40th ILC Session.

ILO (1989, June 27), "Convention concerning Indigenous and Tribal Peoples in Independent Countries", C169, 76th ILC Session.

ILO (1989), "NORMLEX: Information System on International Labour Standards, Ratifications of C169 – Indigenous and Tribal Peoples Convention", No.

169, retrieved from: http://www.ilo.org/dyn/normlex/en/f?p=1000:11300:0::NO::P11300_INSTRUMENT_ID:312314.

International Shoe Co. v. Washington, 326 U.S. 310 (1945).

Judiciary Act of 1789, ch. 20, § 9(b), 1 Stat. 77 (1789) (codified as amended at 28 U.S.C. § 1350 (2006)).

Kessler, F. and Fine, E. (1964), "Culpa in Contrahendo, bargaining in good faith, and freedom of contract: A comparative study", *Harvard Law Review*, 77(3), 401–49.

Killmister, S. (2012), "Why group membership matters: A critical typology", *Ethnicities*, 12(3) 251–69.

Kiobel v. Royal Dutch Petroleum, 569 U.S.__, 133 S.Ct. 1659 (2013).

Kymlicka, W. (1995), *Multicultural Citizenship: A Liberal Theory of Minority Rights*, Oxford: Clarendon Press.

Leff, A.A. (1967), "Unconscionability and the Code – The Emperor's new clause", *University of Pennsylvania Law Journal*, 115(4), 485–559.

Locke, J. (1970), *Two treatises of Government*. (Laslett, P., Ed.). London, England: Cambridge University Press (Original work published 1690).

McGarry, K. (2008), "U.S. patent reform and international public health: Issues of law and policy", *Intercultural Human Rights Law Review*, 3, 299–342.

Minneapolis & St. Louis Railway Co. v. Beckwith, 129 U.S. 26 (1888).

Orozco, D. and Poonamallee, L. (2013), "The role of ethics in the commercialization of indigenous knowledge", *Journal of Business Ethics* (forthcoming), 1–12.

Patterson, E.W. (1964), "The interpretation and construction of contracts", *Columbia Law Review*, 64(5), 833–58.

Reaume, D. (1988), "Individuals, groups and rights to public goods", *University of Toronto Law Journal*, 38(1), 1–27.

Restatement (Second) of Contracts §§ 231, 234 (1981).

Restatement (Third) of Restitution and Unjust Enrichment § 250 (2011).

Roht-Arriaza, N. (1996), "Of seeds and shamans: The appropriation of the scientific and technical knowledge of indigenous and local communities", *Michigan Journal of International Law*, 17, 919–65.

Ruggie, J. G. (2011), "Guiding principles on business and human rights: Implementing the United Nations "protect, respect and remedy" framework: Report of the special representative of the secretary-general on the issue of human rights and transnational corporations and other business enterprises", U.N. Document A/HRC/17/31.

Ruggie, J.G. (2013), *Just Business: Multinational Corporations and Human Rights*. New York, NY: W.W. Norton & Co.

Ryder Truck Rental, Inc. v. Central Packing Co., 341 F.2d. 321 (10th Cir. 1965).

Santa Clara v. Southern Pacific Railroad, 118 U.S. 394 (1886).

Shiva, V. (2000). *Stolen Harvest: The Hijacking of the Global Food Supply*. Cambridge, MA: South End Press.

Snyder v. Massachusetts, 291 U.S. 97, 105 (1934).

Sosa v. Alvarez-Machain, 542 U.S. 692 (2004).

Summers, R.S. (1968), "Good faith in general contract law and the sales provisions of the Uniform Commercial Code", *Virginia Law Review*, 54(2), 195–267.

Trade-Related Aspects of Intellectual Property Rights Agreement (TRIPS) (1995, Apr. 15). Marrakesh Agreement Establishing the World Trade Organization, Annex 1C, 1869 U.N.T.S. 299.

Uniform Commercial Code §§1-203, 2-302 (2002).

U.N. Education, Scientific and Cultural Organisation (UNESCO) (2003, Oct. 17), "Convention for the Safeguarding of the Intangible Cultural Heritage", MISC/2003/CLT/CH/14.

UNESCO, "Convention on the Protection and Promotion of the Diversity of Cultural Expressions of 20 October 2005", CLT-2005/CONVENTION DIVERSITE-CULT REV.2 (2005).

UNESCO (2009, June 15–16), "Conference of Parties to the Convention on the Protection and Promotion of the Diversity of Cultural Expressions", Second Ordinary Session, CE/09/2.CP/210/7.

UNESCO (2010), "Intergovernmental Committee for the Safeguarding of the Intangible Cultural Heritage", 5th Session Nairobi, Kenya, November 2010, Nomination File No. 00425, RL10 – No. 00425, retrieved from: http://www.unesco.org/culture/ich/doc/download.php?versionID=07331.

UNESCO (2011, June 14–15), "Conference of Parties to the Convention on the Protection and Promotion of the Diversity of Cultural Expressions", Third Ordinary Session, CE/11/3.CP/209/Res. (2011).

UNESCO (2013, June 11–13), "Conference of Parties to the Convention on the Protection and Promotion of the Diversity of Cultural Expressions", Fourth Ordinary Session, CE/13/4.CP/Res. (2013).

UNESCO (2012), "Promoting the Convention in International Forums", retrieved from: http://www.unesco.org/new/en/culture/themes/cultural-diversity/diversity-of-cultural-expressions/the-convention/international-fora/.

UNESCO (2014), "Article 21 International Consultation and Coordination, International Coordination – Documents List", retrieved from: http://www.unesco.org/culture/cultural-diversity/2005convention/en/international coordination/documentlist/.

U.N. General Assembly (2007, Sept. 13), "Declaration on the Rights of Indigenous Peoples", G.A. Res. 61/295, Annex, U.N. Doc. A/RES/61/295.

U.N. General Assembly (2012, May 17), "High-level commemoration of the fifth anniversary of the adoption of the UN Declaration on the Rights of Indigenous Peoples", G.A. Res. 66/142, U.N. Doc. A/RES/66/142.

U.N. Universal Declaration of Human Rights (UDHR) (1948, Dec. 10). G.A. Res. 217 (III), U.N. Doc. A/217

U.S. Department of State (2011, Jan. 12), "Initiatives to promote the Government-to-Government relationship and improve the lives of indigenous peoples", announcement of U.S. Support for the United Nations Declaration on the Rights of Indigenous Peoples, retrieved from http://www.state.gov/documents/organization/154782.pdf.

Visual Artists Rights Act, 17 U.S.C. § 106A (2012).

Whiteman, G., and Cooper, H.W. (2000), "Ecological embeddedness", *Academy of Management Journal*, 43(6), 1265–82.

Williams v. Walker-Thomas Furniture Co., 350 F.2d 445, 449 (D.C. Cir. 1965).

World Trade Organization (1999, June 17), *Preferential Tariff Treatment for Least-Developed Countries*, WT/L/304.

World Trade Organization (2000), *Canada – Patent Protection of Pharmaceutical Products, Complaint by the European Communities and their member States, Report of the Panel*, WT/DS114/R.

World Trade Organization (2001, Mar. 12), *European Communities – Measures Affecting Asbestos and Asbestos-Containing Products*, Appellate Body Report, WT/DS135/AB/R (2001).

World Trade Organization (Doha Declaration) (2001), "Ministerial Declaration of 14 November 2001", WT/MIN(01)/DEC/1, 41 I.L.M. 746.

World Trade Organization (2003, June 18), "Council for Trade-Related Aspects of Intellectual Property Rights, Article 27.3(b), The Relationship Between the TRIPS Agreement and the Convention on Biological Diversity, and the Protection of Traditional Knowledge", Communication from Switzerland, IP/C/W/400/Rev.1.

World Trade Organization (2006, Mar. 13), "Council for Trade-Related Aspects of Intellectual Property Rights, Article 27.3(B), Relationship Between the TRIPS Agreement and the CBD, and the Protection of Traditional Knowledge and Folklore", Communication from the United States, IP/C/W/469.

World Trade Organization (2011a, Apr. 21), "Issues Related to the Extension of the Protection of Geographical Indications Provided for in Article 23 of the TRIPS Agreement to Products Other Than Wines and Spirits and Those Related to the Relationship Between the TRIPS Agreement and the Convention on Biological Diversity, Report by the Director-General", WT/GC/W/633, TN/C/W/61.

World Trade Organization (2011b, Mar. 19), "Trade Negotiations Committee, Draft Decision to Enhance Mutual Supportiveness Between the TRIPS Agreement and the Convention on Biological Diversity", Communication from Brazil, China, Colombia, Ecuador, India, Indonesia, Peru, Thailand, the ACP Group, and the African Group, TN/C/W/59.

Wouters, J. and De Meester, B. (2008), "The UNESCO Convention on Cultural Diversity and WTO law: A case study in fragmentation of international law", *Journal of World Trade Law*, 42(1), 205–40.

Yu, P. (2007), "Reconceptualizi ng intellectual property interests in a human rights framework", *U.C. Davis Law Review*, 40(3), 1039–149.

Zagel, G.M. (2005), "WTO and human rights: Examining linkages and suggesting convergence", *IDLO Voices of Development Jurists*, 2(2), 1–36.

8. Conflict minerals and polycentric governance of business and human rights

Jamie Darin Prenkert

During his mandate and since, Special Representative of the Secretary-General on the Issue of Human Rights and Transnational Corporations and Other Business Enterprises ("SRSG") John Ruggie referred to the "Protect, Respect and Remedy" Framework ("PRR framework") and the Guiding Principles on Business and Human Rights ("Guiding Principles") as a polycentric governance system (Ruggie, 2013, p. 78; Ruggie, 2011). Backer (2011), Taylor (2012), and others have done so as well. But what exactly that means has not been very carefully elucidated. This chapter places that description in the context of a deep and varied literature on polycentric governance and evaluates the PRR framework in that light. In particular, the chapter uses as a case study an emerging potential polycentric governance system related to the sourcing of certain minerals from conflicted-affected countries in the African Great Lakes region to explore these issues. The conflict minerals regulatory regime incorporates a notable number of the concerns and opportunities Ruggie highlighted and promoted in the PRR framework and Guiding Principles. The chapter concludes with a recommendation for further study of the business and human rights sector generally, and conflict minerals regulation specifically, in accordance with the polycentric governance literature.

I. BACKGROUND ON POLYCENTRIC GOVERNANCE SYSTEMS

The concept of polycentricity has been utilized in a number of different ways by scholars from a number of different disciplines. This section describes the concept's history and development and then explores its relevance to business and human rights.

A. History and Broad Application

In general, polycentric governance is marked by a regulatory system – sometimes referred to as a regime complex (Shackelford, 2013; Raustiala and Victor, 2004) – that consists of a collective of partially overlapping and nonhierarchical regimes. Nobel Laureate Elinor Ostrom (2010) has said that polycentric systems are "characterized by multiple governing authorities at differing scales rather than a monocentric unit" (p. 552). In a polycentric governance regime, therefore, the state is not the only source or foundation of authority and, in fact, may play little or no role at all (Black, 2008). Instead, a complex array of interdependent actors or decision-making centers, both state and nonstate, which are formally independent of one another, form networks and interact among themselves, each adding some value, while reinforcing each other and compensating for each other's limitations and weaknesses. Each individual actor within the system is typically free from domination by the others and can make its own rules and develop its own norms within its domain of influence. Nevertheless, there is also opportunity within the system for "mutual monitoring, learning, and adaptation of better strategies over time" (Ostrom, 2010, p. 552).

The boundaries of a polycentric governance regime are often marked by the problems or issues with which the various actors share a common concern. In other words, a polycentric system is focused on problem solving but is not defined by any single or particular solution to that problem (Black, 2008). Often, polycentric governance emerges in the face of a collective action problem that the state is either ill-equipped, unwilling, or too slow to tackle. Professor Michael McGinnis (2005) explains that, when facing a collective action problem, a group should be able to address it in the way it sees fit, which can and should include crafting new governance structures that will be able to facilitate the problem-solving process. In this way, a polycentric regime usually involves "bottom-up" rather than "top-down" governance (Shackelford, in press).

It is likely that no one has done more to advance the study of polycentric governance, especially as related to public goods and common pool resources, than Elinor Ostrom, Vincent Ostrom, and their colleagues at the Vincent and Elinor Ostrom Workshop in Political Theory and Policy Analysis at Indiana University. Vincent Ostrom's early work in polycentric governance challenged the prevailing notion in the

1970s and 1980s that the provision of public services, like police and education, was better and more cost-effectively accomplished by slashing the number of departments and districts and consolidating them. Vincent Ostrom's work showed that "no systematic empirical evidence supported reform proposals related to moving the provision of public goods from smaller-scale units to larger governments" (Ostrom, 2009, p. 50). Rather, a series of studies showed, for example, that small- and medium-sized police departments outperformed their larger counterparts serving similar neighborhoods in major urban centers in measures of efficiency and cost (McGinnis, 2009). Though the small and overlapping centers governance seemed inefficient, in practice they performed well.

Elinor Ostrom built on these studies to determine whether polycentric governance regimes could adequately combat collective action problems associated with the provision and regulation of public goods and common pool resources. She challenged the conventional theory of collective action, which held that rational actors would not cooperate to achieve a socially optimal outcome in a prisoner's dilemma scenario like that associated with the tragedy of the commons. Thus, it was thought that only top-down, state-imposed regulations could create the proper incentives for optimal collective action. A series of field studies that she and others conducted on the provision of water resources in California, the design and maintenance of irrigation systems in Nepal, and the protection of forests in Latin America consistently showed that, contrary to the conventional theory, many individuals will cooperate in the face of collective action problems. Local and regional groups of small to medium scale were found to have self-organized to develop solutions to common pool resource problems, despite what the rational choice theory would suggest (Ostrom, 2009). Moreover, in field studies, systems governed polycentrically were often found to have better outcomes than those governed by a central governmental authority (Ostrom, 2012). The polycentric regimes were more nimble, flexible, and invested in guaranteeing success at the local level. And regimes marked by top-down state regulation did not get the kind of local and regional expert input that the polycentric systems did. These observations in the field were consistent with laboratory experiments that found externally imposed regulations that were intended to maximize joint returns in the face of collective action problems actually "crowded out" individuals' voluntary, cooperative behavior (Frey and Oberholzer-Gee, 1997; Reeson and Tisdell, 2008).

Prior to her death, Elinor Ostrom was applying this research – and the institutional analysis and development ("IAD") framework that grew out of it – to the regulation of global climate change. She assumed that sufficient global regulation through treaty or other international legal instrument was either unlikely ever to occur or, certainly, would not be forthcoming in the near future; thus, some alternative means of regulating greenhouse gas ("GHG") emissions would be necessary to address the collective action problem such emissions represent. Ostrom (2010) challenged the prevailing belief that atmospheric conditions and climate, which are *global* public goods, must be addressed on a *global* scale to be effective. Rather, she argued that, because a tremendously large number of actions taken at multiple scales – for example, the household, cities and states, countries, transboundary regional areas, and global levels – affect the amount of GHG emissions, a polycentric system addressing global climate change would incorporate the experience, expertise, and investment of various actors on each of those scales and produce effective, if not perfect, cooperative behavior. This is consistent with the "matching principle" in international law, in that multilevel problems should involve contributions by each of those levels (Adler, 2005).

Thus, problems like those posed by the tragedy of the commons that transcend the Westphalian conception of national jurisdictional boundaries need not be addressed exclusively (or, necessarily, at all) by comprehensive global regulation or international law. Rather, polycentric regulatory action and experimentation by multiple actors at multiple levels linked together by diverse information networks is certainly better than failed or lumbering international initiatives, and likely bring benefits that the top-down regulation cannot.

B. Relevance to Business and Human Rights

SRSG Ruggie recognized similar challenges and opportunities as he undertook his mandate to address human rights and transnational corporations. The likelihood that the corporate responsibility for human rights could be enshrined in some sort of comprehensive and binding instrument of international law or treaty was nil. The Norms on the Responsibilities of Transnational Corporations and Other Business Enterprises with Regard to Human Rights ("Norms") (2003) would have imposed on businesses affirmative duties concurrent with states "to promote, secure the fulfillment of, respect, ensure respect of and protect human rights" within their "sphere of influence." The controversy surrounding the Norms is well known. They failed to get any traction at the United Nations. Ultimately, the U.N. Human Rights Commission took no action on the Norms and instead established Ruggie's mandate. Ruggie recognized that the Norms were both too ambitious and too limited in their scope, that there was no hope of building consensus around an approach that imposed state-like duties with regard to some delimited set of human rights directly on businesses at the level of international law. So, early in his mandate, he made clear his intent to distance his own efforts from the Norms. In his own words, his "first official act was to commit 'Normicide'" (Ruggie, 2013, p. 54). Thus, as with global climate change, it would be folly to look to a top-down approach to regulate transnational corporations with regard to human rights violations and abuses.

Still, globalization has created a dynamic whereby transnational corporations operate beyond the reach of any particular national regulatory system. Governance gaps result from inadequate national regulatory reach, a nonexistent international regulatory framework, and insufficiently organized and empowered nonstate market and social actors. The PRR framework was crafted to address and fill those governance gaps (U.N. Special Representative of the Secretary-General, 2008). They take several forms. Structurally, public governance is fragmented along national territorial lines, while the global economy transcends such territorial boundaries. Even within and among those national jurisdictions, governments lack policy coherence on both vertical and horizontal axes.[1] Finally, states often lack the capacity or will to adopt or implement regulatory measures, because they fear either that they lack the means to enforce them or that they will suffer negative consequences in the global marketplace (Ruggie, 2009). With regard to policy coherence and governance gaps, in 2010, Ruggie identified

> five priority areas through which States should strive to achieve greater policy coherence and effectiveness as part of their duty to protect: (a) safeguarding their own ability to meet their human rights obligations; (b) considering human rights when they do business with business; (c) fostering corporate cultures respectful of rights at home and abroad; (d) devising innovative policies to guide companies operating in conflict affected areas; and (e) examining the cross-cutting issue of extraterritorial jurisdiction. (U.N. Special Representative of the Secretary-General, 2010)

Thus, states clearly have a vital role to play to address the governance gaps, but they cannot by themselves completely close the governance gaps created by globalization.

In the absence of obligatory international law and in light of the governance gaps Ruggie identified, a polycentric system of governance and regulation can thrive. The PRR framework was conceived as just such a polycentric system. When asked about the interaction between the state duty to protect and business's responsibility to respect human rights, Ruggie indicated that the framework and the Guiding Principles reflect a system of polycentric governance. He described it as "an emerging regulatory dynamic under which public and private governance systems each add distinct value, compensate for one another's weaknesses, and play mutually reinforcing roles – out of which a more comprehensive and effective global regime might emerge" (Ruggie, 2011). Referencing the polycentric nature of the framework, Backer (2011) describes it as "an attempt to build simultaneous public and private governance systems as well as coordinate, without integrating, their operations" (p. 43). In other words, the framework serves as a means of providing the information networks and linkages that allow for the multiple actors at multiple levels of society to act as governing authorities within their particular realm of expertise and influence, while reinforcing each other and compensating for each other's limitations and weaknesses. Furthermore, it incorporates the matching principle at both a legal and social regulatory level. The problem of business involvement or complicity in human rights violations and abuses is a multilevel one, ranging from the purely local to the transnational. By complementing the state's duty to protect with business's responsibility to respect human rights, as well as explicating the role that both state and nonstate actors must play in remedying any violations or abuses, the framework anticipates a broad and multilevel approach and provides guidance and expectations for all involved to contribute to addressing the problem at their respective level.

II. CONFLICT MINERALS AND POLYCENTRIC GOVERNANCE

The polycentric nature of the PRR framework is an important and elegant feature of the SRSG's work. Whether it will spawn well-functioning, issue-specific polycentric governance regimes is vital to determine the ultimate success or failure of the framework and Guiding Principles. The remainder of this chapter is devoted to a case study of one potential emerging, issue-specific polycentric governance regime. Because it emulates that polycentric system, incorporates the norms elucidated in the Guiding Principles, and confronts a number of the most troublesome governance gaps, the approach to supply chain transparency and conflict minerals in the Democratic Republic of Congo ("DRC") may well portend how lasting and meaningful the PRR framework and Guiding Principles will be.

A. Background on the Conflict Minerals Issue

Significant swaths of the African continent are rich in natural resources, but poor in stable governance and the hallmarks of civil society and rule of law. In these areas, local communities are often dominated – and even terrorized – by outside interests that seek to extract the value from those resources for their own gain with little regard for the effect on the local peoples. The effects are devastating. Such groups can and do wreak havoc on the local populations and the environment, leave the community without a lucrative source of support, and rob communities of the right to self-determination. These interlopers can range from warlords and terrorists to knights of industry, sometimes (wittingly or not) working in concert.

In the eastern DRC armed rebel groups, as well as some groups loosely affiliated with the official DRC military, profit and fund their operations in part through the domination and control of mineral mines, as well as unauthorized extortive taxation of trade routes and facilities. For example, Schrank (2010) details the interlocking relationships among military and rebel groups that have engaged in this type of exploitation at a cassiterite mine in eastern DRC. In turn, some of these groups terrorize the local populations, taking particular aim at women and girls. They use rape as a tool of control and intimidation. The eastern DRC is perhaps the most dangerous place in the world to be a woman (Peterman, Palermo, and Bredenkamp, 2011).

The origins of the human rights travesty in the DRC are well known. Fighting between and among the armed rebel groups and government forces has led to the deaths of more than five million since the mid-1990s when the aftermath of the Rwandan genocide spilled across the border into eastern DRC (Prunier, 2010). It is a zone of weak or nonexistent governance and nearly constant conflict.

Without a doubt, such conflict is expensive. Thus, the DRC's vast supply of natural resources is also a natural source for rebel groups to tap for funding. The U.N. Security Council adopted a resolution in 2005 recognizing the link between illegal exploitation of natural resources, the illicit trade in those resources, and arms trafficking as a significant factor exacerbating the continuing conflicts in the region (U.N. Security Council, 2005). The armed groups' occupation and exploitation of the mineral mines have provided a rich source of funding for guns, ammunition, and other conflict-sustaining supplies. Along with gems and other precious metals, the DRC has a rich supply of gold, cassiterite, wolframite and coltan. The latter three minerals are refined into the metals tin, tungsten, and tantalum. Gold, tin, tungsten, and tantalum are widely used in numerous industries, but they are particularly important in the production of electronic devices. Cell phones, laptop computers, and digital video cameras, among others, rely on these minerals for their operation. Gold is used for wire coating. Tin is a soldering agent. Tungsten makes cell phones vibrate. Tantalum capacitors store electricity in electronic devices. Although the DRC is not the sole – or even the majority – supplier of these conflict minerals, their abundance has made the DRC a major global supplier (Prendergast and Lezhnev, n.d.). The minerals have been dubbed "conflict minerals" to denote their role in the ongoing conflict and unrest in the Great Lakes Region of Africa, particularly in the DRC.

Artisanal mining is perhaps dangerous enough in and of itself for the miners and the environment. The violence and terror that the military and paramilitary groups inflict on the local inhabitants exacerbates exponentially the difficulties of life in the eastern DRC. Only a multifaceted strategy of international pressure, support, and cooperation at the political, military, social, and economic levels has any hope to produce any long-lasting, successful resolution to the tragedies caused by these entrenched and conflicting interests in the DRC. Yet at least some part of the solution has to address the role that foreign businesses, those up the supply chain from the mines, play in the cycle of conflict and violence. Markets create value in the minerals. That value drives the unauthorized exploitation of the mines and the local populations. Those value-creating markets would not exist without the demand for the products that incorporate the minerals. Although the electronics manufacturers and consumers may be geographically far removed from the DRC mines, it would be short-sighted to ignore their role in any comprehensive strategy for bringing stability to the DRC.

As such, the conflict minerals issue embodies the governance gaps that Ruggie identified as plaguing the business and human rights space. The Congolese Government lacks sufficient capacity to deal with the issue, not least because of its recent history – and, in some parts of the country, current threat – of bloody and devastating violence. Even if the Congolese Government's capacity were not so limited, the complexity of the supply chain for these minerals is such that the challenge presented by legal fragmentation and the conundrum of extraterritorial application of any one nation's laws to a global industry is writ large. The number of actors involved in the process from mine to a finished product is significant; the number of home and host states that are touched by those actors' commercial activities is daunting. The situation presents a classic collective action problem, in that it takes a cooperative comprehensive approach to starve the rebel groups of their sources of income. Defectors who continue to buy from conflict-affected areas fund the rebel groups and undermine governance efforts. Thus, any governance regime needs to be innovative, be adaptive, build trustworthiness and cooperation among the affected actors, and work on multiple scales. Therefore, a polycentric approach is warranted.

In fact, a polycentric governance regime that is focused on supply chain transparency and due diligence and intended to limit the access of rebel groups to the deep pockets of the global market has emerged. The regime incorporates norms that are consistent and, perhaps, inspired by the PRR framework and Guiding Principles (Taylor, 2011). This polycentric regime involves a growing network of state and nonstate regulators, acting interdependently to complement each other and to add value with their strengths while counterbalancing each other's weaknesses.

The causes and continuing dynamics that fuel the instability in the eastern DRC and that lead to the gross human rights abuses are many. Halting the illicit trade in conflict minerals is unlikely, by itself, to remedy all the ills of that region. Nonetheless, the success or failure of the efforts to curb trade in conflict minerals may provide some evidence for how a polycentric approach to issues of business's participation and complicity in violations of human rights will fare.

B. Independent Actors and Decision-making Centers Affecting Conflict Minerals

Although I make no representation that what follows is a comprehensive or complete accounting of all the various actors in this emerging governance regime, it is worthwhile to map some of the activities of the major players at various levels in the process, both state and nonstate. In particular, what follows is a description of initiatives and actors who are directly addressing the issue of conflict minerals. Thus, for instance, I do not describe various aspects of the UN, European, Inter-American, or African human rights regimes (including various treaties relevant to each), which may have ancillary relevance to concerns raised by conflict minerals but not direct impact. That limitation reflects the definition of polycentric governance in the literature, which notes that polycentric governance regimes are focused on solving particular problems (conflict minerals) rather than implementing particular solutions (treaty-making) (Black, 2008).

After charting a rough map of what could be called the conflict minerals polycentric governance regime, I query if there is reason for concern over whether well-intentioned, state-based legislative action by the U.S. Congress will end up "crowding out" what might have been otherwise voluntary cooperative behavior to create a truly effective polycentric system of governance. Or, in the alternative, should the legislation be viewed as an important catalyst for the propagation of the various regulatory and decision-making centers that have developed, bringing about more quickly a fully polycentric regime? Ultimately, careful field study and application of mature analytical tools, such as the IAD framework from the Ostrom Workshop, will be vital to measure the effectiveness of these efforts and to improve and encourage subsequent initiatives. It is not overstatement to suggest that the PRR framework's legitimacy and longevity will likely hang on the success of these types of efforts.

1. National-level state actor: U.S. conflict minerals legislation and SEC Regulation

At the urging of several civil society nongovernmental organizations ("NGOs"), most notably the Enough Project and Global Witness, the U.S. Congress took notice of the conflict mineral supply chain. In 2010, Congress somewhat uncomfortably appended to the Dodd-Frank Wall Street Reform and Consumer Protection Act, the financial reform bill, section 1502, which addresses the conflict minerals problem. Its goal is to starve the armed rebel groups of the essential funding source that comes from trading in conflict minerals (Dodd-Frank, 2011).

Without banning the purchase or use of conflict minerals from the DRC or its neighbors, even if they prove to have funded armed rebels, section 1502 instead incorporates the due diligence and reporting norm that Ruggie says requires companies to "know and show" that they are respecting human rights (Ruggie, 2013, p. 99). Congress chose to force companies to disclose information about their behavior and choices rather than to directly regulate them. Section 1502 regulates the flow of information in three complementary ways (Ochoa and Keenan, 2011). The first affects corporations and their activities. The other two direct other government officers to assist in the compilation and sharing of information related to the conflict minerals trade.

i. Due diligence, reporting, and disclosure Most significantly, section 1502 forces certain companies, consisting primarily of publicly traded technology, automotive, mining, jewelry, and aerospace companies, to disclose to the U.S. Securities and Exchange Commission ("SEC"), and to make available through their websites, information related to their supply chain monitoring and use of conflict minerals. Specifically, the covered companies must disclose whether conflict minerals that are "necessary to the functionality or production of a product" they manufacture originated in the DRC or the countries sharing an internationally recognized border with the DRC (i.e., Angola, Burundi, Central African Republic, Republic of Congo, Rwanda, Sudan, Tanzania, Uganda, and Zambia) (15 U.S.C. § 78m(p)(2)(B)). In addition, the companies must provide "a description of the measures taken … to exercise due diligence on the source and chain of custody of conflict minerals" (15 U.S.C. § 78m(p)(1)(A)(i)). This requirement includes that the company must submit to the SEC a private audit of those efforts, as well as:

> a description of the products manufactured or contracted to be manufactured that are not DRC conflict free … and the facilities used to process the conflict minerals, the country of origin of the conflict minerals, and the efforts to locate the mine or location of origin with the greatest possible specificity. (15 U.S.C. § 78(p)(1)(A)(ii))

To be "DRC conflict free" a product cannot contain minerals "that directly or indirectly finance or benefit armed groups in the [DRC] or an adjoining country" (15 U.S.C. § 78m(p)(1)(D)). This is basically a requirement that covered companies audit their supply chains to ensure that the mines from which the minerals are extracted and/or the trade routes and trading facilities through which the minerals pass are neither under the control of nor financing armed groups.

In August 2012, following an extensive and extended notice and comment period, the SEC issued its final rule on the conflict minerals provision, implementing the Dodd-Frank requirements. The final rule, numbering more than 300 pages, lays out a three-step process for covered companies to determine whether and what to report regarding their use of conflict minerals and the minerals' origin (Conflict Minerals, 2012). Figure 8.1 provides a flowchart of the processes.

The three steps of the rule's approach can be summarized as follows:

First Step: A company must determine if it is subject to the rule.[2] Only those companies whose minerals are necessary to the functionality or production of a product they manufacture are covered. If a company does not fall within this definition, it need not engage in any further investigation or due diligence, make any disclosures, or file any reports under the rule.

Second Step: If a company determines that it is subject to the rule as required in the first step, then it must conduct a reasonable country of origin inquiry. This inquiry must be reasonably designed to determine if the conflict minerals originated

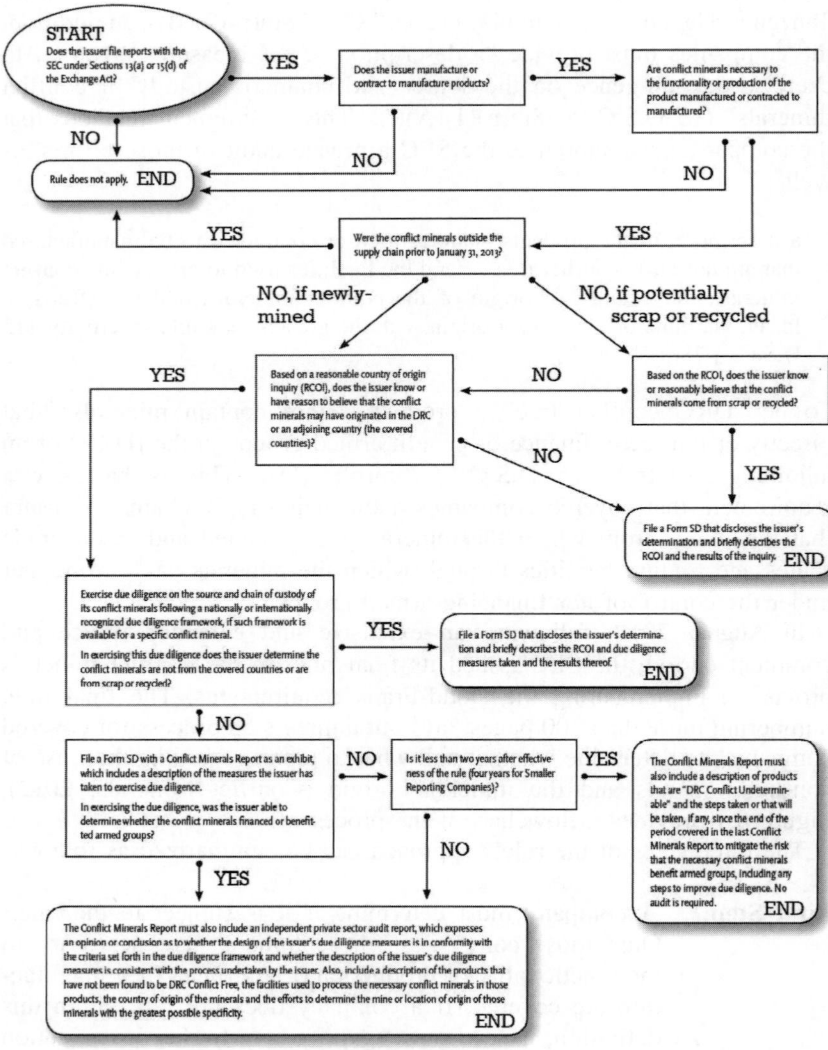

Source: Securities and Exchange Commission (Conflict Minerals, 2012).

Figure 8.1 Conflict minerals flowchart

in the DRC or its neighboring countries and must be done in good faith. The results of this inquiry can be any of the following: (a) a determination that the conflict minerals did not originate in the covered countries; (b) a determination that the conflict minerals are from recycled or scrap sources; (c) an inability to determine the origin of the conflict minerals; or (d) a determination that the conflict minerals *did* originate in the covered countries. A company that determines either of the first two is required to disclose that fact in a new specialized disclosure, Form SD, and to describe the process it utilized in its reasonable country of origin inquiry. Such companies need not proceed to the third step. If a company is unable to determine the origin of the conflict minerals, it too must file a specialized disclosure stating its conclusion and describing its inquiry, but it need not proceed to the third step unless it has reason to believe its conflict minerals may have originated in a covered country and may not be from recycled or scrap sources.[3]

Third Step: A company whose reasonable country of origin inquiry has led to the determination that the conflict minerals originated or may have originated in the covered countries and that they did not come from recycled or scrap materials must exercise due diligence on the source and chain of custody of the conflict minerals and file an extensive report about its due diligence measures along with its Form SD. Ultimately, if the due diligence process reveals that a company's conflict minerals financed or benefited armed groups in the covered countries, the company must disclose as much, presumably subjecting it to significant social and market pressure to avoid such complicity in the future.

The due diligence process must comport with a nationally or internationally recognized framework. Furthermore, the rule requires an independent, external private audit of the report. The objective of the audit is to express an opinion or conclusion as to whether the report describes due diligence measures that comply with an appropriate due diligence framework and whether it accurately describes the due diligence process the company actually undertook.[4]

ii. Government information gathering The second way (following the public company reporting requirements) that the Dodd-Frank Act addresses the conflict minerals issue is that it instructs the U.S. Department of State to develop a strategy to address "the linkages between human rights abuses, armed groups, mining of conflict minerals and commercial products," and to create a map detailing conflict minerals in the DRC. In particular the map is intended to provide up-to-date and publicly available information about what mines, routes, and facilities are considered to be under the control of armed groups. Third, it requires the Comptroller General of the United States and the Secretary of Commerce to provide baseline and ongoing reporting of commercial activities in conflict minerals, including notably by companies not required to file reports with the SEC.

iii. Relation to PRR framework The U.S. conflict minerals legislation reflects a number of challenges and goals of the PRR framework and Guiding Principles. As Taylor (2011) notes, section 1502 is early indication that they have begun taking root. Its incorporation of the know-and-show style due diligence, auditing, and reporting approach quite clearly comport with Ruggie's vision of a human rights due diligence norm. Section 1502 is likely evidence that human rights due diligence has entered the "norm cascade" phase of the norm life cycle in international relations (Finnemore and Sikkink, 1998; Ruggie, 2013).[5] Moreover, the Congress and the SEC are clearly limited in what they can do to extend regulatory efforts extraterritorially. Yet, as Ruggie has argued, domestic measures that force companies that are listed on a country's stock exchanges to report on a variety of risks, regardless of where the risks are incurred, can have extraterritorial implications without charging headlong into the controversial nature of the direct regulation of actors or actions that take place extraterritorially (Ruggie, 2013).

In essence, section 1502 and the SEC's final rule forces the dissemination of information that is otherwise difficult or impossible to discover. Trade in conflict minerals is not prohibited or sanctioned in any way. Rather, the filings and reports by covered companies, the Secretary of State, Comptroller General, and the Secretary of Commerce are intended to distribute information about the use and exploitation of conflict minerals up the supply chain and, ultimately, to the consumer. The SEC rule recognizes that government entities are not always in the best position to extract information on the ground. As such, it anticipates that an independent and interconnected system of public and private regulative actors will need to assist in that work, bringing to bear their greater technical capacities and expertise. In other words, it relies on the development of a polycentric system of which the legislation and regulation are only part. The other components of this network are discussed in the following sections.

2. Subnational level state actor: State and municipal enactments

Following enactment of the section 1502, at least two states and several cities have enacted complementary legislation aimed at reducing their exposure to human rights risks associated with conflict minerals. Maryland's State Procurement and Congo Conflict Minerals Bill (2012) prohibits state government units from knowingly procuring supplies or services from any company that has failed to comply with section 1502. Likewise, California's legislation, an amendment to a public contracting act focusing on the genocide in Darfur, denies companies that are noncompliant with section 1502 the right to bid on contracts to provide goods or services to a state agency (California Public Contracting Code).

The Massachusetts House of Representatives is currently considering a similar procurement bill, prohibiting any "scrutinized company" from bidding or submitting a proposal for a contract for goods or services with a state agency. "Scrutinized company" is defined as a company:

> that is required to disclose information relating to conflict minerals originating in the Democratic Republic of the Congo, or its adjoining countries, pursuant to [section 1502] … , where the [company] has filed an 'unreliable determination,' … reported false information in their report … , or failed to file a report … and which the [SEC] has, upon the completion of the commission's processes, determined that [the company] has made a report that does not satisfy the requirements of due diligence described. (In section 1502 (*An Act Relative to Congo*, 2013))

Some cities, such as Pittsburgh and St. Petersburg, have passed resolutions calling on companies in their cities to engage in due diligence and to take any necessary remedial steps to remove from their supply chains any conflict minerals that fund armed groups. Pittsburg's Proclamation (2011) additionally declared its support for the development of international certification systems to ensure minerals from Central Africa are not contributing to conflict.

These enactments and proclamations reinforce the norms related to due diligence and reporting on conflict minerals. They also address one of the priorities that Ruggie enumerated in his 2010 report to the Human Rights Council to help bridge the coherence-based governance gaps, namely that governments should consider human rights when they do business with business (U.N. Special Representative of the Secretary-General, 2010).

3. National level state actors: Other national laws

Other countries have given some indication of following the lead of the U.S. with regard to domestic legislation like section 1502. For instance, in March 2013, Canadian MP Paul Dewar introduced a bill that would impose due diligence and reporting requirements similar to section 1502. For instance, Bill C-486 (2013) would require Canadian corporations that have "processed, purchased, traded in, used or extracted a designated [conflict] mineral, or contracted to do so" to "exercise due diligence in respect of any extraction, processing, purchasing, trading in or use of designated [conflict] minerals that it carries out in the course of its activities, or that it contracts to have carried out." Such companies would be required to submit reports to the Minister of Foreign affairs and publish them on their websites. The reports would include a description of the due diligence process and would be required to be independently audited by a third party.

Similarly, in March 2013, the Directorate-General for Trade for the European Union commenced a public consultation to explore the possibility of an EU initiative similar to section 1502. A public questionnaire was opened to solicit views on an initiative for responsible sourcing of conflict minerals. The questionnaire sought feedback on whether a due diligence and reporting framework should be adopted. In addition, the questionnaire asked whether an EU conflict minerals initiative should operate in the same manner as the EU Timber Regulation. The consultation was completed in June 2013, and the contributions will be published online. The results of the questionnaire are likely to be used to determine whether and how to reasonably and effectively support ongoing due diligence initiatives related to conflict minerals (Wallerstedt, 2013).

4. Intergovernmental actors: OECD guidance

The SEC rule implementing section 1502 requires that companies use a nationally or internationally recognized due diligence framework to conduct their conflict mineral due diligence. The rule specifies that, at the time of its adoption, the Organisation for Economic Co-operation and Development ("OECD") had issued the only known internationally recognized framework that would allow companies to comply with the rule (Conflict Minerals, 2012). Thus, this section will describe the OECD and its due diligence framework.

The OECD is an intergovernmental economic organization consisting of 34 of the most developed nations in the world who are all committed to democratic government and the market economy. Another 25 non-member countries participate as regular observers or full participants in

OECD committees. Some 50 non-members are less extensively engaged in other OECD activities. The OECD is "a forum in which governments can work together to share experiences and seek solutions to common problems," with the mission to "promote policies that will improve economic and social well-being of people around the world" (About the OECD, n.d.). The OECD, thus, focuses mostly on the generation of knowledge and best practices. Its consensus-based programs are typically non-binding but are meant to be dispersed and adopted to the extent that member and non-member states have the political will to do so. Because of the collective and individual influence and global market power of the member states, OECD programs and standards tend to be adopted broadly and exert significant influence (Backer, 2013).

Relevant to this discussion, the OECD has long provided leadership by example in the promulgation of corporate governance initiatives. For instance, the OECD Principles of Corporate Governance (2004) provide a framework for effective corporate governance, including a chapter devoted to disclosure and transparency. Growing out of this commitment to corporate governance and recognizing the need to provide guidance regarding conflict mineral due diligence in light of the increased attention to the abuses in the DRC, the OECD adopted the Due Diligence Guidance for Responsible Supply Chains of Minerals from Conflict-Affected and High-Risk Areas ("Due Diligence Guidance") in May 2011. Subsequently, in 2012, the Supplement on Gold was developed as a complement to the Due Diligence Guidance, and the Due Diligence Guidance was updated to include references to the Supplement.

The Due Diligence Guidance was developed in concert with representatives of 11 countries of the International Conference on the Great Lakes Region ("ICGLR"), which include Angola, Burundi, Central African Republic, Republic of Congo, DRC, Kenya, Rwanda, Sudan, Tanzania, Uganda, and Zambia. In addition, representatives from industry, civil society, and the U.N. Group of Experts on the DRC consulted in its development. It has received broad-based support from U.N. organizations, including the Security Council; from the ICGLR countries; and at both committee and ministerial levels within the OECD itself. As with most OECD guidance, it is not legally binding, but it has received sufficient OECD endorsement to "reflect[] the common position and political commitment of the OECD members and non-member adherents" (OECD, 2013, p. 4).

The Due Diligence Guidance provides a detailed framework for due diligence for responsible supply chain management of conflict minerals. Due diligence is defined in the guidance as "an on-going, proactive and reactive process through which companies can ensure that they respect human rights and do not contribute to conflict" (OECD, 2013, p. 13). Although a full description of the Due Diligence Guidance is beyond the scope of this chapter, it is worth noting that it provides a five-step framework for risk-based due diligence, which includes: (1) establishing strong company management systems; (2) identifying and assessing risk in the supply chain; (3) defining and implementing a strategy to respond to identified risks; (4) carrying out independent third-party audits of supply chain due diligence at identified points in the supply chain; and (5) reporting on supply chain due diligence. In essence, the Due Diligence Guidance provides the expert guidance for the development and implementation of the due diligence requirements in section 1502 and other regulatory efforts aimed at conflict mineral supply chain management.

Acting independently but with knowledge of the governance efforts of other actors in this space, particularly Congress, the OECD has contributed its broad-based consultation and expertise to provide non-legally binding regulation to the polycentric governance system for conflict minerals. Because the conflict minerals issue represents a challenge to responsible corporate participation in the global economy, the matching principle would suggest that an intergovernmental economic organization ought to be involved in addressing the problems associated with it. However, as discussed in the Conclusion, there is the possibility that the adoption of the Due Diligence Guidance as the only compliant, due diligence, framework under section 1502 will actually stifle the effective functioning of the polycentric governance system by crowding out smaller scale local, regional, or national, due diligence systems that might have been more appropriately tailored to the needs of regulated actors at that scale.

5. Global industry-level non-state actors: GeSI/EICC conflict-free smelter program and IPC due diligence guidance

In addition to state and intergovernmental soft-law actors, purely private industry organizations have been intensely involved in the process of regulating the conflict mineral supply chain. Here I highlight but two examples of organizations that represent collective interests of private commercial interests.

i. Conflict-free smelter program Among the more daunting challenges to implementing any transparency and traceability regime for conflict minerals is the unique nature of the supply chain. To grossly oversimplify a complex process, unrefined minerals and gold come from a huge number of different mines and intermediate sources to smelting companies to be refined into the minerals that are ultimately used in products like electronics. Thus, the smelters represent a choke point in the supply chain. As such, they can play a vital role in helping with the traceability challenges that are inherent in an inquiry of origin process or in performing due diligence. If companies can trace their conflict minerals to specific smelters and those smelters can credibly certify that their inventories of conflict minerals did not finance or benefit armed rebel groups, that substantially lessens the complication of tracing the minerals back to their countries of origin and/or completing the due diligence process. Smelters can do so by knowing where and from whom they source their unrefined stock, keeping track of their inputs, and matching that to their outputs.

Yet, the task is still daunting for any one company to tackle on its own. For instance, after mapping over 90 percent of its supply line for microprocessors between 2009 and 2012, Intel found that it had approximately 200 suppliers, more than 6,000 line items involved, and approximately 140 unique smelters who were engaged in that supply chain (Duran, 2012).

Industry groups have stepped into this gap to assist companies and coordinate cooperative behavior to encourage smelters to be able to credibly assert their conflict free status. Moreover, the groups coordinate cooperative action among mineral buyers and end-users, which helps to lessen the collective action problem that would otherwise arise when noncompliant companies would be willing to source from smelters who do not want to expend the money or effort to become conflict free certified. Without a critical mass of demand and pressure from up the supply chain, insufficient numbers of smelters would have the incentive to cooperate.

In the wake of the move toward conflict mineral regulatory initiatives, the Electronic Industry Citizenship Coalition ("EICC") and the Global e-Sustainability Initiative ("GeSI") joined forces to create the Conflict-Free Sourcing Initiative ("CFSI"). EICC is a coalition of leading electronics companies that coordinate on global supply chain initiatives to improve efficiency and social, ethical, and environmental outcomes. GeSI is a coalition of information and communication technology companies to focus on sustainability issues. Together they spearheaded a working group along with stakeholders in the Automotive Industry Action Group, the Japanese Electronics and Information Technology Industries, and the Retail Industry Leaders Association, among others. This inter-industry working group launched the CFSI in April 2013. It incorporates a Conflict-Free Smelter Program ("CFS Program"), a Conflict Minerals Reporting Template, conflict-free minerals supply chain workshops, conflict minerals training and best practices dissemination, and research on conflict minerals and metals used in the electronics sector (EICC and GeSI, 2013d). By the end November 2013, the growing list of conflict-free tantalum smelters numbered 23 (EICC and GeSI, 2013b), and by early December 2013, 30 gold refiners were certified by the CFS Program (EICC and GeSI, 2013a). While no tungsten smelters had yet achieved compliance, seven tin smelters had gained certification by early November 2013 (EICC and GeSI, 2013c). Compliant smelters and refiners have taken steps to document their sourcing and sales to ensure conflict-free status of their inventories; they also submit to rigorous third-party auditing to ensure their compliance. Thus, becoming conflict-free certified is not cheap.

Individual members of EICC and GeSI developed an "Early Adopters Fund" to incentivize smelters to undergo the certification and audit process. Intel, HP, and the GE Foundation donated $225,000 to the program, which was managed by EICC and RESOLVE, a well-respected NGO that is active in problem solving diverse natural resource, environmental, and public health issues. The Early-Adopters Program promised smelters or refiners that passed their conflict free audit that they would receive reimbursement for half the audit costs, or about $5,000 (Resolve, 2012). This cooperative problem solving is a hallmark of polycentric governance.

ii. IPC due diligence guidelines A number of industry organizations have additionally imparted to their stakeholders education and guidance meant to provide additional support for and uptake of the conflict minerals due diligence norm. As an example of such private stakeholder governance initiative, IPC–Association Connecting Electronics Industries has promulgated Conflict Minerals Due Diligence Guidance. IPC is a global trade organization focused on the electronic interconnection industry. Although its Guidance does little of substance beyond synthesizing the requirements of section 1502 and the guidance provided by the OECD Due Diligence Guidelines, it provides additional education, exposure, and operational capacity to incorporate the investigation, due diligence, and reporting requirements (IPC, 2013).

6. Civil society-level non-state actors: On-the-ground initiatives in the DRC and the Enough Project's conflict-free campus initiative

It should be noted that Ruggie has been criticized for failing to adequately and explicitly include civil society and multi-stakeholder initiatives in the PRR framework (Melish and Meidinger, 2011). He has indicated that their participation is incorporated and assumed in both the second and third pillars of the framework. Perhaps belying that criticism, civil society and NGO activist organizations have had significant influence on the development of section 1502, the complementary state and local legislation, and other initiatives. The Enough Project, for instance, was instrumental in mobilizing grass roots support and providing testimony and anecdotal evidence to support the need for the state-based initiatives. In addition, Enough Project affiliates have spearheaded related small-scale and local initiatives to raise awareness about sourcing of conflict minerals; in particular, the conflict free campus programs that took root at a large number of college and high school campuses, including at 15 campuses where official resolutions encouraging conflict free sourcing have been passed (Participating Schools, n.d.). At the least, these initiatives serve an educative purpose; moreover, they also likely co-opt these educational institutions – themselves influential civil society organizations and market actors – to the polycentric governance project, providing additional opportunities for creative thinking, market pressure, and norm diffusion.

On the other hand, stakeholders on the ground in the DRC have seemingly had less involvement in the conflict minerals regulatory process than one might expect. As the regime has developed, it presents a potential threat, at least in the short term, even to the meager sustenance local populations receive from mining operations, both legitimate and illicit. Indeed, a group of local miners has expressed concern about the effects section 1502 and similar initiatives will have on the ground. Concerns have been raised that the process will have little positive or constructive effect to alleviate the conflict and the concomitant violence and abuse suffered by local populations (Seay, 2012).

There have been initiatives on the ground in the DRC and neighboring countries to assist in traceability efforts from the mine-to-smelter stage of the supply chain. These include the iTSCi Bag and Tag initiative, focused on tin mines; Solutions for Hope, dealing with tantalum mining; and the Public-Private Alliance for Responsible Mineral Sourcing (Resolve, 2012). The extent of their incorporation of in-region communities and organizations is, however, unclear. And, regardless, the instability on the ground in the DRC has made these initiatives difficult to sustain. For example, the iTSCi initiative, focused on piloting tin traceability in mines in a couple of regions in eastern DRC, had to be abandoned when the DRC government suspended mining operations in those regions between September 2010 and March 2011 (iTSCi Project Overview, n.d.).

III. CONCLUSION

The PRR framework and the Guiding Principles have been described by Ruggie and others as creating a system of polycentric governance. The implications of what distinguishes a polycentric governance regime from a state-based monocentric governance regime have not been adequately explored in the literature addressing business and human rights. Legal scholars tend to view the polycentrism of the PRR framework through the lens of international law; however, international relations, political science, and institutional design scholars have explicated and applied the concept far beyond its simple application in federalist legal systems. The interplay among the state responsibility to protect against human rights abuses, business's responsibility to respect human rights, and both state and nonstate actors' duty to address and remedy human rights risks and violations as Ruggie has described them provide a fertile ground for applying that broader polycentric governance literature. In particular, the IAD framework developed by the scholars in the Vincent and Elinor Ostrom Workshop in Political Theory and Policy Analysis could help to analyze the application and implementation of the PRR framework and the Guiding Principles.

In the meantime, there is a possible natural experiment in the emerging polycentric governance regime that is focused on stemming human rights abuses in the DRC related to conflict minerals. In this chapter, I have laid out a case study of that nascent governance system. The conflict minerals regime is an intriguing early application of many of the norms and values that animate the PRR framework and Guiding Principles. It has to grapple with the challenges unique to doing business in a conflict-affected area. It attempts to skirt the concerns that accompany the exercise of extraterritorial jurisdiction over actors engaged in potentially harmful acts beyond the boundaries of the home state by regulating domestic actors in a way that has ripple-effect implications in the foreign jurisdiction. It has done so by incorporating the due diligence norm of the second pillar of the PRR framework to require reporting and disclosure of foreign activities, incorporating Ruggie's "know and show" mantra. It implicates the responsibility of state actors to be cognizant of their human rights risks when doing business with business. And it has relied upon a variety of nonstate actors engaged at various levels and scales to fill out the regime and implement the traceability and due diligence norms. As such its success (or failure) may augur well (or poorly) for the future of the PRR framework and Guiding Principles as a polycentric approach to regulating business and human rights.

Still, it is worth considering whether the conflict minerals regime has been hindered by the central position section 1502 of the Dodd-Frank Act has occupied. As the driver of much of the above-described activity in the conflict minerals space, perhaps the system is more hierarchical than a truly polycentric regime ought to be. If section 1502 dominates and demands the focus and efforts of the other actors in the network, they are then unable to be truly creative in their approach to the problem and are robbed of the ability to make their own rules and develop their own norms within their respective domains of influence. As such, instead of the problem-solving Black (2008) ascribes to polycentric governance systems, perhaps the conflict minerals regime has come to be defined by section 1502's particular solution to the problem. In other words, it is important to determine whether – as occurred in laboratory experiments with externally imposed rules intended to maximize joint returns – section 1502 has "crowded out" alternative creative and cooperative behaviors that would have emerged but for the mandate of an influential state actor. For example, perhaps section 1502 has entrenched the OECD Due Diligence Guidance as the singular standard by which conflict minerals due diligence will be done, even though other local, regional, national, or international organizations might have developed alternative schemes appropriate to their domain of influence.

On the other hand, it might instead be the case that section 1502 provided the vital catalyst to spur cooperative efforts to address the conflict minerals problem. None of the actors described above, save the directly regulated reporting companies, are beholden to Congress on the conflict mineral issue. And Congress is just as reliant on all of them for the due diligence requirement to succeed as anyone. Without the OECD Due Diligence Guidance, for instance, there would be no standard by which the conflict minerals reports could be audited. While the trade groups were no doubt spurred into quick action by the legislation, they have been free from interference from state mandate as to their development of strategies for conflict free smelter certification systems and other traceability initiatives, subjects much more within their domain of influence and expertise than Congress's.

It is clear that this area is ripe for careful application of rigorous theoretical and field work on the optimum design of a polycentric governance system. If the PRR framework and Guiding Principles truly serves as an example and progenitor of polycentric governance, refining the efforts will be vital to its success.

NOTES

1. Vertical incoherence occurs when a state adopts a human rights obligation, for instance through legislation, but fails to give sufficient regard or effort to its implementation. Horizontal incoherence occurs when states regulate in one area in isolation (e.g., securities regulation or labor) with little regard for how that interacts with or effects regulatory efforts elsewhere in the government (Ruggie, 2009).
2. As an initial matter, only companies that are publicly traded via a listing on a U.S. stock exchange are subject to the rule, as only they are governed by the periodic reporting requirements of the Securities and Exchange Act of 1934. Therefore, privately held corporations and, obviously, corporations not listed and traded in the U.S. are not subject to the conflict minerals legislation or the SEC's rule.
3. If such a company proceeds to the due diligence process in the third step and, through that process, determines that the origin of the conflict minerals was not a covered country or that the conflict minerals came from recycled or scrap material, it does not have to complete the third step. Rather, it can simply complete the specialized disclosure and briefly describe its reasonable country of origin inquiry and the due diligence efforts that led to its conclusion that the conflict minerals were not from the covered countries.
4. The rule provides a two-year transition period (four years for smaller companies) during which companies may certify their conflict minerals "DRC conflict undeterminable" either because they are unable to determine whether their conflict minerals that originated in the covered countries financed or benefited armed rebel groups or because their reasonable country of origin inquiry gave them reason to believe the conflict minerals may have originated in the covered countries and the due diligence failed to provide additional clarification as to whether they financed or benefited armed rebel groups. Reports that conclude "DRC conflict undeterminable" during the transition period need not be audited, but must file their report along with a description of steps the company will take or has taken to mitigate the risk that their conflict minerals will benefit armed groups (Conflict Minerals, 2012).
5. In contrast, the relative paucity of nationally or internationally recognized due diligence frameworks that can be used by companies to comply with the SEC rule and the resistance that business groups have exhibited to the due diligence requirement are both evidence that the human rights due diligence norm has not advanced to the internalization stage, where the norm takes on a taken-for-granted quality. Indeed, the National Association of Manufacturers, the Chamber of Commerce of the United States of America, and the Business Roundtable unsuccessfully resorted to the federal court system in an attempt to invalidate the SEC rule (*National Association of Manufacturers v. SEC*, 2013).

REFERENCES

About the OECD (n.d.), *OECD,* retrieved from http://www.oecd.org/about/.

Adler, J.H. (2005), 'Jurisdictional mismatch in environmental federalism', *New York University Environmental Law Journal*, *15*(1), 130–78.

An Act Relative to Congo Conflict Minerals. Massachusetts House Bill No. 2989, doc. no. 599 (January 13, 2013).

Backer, L.C. (2011), 'On the evolution of the United Nations' "protect-respect-remedy" project: the state, the corporation and human rights in a global governance context', *Santa Clara Journal of International Law*, *9*(1), 37–80.

Backer, L.C. (2013, February 2), 'Part 1; The U.S. national contact point – corporate social responsibility between nationalism, internationalism and private markets based globalization', *Law at the End of the Day*, retrieved from http://lcbackerblog.blogspot.com/2013/02/part-1-us-national-contact-point.html.

Bill C-486: An Act respecting corporate practices relating to the extraction, processing, purchase, trade and use of conflict minerals from the Great Lakes Region of Africa. (2013). 1st Reading March 26, 2013, 41st Parliament, 1st Session, retrieved from http://www.parl.gc.ca/HousePublications/Publication.aspx?Language=E&Mode=1&DocId=6062040&File=4&Col=1.

Black, J. (2008), 'Constructing and contesting legitimacy and accountability in polycentric regulatory regimes', *Regulation & Governance*, *2*(2), 137–64.

California Public Contracting Code § 10490 Legislative Counsel of California. Retrieved on May 2, 2013, http://leginfo.legislature.ca.gov/faces/codes.xhtml.

Conflict minerals, 17 C.F.R. pts 240 and 249b (2012).

Dodd-Frank Wall Street Reform and Consumer Protection Act §1502, Pub. L. No. 111-203, 124 Stat. 1376–2223 (2010) (codified in scattered sections of the U.S. Code).

Duran, C. (2012), 'Intel and conflict minerals: a journey of learning, challenges and leadership: progress in driving conflict free sourcing', [PowerPoint slides].

EICC and GeSI (2013a, December 9), 'Conflict-free smelter program: Compliant gold refiners list', *The Conflict-Free Sourcing Initiative*, retrieved from http://www.conflictfreesmelter.org/CompliantGoldRefinerList.htm.

EICC and GeSI (2013b, November 25), 'Conflict-free smelter program: Compliant tantalum smelter list', *The Conflict-Free Sourcing Initiative*, retrieved from http://www.conflictfreesmelter.org/CompliantTantalumSmelterList.htm.

EICC and GeSI (2013c, November 11). Conflict-free smelter program: Compliant tin smelter list. *The Conflict-Free Sourcing Initiative*. Retrieved from http://www.conflictfreesmelter.org/CompliantTinSmelterList.htm

EICC and GeSI (2013d), 'EICC and GeSI launch conflict-free sourcing initiative', [Press release], retrieved from HTTP://EICC.INFO/DOCUMENTS/PRCFSILAUNCHFINAL.PDF.

Finnemore, M. and Sikkink, K. (1998), International norm dynamics and political change', *International Organization*, *52*(4), 887–917.

Frey, B.S., and Overholser-Gee, F. (1997), 'The cost of price incentives: an empirical analysis of motivation crowding-out', *American Economic Review*, *87*(4), 746–55.

IPC (2013, February 12), 'New IPC guide spells out electronic manufacturers' conflict minerals due diligence obligations', retrieved from http://www.ipc.org/contentpage.aspx?pageid=new-ipc-guide-spells-out-electronics-manufacturers-conflict-minerals-due-diligence-obligations.

iTSCi Project Overview, *ITRI*, retrieved from https://www.itri.co.uk/index.php?option=com_zoo&task=item&item_id=2192&Itemid=189.

Maryland State Procurement and Congo Conflict Minerals Bill, Md. State Procurement and Congo Conflict Minerals Act, Md. State Fin. & Pro. Code § 14-413 (2013).

McGinnis, M.D. (2005, June), 'Costs and challenges of polycentric governance', retrieved from Vincent and Elinor Ostrom Workshop in Political Theory and Policy Analysis website: http://www.indiana.edu/~workshop/papers/mcginnis_berlin.pdf.

Melish, T.J. and Meidinger, E. (2011), 'Protect, respect, remedy and participate: "new governance" for the Ruggie framework', in R. Mares (ed.), *Business and Human Rights at a Crossroads: The Legacy of John Ruggie* (1–34). Leiden and Boston: Martinus Nijhoff.

National Association of Manufacturers v. SEC, Civil Action No. 13-CV-635(RLW) No. 12-1422 (D.D.C. July 23, 2013).

Ochoa, C. and Keenan, P.J. (2011), 'Regulating information flows, regulating conflict: an analysis of United States conflict minerals legislation', *Goettingen Journal of International Law*, *3*(1), 129–54.

OECD (2004), 'Principles of corporate governance', Paris: OECD.

OECD (2013), 'Due diligence guidance for responsible supply chains of minerals from conflict-affected and high-risk areas', Paris: OECD.

Ostrom, E. (2009, October), 'A polycentric approach for coping with climate change', (World Bank Policy Research Working Paper No. 5095).

Ostrom, E. (2010), 'Polycentric systems for coping with collective action and global environmental change', *Global Environmental Change*, *20*(1), 550–7.

Ostrom, E. (2012), 'Polycentric systems: multilevel governance involving a diversity of organizations', in E. Brousseau, T. Dedeurwaerdere, P. Jouvet, and M. Willinger (eds.), *Global Environmental Commons* (pp. 105–25). UK: Oxford University Press.

Participating schools, 'Raise Hope for Congo', retrieved from http://www.raisehopeforcongo.org/content/participating-schools.

Peterman, A., Palermo, T., and Bredenkamp, C. (2011), 'Estimates and determinants of sexual violence against women in the Democratic Republic of Congo', *American Journal of Public Health*, *101*(6), 1060–7.

Prendergast, J., and Lezhnev, S. (n.d.), 'From mine to mobile phone: the conflict minerals supply chain', (White paper). Enough Project, retrieved from: http://www.enoughproject.org/files/publications/minetomobile.pdf.

Proclamation. (April 19, 2011), City Council of Pittsburgh, Pennsylvania. File no. 2011-1639, retrieved from: http://pittsburgh.legistar.com/LegislationDetail.aspx?ID=873982&GUID=53DB676C-7643-4948-A56D-6731D4925634.

Prunier, G. (2010), *Africa's World War: Congo, The Rwandan Genocide, And The Making Of A Continental Catastrophe*, Oxford, UK: Oxford University Press.

Raustiala, K., and Victor, D. (2004), 'The regime complex for plant genetic resources', *International Organization. 58*(2), 277–309, doi:10.10170/S0020818304582036.

Reeson, A.F., and Tisdell, J.G. (2008), 'Institutions, motivations and public goods: an experimental test of motivational crowding', *Journal of Economic Behavior and Organization*, *68*(1), 273–81.

Resolve (2012, April 3), 'Intel, HP, GE Foundation create fund to encourage participation in conflict-free smelter program', [press release], retrieved from http://www.resolv.org/wp-content/uploads/2012/04/cfs-early-adopters-fund-launch-press-release-final.pdf

Ruggie, J.G. (2013), *Just Business: Multinational Corporations and Human Rights*, New York, NY: W.W. Norton & Co.

Ruggie, J.G. (2011), 'Berne declaration interview with John Ruggie', retrieved from http://www.business-humanrights.org/media/documents/berne-declaration-interview-ruggie-nov-2011.pdf.

Ruggie, J.G. (2009, January), '*Keynote Address*', presented at the third annual responsible investment forum, New York, NY, retrieved from: http://198.170.85.29/Ruggie-address-to-Responsible-Invest-Forum-12-Jan-2009.pdf.

Schrank, D. (2010, Fall), 'Tin fever', *Virginia Quarterly Review*, *86*(4), 24–47.

Seay, L.E. (2012), 'What's wrong with Dodd-Frank 1502? Conflict minerals, civilian livelihoods, and the unintended consequences of western advocacy', Center for Global Development Working Paper No. 284, retrieved from Center for Global Development website: http://www.cgdev.org/sites/default/files/1425843_file_seay_dodd_frank_final.pdf.

Shackelford, S. (in press), 'Governing the final frontier: a polycentric approach to managing space weaponization and orbital debris', *American Business Law Journal*.

Shackelford, S. (2013), 'Toward cyber peace: managing cyber attacks through polycentric governance', *American University Law Review*, *62*(5), 1273–364.

Taylor, M.B. (2011), 'The Ruggie framework: polycentric regulation and the implications for corporate social responsibility', *Etikki i praksis: Nordic Journal of Applied Ethics* *5*(1), 9–30.

U.N. Document, 'Norms on the responsibilities of transnational corporations and other business enterprises with regard to human rights', U.N. Document E/CN.4/Sub.2/2003/12/Rev.2 (2003).

U.N. Security Council (28 October 2005), 5296th Meeting, Resolution 1635 (2005) [On the Situation Concerning the Democratic Republic of Congo*]*. (S/RES/1635)..

U.N. Special Representative of the Secretary-General (2008, April), 'Protect, respect, remedy: a framework for business and human rights: report of the special representative of the secretary-general on the issue of human rights and transnational corporations and other business enterprises, delivered to the human rights council', U.N. Document A/HRC/8/5.

U.N. Special Representative of the Secretary-General (2010, April), 'Business and human rights: further steps toward the operationalization of the "protect, respect and remedy" framework: report of the special representative of the secretary-general on the issue of human rights and transnational corporations and other business enterprises, delivered to the human rights council', U.N. Document A/HRC/14/27.

Wallerstedt, K. (2013, April 4), 'EU and Canada consider conflict minerals rules', *3e Company Blog*, retrieved from http://3ecompany.com/blog/?p=172.

9. Feeding the world beyond 2050: A coordinated approach to preserving agricultural innovation and the human right to food

Daniel R. Cahoy

In 2005, the United Nations' Food and Agriculture Organization (FAO) held a meeting on the outlook for agricultural production in the year 2050. The resulting studies have been periodically updated, most recently in 2012 (Alexandratos and Bruinsma, 2012). The object was to identify issues and dangers in future food supplies, but also more broadly to assess whether we can meet global needs in 50 years. One conclusion was that the ability of the world to sustain continued population growth is highly connected to the likelihood of future advances. We simply cannot feed a predicted global population of over 9 billion people in 2050 with current agricultural technology (some of which was actually developed hundreds of years ago). In addition, the threat of climate change means that many growing regions will experience the pressure of hotter, more arid environments. The ability to ameliorate those challenges with technology may be the only way to sustain an adequate supply of food. Technology is as connected with future agriculture as physics is with space travel.

Thankfully, technology has a proven record of advancing agricultural production. While the use of technology in agriculture spans human history – encompassing animal and plant selection, breeding and other growth and reproduction strategies (Nicholson, 2003) – the advent of new technologies permitting manipulation on a genetic level has accelerated the rate of change dramatically. The impact has similarly expanded and it is fair to say that modern life is highly dependent on high technology means of producing food (Charles, 2002).

Of course, advances in food-related technology are generally not the result of altruism. A profit potential underlies much of the recent growth. Although government funding can facilitate a floor for basic research, private investment is critical to the creation of advanced commercial products and markets. However, it is understood that the investment in innovation may produce insufficient returns if competitors are able to utilize resulting inventions from the outset. Therefore, innovators seek a legal means of excluding others from valuable innovation for as long as possible. The primary mechanism for such protection is intellectual property (IP) rights.

Intellectual property protections are provided by a variety of different types of legal regimes, and in the context of agricultural technology, patents and trade secrets are particularly important players. Given the investment necessary to invent in the biotechnology arena, IP rights are viewed as essential assets (Nicholson, 2003). But the application of IP rights can have a negative side as well. When important innovations are locked up from general public access, even for a short period of time, the result may be increased prices and reduced access. Age-old practices like saving seeds for future planting may be newly curtailed. Individual farmers and developing regions may be disadvantaged if access is not reasonably available. Biodiversity could be compromised through the use of narrower, proprietary technologies. In general, there is a balance to be achieved between innovation incentives and access to technology, and the application of IP rights to agricultural production creates one of the most central battlefields.

Limitations on access to agricultural technology may contravene our desire to satisfy essential human needs. Food is something so basic to existence that it is described in the language of human rights. Article 25 of the Universal Declaration of Human Rights (UDHR) states that "Everyone has the right to a standard of living adequate for the health and well being of himself and his family, including food … ." Article 11 of the International Covenant on Economic, Social and Cultural Rights (ICESCR) includes similar language with the accompanying obligation to "ensure an equitable distribution of world food supplies in relation to need." Because IP may pose a barrier to access and distribution of food, such human rights may be at stake (UN Special Rapporteur on the Right to Food (SRRF), 2009). But this conflict has only recently begun to receive consideration.

The resolution to the human rights and invention-incentive conflict will likely emerge only as the result of interactions of multiple stakeholders. Governments must consider when human rights needs should trump property incentives. Firms should utilize mechanisms that increase access and preserve profit. And investors and activists should credit business behavior that considers human rights implications. A roadmap for evaluating human rights concerns and business needs can be found in the work of the Special Representative to the UN Secretary General (SRSG) John Ruggie. Appointed to produce a workable (and broadly acceptable) set of considerations in 2005, Ruggie and his team generated several reports culminating in the 2011 Guiding Principles (UN SRSG, 2011). The Principles create responsibilities for governments, firms and other stakeholders to ensure that protecting human rights is shared activity. While the consideration of IP constraints does not appear to have been at the forefront of considerations when the Principles were drafted, there is much in the decision criteria that is applicable.

This chapter begins by providing an overview of the need for new technology and the application of IP to protect agricultural innovation. It considers the most important rights in international markets and describes their advantages and challenges when applied to food. Next, the chapter considers the access issues created by IP. It frames the concern in the context of the human right to adequate food. The chapter then considers how the Guiding Principles can help ensure that the human right to adequate food can be satisfied in the current trade-oriented international IP framework. The chapter concludes that IP impacts on the future of food production could be significant and it is better to plan for the relief valves now rather that wait for problems to arise.

I. RISING FOOD PRESSURE AND THE IMPORTANCE OF TECHNOLOGY

From the beginning of recorded history, the challenge of attaining sufficient supplies of food and water has been a primary focus of society. When periods of relative food stability did exist, more complex societies could form (Miller and Wetterstrom, 2012). But when political chaos and disease suppress organized production and plentiful food sources, humans fall back to focusing on subsistence agriculture as the core reason for societal interaction. Learning, invention and communication become transfixed on survival, and food is the center. It is no accident that food is the core of a society's culture and identity.

In recent years, the world has achieved an amazing degree of productivity in agriculture. More food is produced each year (FAO, 2013a) and the demands of the world's population could theoretically be satisfied (if not for other issues that prevent fully equitable food distribution). But the status quo is not sufficient for the future. The world's population continues to rise, and the food production must continue to grow as well. The FAO estimates that food production will increase by 60 percent to feed the population in 2050 (Alexandratos and Bruinsma, 2012). Other estimates are even higher. In any case, it is clear that productivity must increase.

A. Will Current Food Production Methods Fail us in the Future?

Today, there are warnings that our fortune with food may not last. The world's growing population demands greater production from the land. Some countries have little room to expand agricultural use and must depend on greater production or food imports. Moreover, for some types of food, like essential cereal crops, production fluctuates year to year (FAO, 2013b). Perhaps the world cannot keep up.

Some say that we have already experienced a global food shortage event in the new millennium. A shockwave reverberated around the world in 2008 when food prices for basic cereals rose along energy prices (UN-DESA, 2011). Many believed that the use of foodstocks for biofuels were to blame. Although biofuels – particularly those made from corn – are not derived from the same crops that produce human food, a connection could be intuited. Unrest ensued and calls for greater food security erupted. The lasting impact turned out to be relatively minor, and the crisis may have been exaggerated to some extent. Nevertheless, the strong reaction is a warning for the future.

Of course, warnings about adequate food for a growing population are not new. Over 200 ago, Thomas Robert Malthus forewarned of an earth doomed to face starvation as population swarmed capacity (Malthus, 1798/2008). But these predictions did not come true. Malthus could not have known the extent to which modern agriculture would transform the productivity of farmland. Food production has increased dramatically over the last 50 years, and there is a perception that it could continue to keep up should the current environment persist. While there is certainly starvation and malnutrition in the world, the perception is that such suffering is most often caused by distribution problems and outright criminal behavior. The FAO has stated that, if current trends persist, it is in fact likely that we could meet the 60 percent production increase needed by 2050 (Alexandratos and Bruinsma, 2012).

But the unknowns are frightening. Most concerning is the possibility that climate change could radically alter the environment (Gillis, 2013). As the earth warms, formerly fertile lands may become arid. Conversely, altered weather patterns may lead to flooding of healthy farmland, foster disease or disturb normal crop growth patterns. In addition to a morphing climate, limits on available water could interfere with necessary irrigation. Currently, the greatest demand on the water supply is agriculture.

But demand on existing water supplies in many areas may force leaders to shift away from local food irrigation in favor of water used for human consumption. And finally, the supply of energy in the future is an open question. Energy and modern agriculture are highly connected. The natural gas revolution in the U.S. has relieved some pressure, but developing countries like China and India appear to be more than making up for any savings. The possible pitfalls may sound like a far-fetched parade of horribles, but some believe we are already beginning to see effects.

B. Technology to the Rescue

In the same way that new farming methods, better seeds and agricultural chemicals transformed food production in the last 100 years, many believe that technology can once again be our savior. Invention can play an even bigger role in increasing production from each piece of land. For example, it is possible to genetically engineer some types of plants to be more resistant to heat and drought. Better resistance to insects and weeds can allow more to grow on less land. More efficient water transportation methods can preserve irrigation in water-challenged environments. And environmentally friendly fuels can create sustainably energy for planting, harvesting and transport. Even in the face of great environmental pressure, the products of a serious research and development program may continue to boost production.

Will technology suffice? In a review of existing research on the use of technology to close "yield gaps" (the difference in the yield potential for land and the actual yield), Fischer, Byerlee and Edmeades (2011) considered the impact on rice, wheat and maize. They concluded that there are certainly gains to be made with technology that have not yet been realized. Fischer et al. state that genetic enhancement for climate stress tolerance in addition to conservation tillage and conventional breeding could do much to close the gap and increase productivity.

Although there is reticence to a more liberal use of genetic modification, it is likely that greater acceptance will follow need. Fischer et al. suggest that promoting genetic technology should be a policy initiative. The same follows with other technologies that can contribute to food production. Because we may have reached a point of diminishing returns on traditional agriculture methods and materials, high technology will be necessary if future pressures occur as predicted. The issue then turns to technology ownership and access. Who will control the future technology of food?

C. Building a Comprehensive Fence with Property Rights

The useful inventions that underlie technological progress can be protected by the most powerful and fundamental of IP rights: the patent. Patents are granted under the legal systems of almost every nation. In fact, participation in the global economy is strongly linked to the offering of a fairly standard array of patent rights. Since 1883, with the signing of the Paris Convention for the Protection of Industrial Property, nations have come together to harmonize their approaches to IP. With the recent adoption of the Trade-Related Aspects of Intellectual Property Agreement (TRIPS), which is a core criterion for membership in the World Trade Organization, the availability of patent protection has become even more standardized (TRIPS, 1994).

Generally stated, patents protect new and useful inventions, which may include articles of manufacture, methods or systems, and improvements to existing technology. Creating an incentive to fund research and development is the intellectual core of the patent system. Through the conveyance of a property right that permits an owner to charge monopoly rents, a sufficient return on investment that justifies research and development (R&D) risks may be realized. However, it is important to note that patents have an additional societal advantage, one that is not necessarily appropriable by the owner. Patents are extremely effective in disseminating information. The public nature of granted patents ensure that the information claimed (as well as contextual background) is available for all to see. Moreover, the relatively short patent term ensures that inventors eventually dedicate their creation to the public. In the short term, they also encourage designing around, which is also assumed to accelerate technological development.

Firms, universities and individuals are increasingly relying on patents as a means of protecting innovation in agricultural biotechnology. The impact of patents in the field has expanded in recent years, and the trend is international in nature (SRRF, 2009). It is clear that a basic competence in patents is now required to navigate the modern agricultural landscape.

What is the result of the increasing prevalence of utility patents in agricultural biotechnology? In short, the market has been transformed. Utility patents have the capacity to convey great power in green biotechnology for two important reasons: (1) the nature of invention is more siloed, similar to broader fields of biotechnology and pharmaceuticals and (2) there is significant consolidation of rights that permits a few large firms to use them more effectively dominate the market (Cahoy and Glenna, 2009). In general, there is less product cross-over in inventions.

Or, considered inversely, an agricultural biotechnology product is generally covered by only a few patents as opposed to the hundreds that apply to mobile communications technology products like cell phones. This means that the relevant patents for a particular application can be more readily identified. Additionally, patent rights overall are more consolidated, meaning that large players have a great ability to manipulate the environment. The impact of these two factors is that agricultural biotechnology products that are available are highly constrained by IP rights. Additionally, products in the field are developed with less competition and are sold in a market with fewer alternatives.

Ultimately, the patent connection may result in higher prices for consumers, which is the downside of the propertization of agricultural biotech innovation. In addition, coordination problems can result notwithstanding the fact that agricultural biotechnology is nominally more consolidated than other fields. Although patents may provide the fuel for the most far-reaching and world-changing agricultural inventions, those same rights can keep such inventions out of the hands of the most vulnerable populations. Thus, any discussion of the benefits of patents should include some consideration of the access limitations.

One often-cited example of patent barriers is the underutilization of a genetically engineered crop known as golden rice (Potrykus, 2010). The rice was specifically engineered to provide high levels of Vitamin A, which would provide substantial nutritional benefits to populations in developing nations. However, the maze of 70 patents covering the technology, owned by multiple parties, created licensing issues that made the product significantly less attractive. Eventually, licenses were obtained and pooled, but regulatory hurdles delayed the production of the rice. To date, golden rice has had very little global impact.

In most countries, an additional protection available for plants and their respective germ plasma is plant variety protection. This unique form of IP is directed to the phenotypic distinctiveness of asexually reproduced plants. Plants of a particularly morphology and appearance are protected from sale, production, export, etc., without the authority of the breeder. Stemming from the UPOV treaty in 1961 (International Convention for Protection of New Varieties of Plants, 1961 (UPOV)), several nations adopted protection for new varieties of plants in order to create incentives for breeders.

One of the most important reasons to consider plant variety protection is that some countries exclude such material from patent rights. Most notable is the European Patent Convention, which does not allow utility patents on plants (Convention on the Grant of European Patents, 2010

(EPC), art. 53(b)). Importantly, plant variety protection generally contains several enforcement exceptions that do not exist in traditional patent law such as seed saving. Seed saving occurs when a farmer retains seeds from a previous year's harvest to propagate future crops. It is potentially a way to keep costs down for individual famers, and particularly relevant when protected seeds are used to grow foods. However, seed saving is an optional exception under the 1991 revision of UPOV (UPOV, 1991). Many countries have created legislation that complies with this revision, and others have considered it. The U.S. currently permits seed saving (Plant Variety Protection, 2006, § 2543), but this protection is somewhat hollow given the preference for patent protection over germ plasm. Moreover, companies are not sitting still on UPOV exemptions. The economic consequence of such rights has prompted companies to consider implementing stopgaps such as hybrid or terminator (or GURT) technology that precludes simple saving (Torrance, 2012).

Additional property rights impacting food include trade secret protection (NCCUSL, 1986) and narrow plant patents covering cultivated plants capable of asexual reproduction (e.g., Plant Patent Act of 1930). Together, such rights can convey great control of the agricultural marketplace.

II. HOW A CONFLICT ARISES BETWEEN FOOD INNOVATION AND ACCESS

Global trends point to the increased interaction of IP rights and agricultural biotechnology. More innovations are subject to patent rights, and those rights are being extended to more countries around the world (OECD, 2008). Despite the cautions, there appears to be a greater effort to propertize agricultural innovation. In many cases, the concern is emerging after the rights are set in place. Intellectual property rights are privately owned, and an understanding of how such rights impact the public space is an understudied and in many cases poorly understood phenomenon. But despite the lack of oversight, the ascendancy continues.

The closer relationship may have benefits in terms of increased output and firm profits, but also increased risks in terms of access. Policy makers will have to determine the extent to which greater exceptions are necessary to provide low-cost access or address emergencies. The significance of these assessments will only increase as the world faces increased pressure from population growth and climate change. It is therefore critical that the convergence of IP and agricultural technology becomes the subject of study at national and global levels. Reaction should come from a standpoint of social good, which at base is the rationale supporting the existence of IP rights in the first place.

A. Systematic Replacement of Unprotected Food Sources

One of the most amazing aspects of the biotechnology revolution in agriculture is the speed at which conventional crops can be replaced. According to the USDA's Economic Research Service, genetically modified soybeans constitute over 90 percent of planted crops in the U.S. (USDA, 2012). Cotton and corn are over 70 percent (USDA, 2012). The situation is less striking in the rest of the world where genetically modified foods have faced greater resistance. But it is fair to say that adoption of genetically modified crops and other proprietary enhancement/control technologies is spreading across the globe (Endres and Goldsmith, 2007).

A concern with the increasing dominance of proprietary technology is that non-modified crops and food will slowly dwindle. Farmers may be left with little choice but to purchase proprietary materials, particularly in times of crisis. The problem can even be recapitulating, as less genetically diverse proprietary food supplies are more likely to be impacted by disease or climate change, requiring the use of replacement proprietary technology. Essentially, as the production of food becomes a more corporate endeavor, it is likely that high technology enhancements will become so integrated that they are impossible to avoid. Utilization of IP is the default rather than the exception.

B. Possibility of Increased Prices as a Result of High Technology Dominance

The nature of IP is competition exclusion and the natural consequence of such exclusion is increased prices. Indeed, the potential for monopoly pricing is generally deemed the reward for engaging in innovation. Moreover, many innovators at least claim to count on the profits from a price premium to fund their broader R&D programs. Rather than a windfall, higher prices are supposed to be the return that justifies the investment.

The exchange is that, following the expiration of the property right, the public gains access to the invention and can utilize it without the need to compensate the inventor. The short-term pricing barrier is replaced by a long-term contribution to knowledge that might not have occurred if not for the profit incentive (Landes and Posner, 2003). Of course, that theory is based on the idea that inventors create in anticipation of gaining rights rather than simply seeking coverage for those ideas that would have been produced in the normal course of business. Many question the extent to which the ideal situation occurs in practice (and it is likely that the answer is industry-dependent).

At any rate, in the short term, it is generally acknowledged that IP leads to higher prices and less public control over uses. The correlation has been most commonly demonstrated by the drop-off in prices following patent expiration. In the pharmaceutical industry, the price differences before and after generic entry are significant (Huckfeld and Knittel, 2011). The price differential is likely to be substantially less in industries that are not so patent dependent when alternatives exist. Currently, the food industry may be largely in the non-patent influenced state. But that state is likely to change as technology becomes more integrated.

One common complaint against monopoly pricing in the context of essential goods is that a decent return on investment could often be captured at a level lower than market demand. In other words, if one were to take into account the actual firm inputs as well as the contribution of public research investment, the *necessary* recoupment price may be less than the market value. Such arguments are often put forward in the context of essential medicines but they reasonably apply to advanced food technology as well. Governments often fund basic research, and the private IP owner's contribution to R&D may be only a percentage of the total sunk costs. Thus, the "reasonable" price may be significantly less than the value to the public. However, there are at least two cogent counterarguments. One is that the majority of overall R&D spending in agriculture is provided by the private sector, suggesting that government investment is not the central contributor (Alston, James, Anderson and Pardey, 2010). Another is that one success can fund many failures. A rational R&D program invests in IP like a lottery ticket – firms hope for a small percentage of successes that can command the highest prices in order to support a broader product portfolio. From that perspective, companies are morally justified in squeezing every penny out of the buying public.

Another influence on high prices is the fact that effective bargaining may be suppressed by multi-firm interactions. Intellectual property barriers can come from disparate sources and be difficult to address through single-company negotiation. One product may employ many different technologies, and several companies may own those technologies. This concept of overlap can lead to gridlock that can preclude certain innovations from coming to market (Heller, 2010). More commonly, companies are willing to license, but the stacking of various rights can create a fee base that is not easily reduced in response to emergent need.

C. The Danger of Exhaustion and Access Limitation

An IP owner is not, of course, required to charge higher prices to everyone. In fact, there are many examples in which IP owners provide low-cost options for those of limited means. For example, in the context of pharmaceuticals, companies often manage discount programs that deliver low-cost drugs to impoverished citizens of least developed countries (Buckley, 2011). Outright donations occur as well. It is entirely reasonable to assume that, no matter how connected IP rights become with food, access will still exist for many.

One reason for low-cost options is of course simply the fact that market conditions demand it. IP owners are aware of the profit potential in emerging markets. But capturing those profits generally involves offering products at prices significantly below those set in developed markets. Firms may even choose to license local manufacture and distribution in order to gain greater access to markets. In many cases, this may be an attempt to generate additional profits, but in others, it may simply be evidence of forgoing profits in some markets in the name of good global citizenship.

The willingness of IP owners to provide low-cost options is generally highly related to market segmentation. In other words, the ability to engage in legal price discrimination ensures that profits in developed markets can sustain the company. If discounted products from developing countries are imported into the developed market, they can undermine the firm's profit scheme. Note that this is true even if the discounted products are not "generic," but rather produced by the IP owner itself. The ability to segment pricing is key to access in the face of strong IP rights.

Interestingly, the extent to which price discrimination is possible differs from country to country. The power depends on the IP owner's ability to enforce rights locally over goods first sold abroad. This ability conflicts with the principle of "exhaustion": the notion that once a product embodying an IP right is sold, it may then be resold without further restraint (Cahoy, 2011). Due to this principle, price discrimination within a single country is often difficult to accomplish without additional access barriers. However, exhaustion is not as powerful internationally. Some countries like the U.S. may follow a policy of national exhaustion. Others, like the EU, follow a policy of regional exhaustion. If a sale occurs outside of the country or region, the rights are sill in full force within the country or region and low-cost importation can be restricted.

There is a considerable backlash against limiting exhaustion and there are signs that its future enforcement may be in danger. Many believe that when a sale compensates an IP owner, no further compensation is required simply because the product moves across borders. The U.S. has been the stage for one of the most recent curtailments of exhaustion principles in the context of copyright. In *Kirtsaeng v. Wiley* (2013), the Supreme Court reviewed the case of a college student who imported textbooks from overseas for sale in the U.S. The textbooks contained generally the same written material as those marketed in the U.S., but were sold for a significant discount overseas. The publisher, Wiley, asserted that importing the textbooks violated its U.S. copyrights that were not exhausted overseas (through a doctrine known as "first sale" in copyright). The Supreme Court disagreed and held that a product sold under the authority of the copyright owner in another country exhausted the rights of the owner in the U.S. It is reasonable to consider whether the Supreme Court's reasoning could apply to rights like patents. Patent exhaustion is a common law rule in the U.S., and it is possible that the Supreme Court's recent view may signal a change in legal doctrine that embraces a principle of international exhaustion.

Even more complicated in the context of self-replicating technologies like many in agricultural biotech is the notion that new generations may be considered new copies. According the recent Supreme Court decision in *Bowman v. Monsanto* (2013), such new copies are not subject to the exhaustion triggered by the sale of the previous copy. The case involved a farmer who purchased patented "Roundup Ready" soybean seeds from a grain elevator outside Monsanto's usual licensing system. Typically, such seeds would be used as animal feed or for industrial use. However, Bowman planted the seeds and selected those with the patented genetic trait by applying Roundup. He then collected the seeds for further planting. Monsanto argued that such use is merely unauthorized "making" of the invention in violation of the patent right. The Supreme Court agreed, finding that control over future propagation is important to maintaining invention incentives in products like seeds. The case's applicability to other self-replicating products is less clear (and specifically not decided in the opinion) (p. 1769).

It is possible that the consequences of a loss of price discrimination power would be lower prices for all. That is certainly what many expected in the wake of the *Kirtsaeng* decision. However, it is also likely that IP owners will simply charge higher prices across the board or restrict sales in countries in which the market cannot bear developed-country prices. The result may be significantly less access. Such a future would be problematic for something as essential as food, and the need to address access restrictions will become more pressing.

D. Patents May Preclude Follow-On Innovation in Food

New varieties of crops, better agrochemicals and more efficient production systems may only arise through experimentation and the desire to build upon existing technology. However, when patents cover the foundational technology, researchers and end-users may face a wall. The failure to provide a means for those other than the right holder to improve and recombine technology can create a powerful access barrier (Murray and Stern, 2007). It is insidious as well, because it is impossible to know what outcome would result if third-party use was better supported.

In the U.S., the patent statute does not contain an explicit experimental use exception. The courts have carved out a common law exception, but it has been severely limited since the U.S. Court of Appeals for the Federal Circuit's decision in *Madey v. Duke* (2002). That case found a university liable for infringing a former employee's laser patent on the basis that the business of the university is research, thus continued academic use is not simply idle experimentation. Most experimental uses that have a commercial effect – presumably including agribusiness applications – will not be immunized.

Other countries have more robust experimental use defenses, and perhaps this limitation is not as burdensome as restrictions from primary patent use rights (SRRF, 2009). Moreover, the UPOV treaty contains an experimental-use exception. Experimental-use restriction, where it exists, can be viewed as simply another layer on top of the other IP limitations that can restrict access to food.

E. Inadequate Relief Valves

One could argue that limiting access to protected technologies is irrational so long as consumers are willing to pay some price. Generating some profit, no matter how small, seems more desirable in almost every case. However, the interplay of other markets and the loss of discrimination may indeed create incentives for companies to limit sales in some cases. Additionally, when a firm considers its overall product portfolio, it may reasonably choose to favor high-profit products by attempting to limit access to low-cost alternatives. It is possible that companies occasionally use IP rights to bury some technologies. When the technology relates to an item as essential as food, the impact is potentially greater. Even beyond pure exclusion, high prices can create a barrier to access that threatens vulnerable populations. To many, pricing presents the greater challenge, and it is why generic entry is so often welcomed in the pharmaceutical industry.

To guard against undesirable exclusion, IP rights have built-in relief valves. In the context of patents, compulsory licensing for reasonable remuneration can provide a path for greater access. Article 31 of the TRIPS Agreement (1994) permits use without the authorization of the patent owner. It contains some broad rights exceptions, including "national emergency" and "public non-commercial use." TRIPS requires licensing countries to pay adequate remuneration in the context of a license, but the adequacy of such remuneration has never been challenged at the WTO.

Article 17 of the UPOV treaty (1961) on plant variety protection permits contracting parties to restrict the breeder right for the "public interest." In such cases, "equitable remuneration" is required. The U.S. has specifically enacted this compulsory license exception at 7 U.S.C. § 2404, which empowers the Secretary of Agriculture to issue licenses to be compensated at a reasonable royalty at least.

The Convention on Biological Diversity does not explicitly include a provision permitting compulsory licenses. However, Article 16 declares that access and transfers of the technology to developing countries "shall be provided and/or facilitated under fair and most favorable terms." Many read that language to provide a *de facto* compulsory license right, if not an actual legal mechanism.

Thus, IP relief valves exist. But, unfortunately, the relief valves may be inadequate in the context of food technologies. TRIPS permits use within the licensing country but not export. That limitation denies access to a member state that cannot produce the invention domestically. In the context of pharmaceuticals, this limitation was relaxed to allow coordinated export from countries with production resources (WTO, 2003). But it is restricted to pharmaceuticals. To the extent that a country needs to import patented agricultural technology from another country with production capability, the flexibility does not exist. It seems that the breeder's right under the UPOV treaty may permit cross-border collaboration so long as two countries consider it to be in the "public interest." But this interpretation has not apparently been tested.

Beyond the technical exceptions of patent and plant variety protection, the greater limitation is firm pressure against compulsory licensing. Companies and industry groups have in the past treated compulsory licensing as a "breaking" of the rights structure. The US Trade Representative has placed countries on its Special-301 list for inadequate intellectual property protection as a consequence (USTR, 2013). The reaction has somewhat dampened in the essential medicines context due to the extreme pressure of NGOs. However, it is not clear that food technology will necessarily be given such a pass.

III. A COORDINATED APPROACH TO RESOLVING FOOD ACCESS WITH THE GUIDING PRINCIPLES

Historically, governments have been the primary actors for addressing human rights issues such as access to adequate food. But recently, it has become clear that firms can also be important players and can aid in the process, although, they share responsibility and culpability as well. A recent attempt to understand how business and government can coordinate was commissioned by the UN Human Rights Council from Harvard Professor John Ruggie. The resulting reports, produced over a period between 2005 and 2011, constitute the most comprehensive, road-tested and accepted framework to date. It seems reasonable to consider how one might apply this general framework to help resolve the IP–food access debate.

Although Ruggie's reports do not directly address IP issues, they contain action items that clearly apply. Following his prescriptions would lead to more effective protection and stronger participation by the business community. The work calls for government action that would encompass much of the same mechanisms articulated in the access to medicines debate. But it also calls for firm action to proactively identify issues and address them in a manner that minimizes human rights impacts. This shared understanding could be a watershed if actually employed to prepare the world for a future crisis in food.

A. John Ruggie Engages the Business Community as a Human Rights Partner

The notion that firms have human rights responsibilities is a somewhat recent development in international policy. Early efforts were of course directed to simply getting governments to acknowledge responsibility. Following World War II, the UDHR provided a strong but aspirational articulation of human rights principles. Subsequently, more formal national responsibilities resulted from two treaties: (1) the ICESCR, 1966, and (2) the International Covenant on Civil and Political Rights (ICCPR, 1966). Together, these three documents form the international "Bill of Human Rights." However, because the Covenants are agreements between governments, they do not directly impact business behavior. And so questions have arisen as to whether formal business responsibilities for human rights even exist.

While the 1970s brought the Code of Conduct for Transnational Corporations as a statement of firm ideals, it was the 2002 Norms on the Responsibilities of Transnational Corporations and Other Business Enterprises with Respect to Human Rights (UN, 2003) that tried to cement responsibility in the business community. The U.N. Economic and Social Council (ECOSOC) released the Norms to much praise from many governments and human rights advocates. However, they were widely opposed by the business community for their burdensome or ambiguous obligations and the fact that they were created without any sense of buy-in from industry. Eventually, they were declared to have no legal standing (OHCHR, 2004).

Against this backdrop, John Ruggie was engaged as SRSG to clarify standards across interest groups. It quickly became clear that there was little in the way of a shared understanding between NGOs, business and governments about firm responsibility, and Ruggie was compelled to start from scratch. After conducting significant research on evolving human rights standards by engaging the interested parties (Phase I), Ruggie provided an encapsulating framework (Phase II). The framework includes three basic principles: Protect, Respect and Remedy. More specifically, it is (1) the "state responsibility to *protect* against human rights abuses by third parties," (2) the "corporate responsibility to *respect* human rights," and (3) the obligation to provide victims "*access* … to effective remedies" (UN SRSG, 2008). The framework received widespread praise and support, including from members of the business community.

In 2010, Ruggie received the mandate to "operationalize" his framework with specific guidance and recommendations. The Guiding Principles on Business and Human Rights were the result (UN SRSG, 2011). Released in 2011, the report lists 31 sub-principles, each falling within the Protect, Respect and Remedy framework. They are intended to encompass various aspects of business behavior and human rights impacts. All of the principles may not be relevant to a given firm, but it should be possible to review them and identify what guidance is appropriate. Perhaps more importantly, the Guiding Principles provide a shared language that can be used to frame government, industry and third-party interactions.

Although some specific activities are envisioned in the Principles – such as sourcing materials from regions of conflict – the specific contexts of the human right to food or IP access limitations are not mentioned. However, one can find direction in at least three principles. The first, under "Operational Principles," is number 3(a), the state duty to:

> [e]nsure that other laws and policies governing the creation and ongoing operation of business enterprises, such as corporate law, do not constrain but enable business respect for human rights … . (UN SRSG, p. 8, 2011)

This appears applicable to IP rights and access. Granting IP rights does not impact third-party human rights directly; as a negative right, it does not permit one to exercise positive power over another. However, as described above, IP can operate to create human rights issues when access is retrained by availability or cost. This may happen through the primary owner or a downstream licensee. Thus, Guiding Principle 3(a) suggests that states should enact an enforcement regime that allows for human rights relief valves like compulsory licensing.

The next relevant Principle concerns business activity. Principle 13 states that businesses are required to:

> (a) Avoid causing or contributing to adverse human rights impacts through their own activities, and address such impacts when they occur;
>
> (b) Seek to prevent or mitigate adverse human rights impacts that are directly linked to their operations, products or services by their business relationships, even if they have not contributed to those impacts. (UN SRSG, p. 14, 2011)

This suggests that the human rights aspects of IP enforcement should be taken into account by firms. Where enforcement would limit access to a level that human rights are impacted, a firm should investigate options for alleviating the harm. This is true whether access is limited by price or availability.

One mechanism available to firms to increase availability is price discrimination. While it sounds like a negative, it also has the effect of increasing sales by making products available to some consumers who would not pay a premium price. Selling to vulnerable populations at low cost (or no cost) may improve access and not significantly impact profits. In addition, note that, to the extent that price discrimination is squelched by exhaustion, this action of the firm under Principle 13 implicates additional action by the state under Principle 3.

Other Principles relevant to IP-human rights conflicts relate to a firm's due diligence. Principle 17 describes due diligence generally, and Principles 18 and 19 relate to identification (with the help of third parties, if necessary) and reporting. Although assessment and reporting may seem passive, by identifying problems firms are much more likely to be inclined to act. Transparency is acknowledged as a useful tool in financial and sustainability reporting. Even firms with the best of intentions may discover issues of which they were not aware.

With those principles in mind, one can articulate more specific strategies to achieve those goals in the context of IP. The most complex duties rest on states. But arguably the most powerful measures lie in the hands of firms.

B. Ensuring that Intellectual Property Law does not "Constrain but Enable Business Respect for Human Rights"

The key for the government role in resolving the conflict between IP incentives and access needs is to return to the economic grounding of the rights. If innovators can be compensated, there is no need to limit access. The disconnect in IP and food is the availability of a mechanism that will ensure that innovators are compensated by those who can pay while providing the lowest-priced access for vulnerable populations. Creating a system for need (human rights)-based compensation would provide a significant safety net and go a long way toward addressing human rights concerns.

Three steps outline the essential aspects of an effective human rights-based relief valve. The first is a means of identifying the controlling rights through IP landscaping. In many cases, rights have been infringed innocently, and in others rights have been avoided unnecessarily. The second step is the incorporation of a rights-based compensation mechanism for compulsory licensing of patents and plant varieties. The fact that the current regime has no such guidance provokes great ire among IP rights holders. The final step is the assurance of national exhaustion to facilitate price discrimination. Patent and plant variety owners are most likely to enable low-cost access if it will not undermine their primary markets.

1. Identifying the technology and tracking the rights

Somewhat unintuitive is the fact that a lack of knowledge of who owns what can actually be an initial, substantial access barrier. When thickets of rights exist, it can be difficult to figure out any non-infringing path. Moreover, when one does wish to purchase or license, the possibility that multiple IP owners will converge and stack royalties is a significant problem. An understanding of the rights landscape is therefore essential to resolving any access barriers.

Compared to other fields, there has been substantial progress in mapping the patent rights environment for agricultural technologies. Academics and governments have generated patent collections (e.g.,

Cahoy and Glenna, 2009). Perhaps more importantly, non-government organizations have tried to undertake a broad role to facilitate rights indemnification. One of the most prominent of these organizations is Public Intellectual Property Resources for Agriculture (PIPRA). In addition to providing basic IP information and assisting in licensing, PIPRA provides patent landscapes to clients such as developing countries and other non-profit organizations. Another organization called Cambia has generated multiple agricultural biotechnology landscapes and has launched an Initiative for Open Innovation (IOI). The goal of IOI is to make the world's patent systems more inclusive and transparent.

To date, existing landscape efforts have not focused on a tracking system that includes diverse rights like plant varieties and patents in the same maps. But such convergence is possible and made much easier by recent advances in technology as well as patent information disclosure. To ensure the proper balancing between innovation and food rights, mapping systems should be made more robust and user friendly.

2. No fault licensing as the predominant model

The most formal international compulsory licensing system is articulated in the TRIPS Agreement. The greatest problem with it is that it is focused on justifications for its invocation. Countries feel obligated to demonstrate a need to engage in unauthorized IP use. In the context of pharmaceuticals, the justification has now been pre-loaded into the system and stakeholders are loath to question a decision that leads to greater access to essential medicines. But this relaxation in scrutiny is narrow. Additional justifications must be created for new technologies.

Unfortunately, it is not so easy to carve out a "Doha Declaration"-like exclusion for food. The technology involved in food production is multifaceted and hard to succinctly define. It could include genetically modified seeds or germ plasm, but it could also include agrochemicals, irrigation systems, preservation systems and a host of other technologically diverse inventions. There is also significant crossover to other fields. Creating an IP exception for food is much more complicated than a specific good like pharmaceuticals and there will almost always be arguments about what should be included.

Moreover, IP exceptions always raise concerns about when an appropriately emergent situation exists. What kind of food emergency should justify compulsory licensing? Given that food production varies from year to year due to drought, disease and war, it could be very difficult to distinguish between the extraordinary needs of one developing nation compared to the standard agricultural challenges of another.

The better path forward is to create a no-fault licensing regime that does not ask for justification. Rather, it compensates according to need. In most cases, licensing would not offer substantial advantages over negotiating with the IP owner. However, when a core human right like access to food is concerned, compensation could be attenuated to provide a discount. Such attenuation would require a somewhat structured balancing scheme.

3. Parallels to the recent FRAND debate

To a great extent, the idea of increased access coupled with special need and great societal benefit is captured by the current discussion of how to address standards-essential patents. Such patents cover technology that is adopted by multiple companies with the understanding that the owners of related patents will allow access on fair, reasonable and non-discriminatory (FRAND) terms. The issue that has generated the most attention is whether FRAND-committed patents can be used to enjoin an infringer (Blind and Pohlmann, 2013). More courts and adjudicating agencies are determining that injunctions are generally not appropriate enforcement mechanisms. Absent some indication that a defendant refuses to pay any license fee, the patents should be made available at a fair rate.

This scheme can be related to IP over food. In general, such rights can be used to exclude. But under certain circumstances, when need is great and a means of compensation is possible, a licensing system based on fair, reasonable and non-discriminatory terms could be employed in a manner that would not destroy incentives. Clearly, how one sets the terms is a key factor. And that is where the intersection between IP and human rights becomes extremely important.

4. Balancing compensation needs with human rights

Even if one agrees with the notion of a preferred licensing scheme in times of need, how fairness should be determined is not necessarily clear. Although it has not been the primary focus of IP-human rights balancing, it is possible to imagine human rights attenuation to compensation that would create more satisfactory solutions. The author has previously articulated the idea in the context of essential medicines and it is excerpted here (Cahoy, 2011). It applies equally to the future of food.

Given that the primary issue in compulsory licensing is income, it makes sense to focus on the royalty aspects of TRIPS. This provides a great deal of flexibility. The section of TRIPS addressing remuneration is set forth in very vague terms, which means that a modification could easily be layered on top. No formal system need be disassembled, and no real expectations exist that must be revised.

TRIPS Article 31 requires only that remuneration be "adequate." Does "adequate" mean sufficient to cover lost sales, production, or R&D costs, or is it simply a rule-of-thumb amount that has been allocated in other contexts? TRIPS is silent on this account. However, this silence provides an opportunity. The incorporation of some means of determining when remuneration is adequate would solve the inconsistencies noted above. It could distinguish between a circumstance in which there is no access in an emergency from one in which a country engages in purely opportunistic licensing. Moreover, the involvement of a dispute resolution panel would ensure some degree of objectivity.

A human rights assessment could provide some indication of when a less-than-market royalty payment is necessary. Although human rights obligations are not accepted by every nation – notably, the U.S. has refused to ratify what could be considered the most important treaty relating to cultural and social rights, the ICESCR – there is more agreement here than meets the eye. The fundamental principles of human rights seem to underlie almost every nation's pronouncements regarding access to inventions, and all nations actually do respect at least some of these obligations. The disagreement appears to be on when human rights are truly at stake and what mechanisms are necessary to "respect, protect and fulfill" them. It seems likely that most nations would agree to a human rights analysis as a set of balancing principles if such an analysis were complete enough to consider all interests. In cases where there is a deep objection to the language of human rights, an argument that the relevant principles are part of customary international law may carry some weight.

The first step in the process would be to determine what human rights are implicated in a given compulsory licensing decision. Where patented inventions are concerned, the right to health is a primary candidate for remuneration consideration. According to Article 25 of the UDHR, "[e]veryone has the right to a standard of living adequate for the health of himself and of his family, including food, clothing, housing and medical care and necessary social service." That basic broad principle was ratified by many of the developed country members of the TRIPS agreement, including the U.S. However, it is not binding and is reasonably subject to interpretation. More specific is the ICESCR, which requires members to "improve methods of production, conservation and distribution of food by making full use of technical and scientific knowledge … ." This agreement has binding obligations and could plausibly cover access to food-related technologies in a time of crisis (Dumas, 2010; Straub,

2006). The list of non-ratifying countries is somewhat problematic, with the most important holdout being the U.S. But the underlying notion of this rights obligation is generally supported by public policy and law, even in the U.S.

The ICESCR's right to food has been interpreted by the U.N. Committee on Economic, Social and Cultural Rights in its Comment 12 issued in 1999 (CESCR, Comment 12). Its focus is on food distribution and deprivation rather than IP barriers. However, compulsory licensing under the ICESCR has been subject to detailed interpretation in the context of medicines, and the text could be carried over to food. According to the Comment 14 issued in 2000 regarding the right to health, parties have several "core" obligations that include access to food. As a starting point, a remuneration regime that stands as a barrier to these core obligations by making them economically unobtainable is problematic.

A counterweight to the human right to health is, to some extent, the right to profit from one's invention. This right is often ignored or at least highly subjugated to other human rights. According to UDHR, Article 27, "[e]veryone has the right to the protection of the moral and material interests resulting from any scientific, literary or artistic production of which he is the author." Again, this is reflected in ICESCR, Article 15, which describes the "right of everyone … [t]o benefit from the protection of the moral and material interests resulting from any scientific, literary or artistic production of which he is the author." This seemingly strong statement has been tamped down by the Commission, which noted that the human right to benefit from IP is not coextensive with legal right contained in IP laws. Rather, the human right is tied into a personal interest. This is similar to the natural rights or Lockean perspective on IP prevalent in earlier common law jurisprudence and scholarship. One aspect this perspective makes clear is the necessity for alienation of the property – as opposed the human right – which necessarily feeds into the adequate remuneration issue. The ability to be fairly compensated for a scientific production is strongly connected to its alienability. In addition to ICESCR rights for IP specifically, there is a right to property accepted in non-binding human rights documents like the UDHR and the Declaration on the Rights and Duties of Man. These could be informative in providing some interpretative context to a compulsory licensing remuneration valuation.

Considering these rights, one can see the evolution of a balancing test. First, there is an internal human rights balancing test. One assesses the current state of access to the technology and asks, does pricing play a role in reducing access such that a core food-access obligation is impacted? One also considers what impact the remuneration discount would have on the right to benefit from the invention. Second, there should be an external innovation incentive policy balancing. What impact would a royalty reduction have on the overall innovation environment? In some cases, where there is great need for food access supported by human rights principles, and little impact on investment returns, the reduction in remuneration from market levels may be great. In others, where access is not a problem and profit would be dramatically affected, remuneration reduction will be small. This construction essentially formalizes what advocates on all sides have been saying for years.

Clearly, using a broad system like this would not yield complete predictability, but it would compel actors to articulate a case for their plan and have some understanding of when rules will bend in their favor. An understanding of which interests the law favors, in turn, fosters negotiation whenever possible. If one creates enough certainty in the commercial and regulatory landscape, a private market will fill in the spaces unless impeded by some other barrier. In such a case, compulsory licensing can be used to address the deficiency.

Key to a human rights-linked remuneration attenuation system is the participation of an international decision-making body, namely the WTO Dispute Settlement Body. While this entity has been growing more active in recent years, deciding a number of issues related to TRIPS, it has never commented on remuneration. It is reasonable to assume that additional expertise would be necessary. But such expertise is not unattainable, or even unusual in the field of IP compensation. In every infringement case, courts and lay juries are required to make an *ex post* determination of damages in view of a number of complex factors. There is no reason to assume that a WTO body would be unable to do the same, and perhaps issue some measure of guidance in the form of advisory opinions. In addition, it is likely that a political process could be included to ensure that royalty rules capture all of the relevant interests, as in the U.S. copyright royalty setting. Though one could argue that such a process is already guaranteed by the WTO's own negotiation structure, the long and contentious debate leading up to the Paragraph 6 (access-to-medicines) amendment suggests that there may be better alternatives.

Of course, functionally, a remuneration attenuation system must also be implemented in national laws. The WTO Dispute Settlement Body's power extends only to sanctions for countries that do not fulfill their obligations under TRIPS and other aspects of GATT. To comply, a country would be required to establish a process for ensuring the relevant human rights and innovation considerations are taken into account in setting royalties. Theoretically, any country that has a process for expropriating property already has the outline in place, and certain specifics relevant to patents would simply need to be incorporated.

What about countries such as the U.S. that do not adhere to ICESCR? Would a remuneration attenuation regime based on such principles be subject to serious objections? This would likely be the case if the regime was imposed on a given country, but such implementation is actually never required. Attenuating remuneration is a voluntary relaxation of IP obligations, and as with other flexible provisions in TRIPS, countries may impose stronger property standards. The U.S. already has jurisprudence in place for government compulsory licenses, and courts could add this tweak related to human rights without the need for legislative revision.

5. Compensation cannot be eliminated

One might ask, why utilize a graduated system that in many cases demands developing countries make some payment for access to food IP? Perhaps a better alternative would be to permit all but developed nations to simply exclude food-related inventions from protection. If we simply determine property and the right to food to be incongruous, why not focus on its preservation in the countries that provide the majority of profits?

With no attenuation or preservation of compensation, the result may be avoidance of those markets with no protection. Companies may market only in high-value countries or provide products that are of little interest to the developing world. At this stage, there appears to be a real interest in the profit potential in new markets in Asia, Africa and South America. That interest might be chilled if the rights regime means essentially abandoning the information protection.

Perhaps the simplest analogy is in the context of U.S. contract law and the concept of necessaries for those who lack capacity. Individuals who do not possess the capacity to contract – most prominently minors – may nevertheless enter into agreements and avoid them within a reasonable time after capacity is attained (ALI, Restatement (Second) of Contracts, 1981). That rule, standing alone, is fine for purveyors of electronics and other non-essential good. And the logical reaction is also fine: many merchants of goods and services might refuse to deal with minors. However, we realize that such a result is unacceptable when essential goods are concerned. To ensure that merchants continue to transact in essential goods or "necessaries" with minors, we ensure that minors are obligated to pay the reasonable value for what they receive. That same rationale applies to IP and food. If we wish firms to develop and disseminate food technology to markets with vulnerable populations, there must be a minimal incentive and a guarantee that investment will not be lost.

However, for an open licensing regime to function, one limitation vaguely supported in TRIPS must be enhanced: national or regional exhaustion. National patent exhaustion is the principle that a sale in one country exhausts the patentee's right in only that country. It is an essential component of limiting parallel importation between countries that in turn preserves tiered pricing.

Of course, national exhaustion seems overly strict when it precludes parallel importation between countries at a similar development stage. It may be largely impractical as well. This is the idea behind the Paragraph 6 rule permitting trade of licensed pharmaceuticals between least-developed countries (WTO, 2003). This principle could be extended to provide for economic regional exhaustion in the context of food (or more generally).

C. The Firm's "Respect" Responsibility: "Avoid Causing or Contributing to" Food Access Problems

The complexities and diplomacy involved in administering a compulsory license regime make it important to plan, but difficult to impose. Even if there is a broader agreement in the business community that such licenses can be imposed fairly, they are still likely to be used only rarely. In contrast, firms have a great deal of power to make decisions concerning access that are immediately effective and even more likely to preserve a profit structure. In the access to medicines debate, the willingness of firms to voluntarily engage in low-cost licensing is chronically understudied, yet it is probably the source of most of the cheap versions of any drug still under patent. By following the Ruggie Guiding Principles, firms can take control of the access issue and benefit from the goodwill for helping to provide greater access to food.

1. Anticipate, assess and address

If one were to summarize firms' IP responsibilities under the Ruggie Principles, the phrase "just look around" would be accurate. Many of the conflicts that companies create are the result of simply being unaware of the impact of their pricing and marketing strategies coupled with an unnecessarily defense position when it comes to firm assets. Conversely, firms that take the initiative to provide access where barriers exist yield more positive public perceptions as well as the potential for increased profit.

A good model is provided by the actions of certain members of the pharmaceutical industry in the context of essential medicines. In the early 1990s, there was much concern about the high cost of medicines for AIDS treatment in particular. As AIDS infection reached a level of global crisis, advocacy groups and eventually governments focused on patented medicines as a key barrier to treatment. Calls for relaxing patent barriers ensued and eventually the Trade-Related Aspects of Intellectual Property Agreement (TRIPS) was amended to permit greater compulsory licensing. However, before compulsory licensing became prominent, many companies voluntarily lowered prices in developing countries or even offered medicines for free (Buckley, 2011). As a general matter, access to the most advanced AIDS medicines in least-developed and developing countries is probably primarily through such programs.

Certainly, there was self-interest in pharmaceutical companies engaging in low-cost or free drug distribution. Generally speaking, preserving a positive public perception comes only at the cost of a relatively low-profit market segment. But the point is that voluntary access also is much more in line with the Ruggie principles of ascertaining the human rights impact of a firm's actions and acting to minimize it. If applied in the context of food-related IP prospectively (rather than after a public outcry ensues), firms and broader stakeholders will benefit.

2. Partner with states and the NGO community to better predict problems

Firms are limited in the knowledge they can gain through their own global operations. It is always possible that a firm that is causing harm through its marketing and sales strategies is substantially ignorant of the impact. For that reason, it can be very useful to engage interested stakeholders like NGO groups (e.g., Oxfam International) to identify problems that could be ameliorated by the firm. Ideally, a non-confrontational partnership could be created that would allow the business and NGO communities to work together to voluntarily address human rights considerations. This is in keeping with firm responsibilities under the Ruggie principles, if not explicitly required.

IV. CONCLUSION

It appears increasingly true that the future of food is tied to IP. With growing populations and increased stress on the environment, the need for access to food IP may be more important with each passing year: and access means it is necessary to address the fundamental human right of adequate food supplies.

Such issues have been addressed in the context of essential medicines. However, the diversity of technologies involved in food production as well and the different types of overlaying rights creates a more complicated situation. To ensure a bright future for the global food supply, access to food IP must be particularly investigated and addressed. The integration of human rights balancing can provide a novel, fair means of taking into account the interest of various stakeholders. This discussion must take place soon, as global food supply pressures show no signs of alleviating soon.

REFERENCES

Alexandratos, N. and Bruinsma, J. (2012), "World Agriculture Toward 2030/2050: The 2012 Revision", ESA Working Paper No. 12-03. Rome, FAO.

Alston, J.M., Andersen, M.A., James, J.S. and Pardey, P.G. (2010), *Persistence Pays: U.S. Agricultural Productivity Growth and the Benefits from Public R&D Spending*. New York: Springer.

American Law Institute (ALI) (1981), *Restatement (Second) of Contracts* § 12.

Blind, K. and Pohlmann, T. (2013, Sept.), "Trends in the interplay of IPR and standards, FRAND commitments and SEP litigation", *les Nouvelles*, 177–81.

Bowman v. Monsanto, __ U.S. __, 133 S.Ct 1761 (2013).

Buckley, M. (2011), "Looking inward: Regional parallel trade as a means of bringing affordable drugs to Africa", *Seton Hall L. Rev.*, 41(2), 625–99.

Cahoy, D. (2011), "Breaking patents", *Michigan Journal of International Law*, 32(3), 461–509.

Cahoy, D. and Glenna, L. (2009), "Private ordering and public energy innovation policy", *Florida State University Law Review*, 36(3), 416–58.

Charles, D. (2002), *Lords of the Harvest: Biotech, Big Money, and the Future of Food*. New York: Basic Books.

Dumas, G. (2010), "A greener revolution: Using the right to food as a political weapon against climate change", *New York University Journal of International Law & Politics*, 43(1), 107–58.

Endres A.B. and Goldsmith P.D. (2007), "Alternative business strategies in weak intellectual property environments: A law and economics analysis of the agro-biotechnology firm's strategic dilemma", *Journal of Intellectual Property Law*, 14(2), 237–68.

Convention on the Grant of European Patents (EPC), Oct. 5, 1973, as revised Nov. 29, 2000. (2010). *The European Patent Convention* (14th ed.), Munich, Germany: European Patent Office.

Fischer, T.R., Byerlee, D. and Edmeades, G.O. (2011), "Can technology deliver on the yield challenge to 2050?" in Conforti, P. (ed.), *Looking Ahead in World Food and Agriculture*, Rome, Italy: UN Food and Agriculture Organization.

Gillis, J. (2013, Nov. 11), "A jolt to complacency of food supply", *New York Times*, p. D3.

Heller, M. (2010), *The Gridlock Economy: How Too Much Ownership Wrecks Markets, Stops Innovation, and Costs Lives*. New York: Basic Books.

Huckfeldt, P.J. and Knittel, C.R. (2011), "Pharmaceutical use following generic entry: Paying less and buying less", *NBER Working Paper 17046*.

International Covenant on Civil and Political Rights (ICCPR) (1966, Dec. 16). 999 U.N.T.S. 171, S. Treaty Doc. No. 95-20.

International Covenant on Economic, Social and Cultural Rights (ICESCR) (1966, Dec. 16). 999 U.N.T.S. 3.

International Union for the Protection of New Varieties of Plants. International Convention for the Protection of New Varieties of Plants (UPOV) (1961, Dec. 2). 33 U.S.T. 2703, 815 U.N.T.S. 89.

Kirtsaeng v. John Wiley & Sons, Inc., __ U.S. __, 133 S.Ct. 1351 (2013).

Landes, W. and Posner, R. (2003), *The Economic Structure of Intellectual Property Law*. Cambridge, MA: Belknap Press.

Madey v. Duke, 307 F.3d 1351 (Fed. Cir. 2002).

Malthus, T. (2008), *An Essay on the Principle of Population*, (G. Gilbert (ed.), Oxford, UK: Oxford University Press, (original work published 1789).

Miller, J.F. and Wetterstrom, W. (2012), "The beginning of agriculture: The ancient Near East and North Africa", in K.F. Kiple and K.C. Ornelas (eds), *The Cambridge World History of Food* (pp. 1122–39). Cambridge, UK: Cambridge University Press.

Murray, F. and Stern, S. (2007), "Do formal intellectual property rights hinder the free flow of scientific knowledge? An empirical test of the anti-commons hypothesis", *Journal of Economic Behavior & Organization*, 63(4), 648–87

National Conference of Commissioners on Uniform State Laws (NCCUSL) (1986). Uniform Trade Secrets Act with 1985 Amendments.

Nicholson, D. (2003), "Agricultural biotechnology and genetically-modified foods: Will the developing world bite?" *Virginia Journal of Law and Technology*, 8, 7–65.

Office of the High Commissioner for Human Rights (OHCHR) (2004, Apr. 20), "Responsibilities of Transnational Corporations and Related Business Enterprises with Regard to Human Rights", U.N. Doc. E/CN.4/DEC/2004/116.

Organization for Economic Co-Operation and Development (OECD) (2008), "2008 Compendium of Patent Statistics", retrieved from http://www.oecd.org/science/innovationinsciencetechnologyandindustry/37569377.pdf.

Plant Patent Act of 1930, 35 U.S.C. §§161–164 (2006).

Plant Variety Protection, 7 U.S.C. § 2543 (2006).

Potrykus, I. (2010), "Lessons from the "Humanitarian Golden Rice" Project: Regulation prevents development of public good genetically engineered crop products", *New Biotechnology*, 27(5), 466–72.

Straub, P. (2006), "Farmers in the IP wrench – How patents on gene-modified crops violate the right to food in developing countries", *Hastings International and Comparative Law Review*, 29(2), 187–213.

Torrance, A. (2012), "Planted obsolescence: Synagriculture and the law", *Idaho Law Review*, 48(2), 321–50.

Trade-Related Aspects of Intellectual Property Rights Agreement (TRIPS) (1994, Apr. 15). Marrakesh Agreement Establishing the World Trade Organization, Annex 1C, 1869 U.N.T.S. 299 (1994).
United Nations (2003), "Norms on the responsibilities of transnational corporations and other business enterprises with regard to human rights", U.N. Document E/CN.4/Sub.2/2003/12/Rev.2.
UN Committee on Economic, Social and Cultural Rights (1999), "General Comments 12 – The right to adequate food", UN Document E/C.12/1999/5.
UN Committee on Economic, Social and Cultural Rights (2000), "General Comments 14 – The right to the highest attainable standard of health", UN Document E/C.12/2000/4.
UN Dept. of Econ, and Social Aff. (UN-DESA) (2011), "The Global Social Crisis", UN Document ST/ESA/224.
UN Food and Agriculture Organization (FAO) (2013a, Nov. 27). FAOSTAT, Production, retrieved from http://faostat.fao.org/site/339/default.aspx.
UN Food and Agriculture Organization (FAO) (2013b, Nov.), "Food Outlook: Biannual Report of Global Food Markets", retrieved from http://www.fao.org/docrep/019/i3473e/i3473e.pdf.
UN Special Rapporteur on the Right to Food (SRRF) (2009, July 23), "The Right to Food: Seed Policies and the Right to Food: Enhancing Agrobiodiversity and Encouraging Innovation", UN Document A/64/170.
UN Special Representative of the Secretary-General (SRSG) (2008, April), "Protect, respect, remedy: A framework for business and human rights: report of the special representative of the secretary-general on the issue of human rights and transnational corporations and other business enterprises, delivered to the human rights council", UN Document A/HRC/8/5.
UN Special Representative of the Secretary-General (SRSG) (2011, March), "Guiding Principles on Business and Human Rights: Implementing the United Nations "Protect, Respect and Remedy" Framework", UN Document A/HRC/17/31.
Universal Declaration of Human Rights (UDHR) (1948, Dec. 10). G.A. Res. 217 (III), U.N. Doc. A/217.
U.S. Department of Agriculture (USDA) (2012, July 5). "Recent trends in GE adoption", retrieved from http://www.ers.usda.gov/data-products/adoption-of-genetically-engineered-crops-in-the-us/recent-trends-in-ge-adoption.aspx
U.S. Trade Representative (USTR) (2013, May), "2013 Special 301 Report", retrieved from http://www.ustr.gov/sites/default/files/05012013%202013%20Special%20301%20Report.pdf.
World Trade Organization (WTO) (2003, Sept. 1), "Decision of the General Council, implementation of paragraph 6 of the Doha Declaration on the TRIPS Agreement and Public Health", WT/L/540.

Index